D1360499

THE GREEK REVOLUTION OF 1821

The transition from slavery to freedom

Vassilios Moutsoglou

THE GREEK REVOLUTION OF 1821

CONTENTS

The Greek Revolution of 1821

FOREWORD

Although many political, economic, social, and ideological revolutions had already taken place before, the Greek Revolution of 1821, in many aspects, introduces an unprecedented perspective in relation to the era in the history of nations. A Christian people enslaved for centuries by a very powerful Muslim conqueror manages under particularly adverse external and internal circumstances to acquire a cultural identity, to realize its national status, to take up arms and rebel against its oppressors, at a time in which the notion of nation-states, if not entirely unknown, was in its infancy. In contrast to the Serbian revolution that was a peasant uprising, where the idea of national unity was only subsequently incorporated, the Greek Revolution follows a diametrical path.[1]

A revolution is a set of situations and actions. Reference to these is requisite in describing and understanding the events. The object of this study focuses on the causes and the evolvement of the Revolution of 1821. The analysis is done with a contemporary look, mainly by the synthesis of results of previous historical research. In some instances, the versions of Greek and Turkish historians clash, with the narratives of the two sides contradicting each other. Moreover, occasionally, the blur of ideological analyses obscures the facts to the extent it may require resorting to common sense for their clarification.

---

[1] Jacques Ancel : Peuples et Nations des Balkans, 1930, Nouvelle Edition, Paris, 1992, p. 157 (in French).

It has been attempted to ascribe one-dimensional views to the main cause of the explosion of the Greek Revolution. Some historians attribute it to the wretched conditions of slavery, while others consider that it was brought about as a result of the European Enlightenment and ideals of the French Revolution. Some claim that the Greek intellectuals "discovered" and exploited the admiration that Europeans nurtured for ancient Greece, some attribute it to the spiritual flourishing and maturation of Hellenism, and others to the work of the Society of Friends (Filiki Etaireia). Perhaps the most sensible explanation for the causes of the Greek Revolution is that it is the composition or the resultant of all of these.

This study also provides the opposing side's rationale, by examining how the Ottoman administration saw the revolutionary moves against it while citing views of modern Turkish historians who attempt to interpret the Revolution by integrating it in the history of the Ottoman Empire. Therefore, in the context of the Greek Revolution, the history of the Empire is also taken into consideration in exploring the causes of the policy that the Sublime Porte followed.

The Ottomans, despite the gradual collapse of their empire, were a force to be reckoned with. The Ottoman oppressors may have been open to corruption by bribery and venality and may have been violent and arrogant, but they were neither ignorant nor disorganized. They were not powerless, nor cowards and did not lack virtues, especially soldierly but also those related to their religion and nation, as they perceived them. Not only starting a war against them but even the thought that an enslaved nation could take arms with the purpose of its secession and independence, under the circumstances that prevailed, were out of time and place. The study of the

10

regime in force during the difficult years of Turkish domination is necessary for the understanding of the Greek transition process. In the context of the pre-revolutionary status quo, the social, economic and administrative conditions are investigated through the prism of the analysis of the concerns and hopes as well as the feelings that govern the Greeks on the eve of the Revolution. An attempt is also made to identify the causes of the internal conflicts in the ranks of the Greeks during the Greco-Ottoman war, which did not arise in their entirety as a result of emerging conditions attributed to the Revolution, but they had already partly existed.

Constantinople, the capital of the nation, holds a special place in the history of Hellenism of that era. Constantinople or City (Polis) as it was called, remained the center of the Greeks under the Ottoman Empire, and after the Revolution became a second national pole. A survey of the governing establishment of the Greeks under the Ottomans, explains the roots of the reservations held by a segment of Greeks about the Revolution. However, the Greeks of Constantinople were used as hostages not only during the Revolution of the nation but also later, in the 20th century, during the Cyprus controversy.

The narration naturally finds its way into the history of the Ottoman Empire and in its relations with the reborn Greek nation. It dwells upon the involvement of the Great Powers of the time in the events and the influence exercised by their aspirations, the actors of the drama, and finally the interactions of the relationships that arose from the activities of the international community.

Along with the battles, the Revolution evolves also on a political and diplomatic level. The study omits detail references to the chaotic situations arising from internal conflicts; they are not actually part of the transition. Nor does it delve into the war events in Peloponnese and elsewhere after the eruption of the Revolution limiting itself only to their outline. This was no longer a revolutionary conflict but a normal war between two organized states, one constitutional and one autocratic. In this war, the Greeks defeated the Ottomans with the help of their allies, their freedom was not granted to them as discerned by the Ottoman rendition of the events, but it was gained via battles with their opponents who also benefitted from alliances with both Muslim and European nations. The Ottoman positions of the time, as recorded, seem arrogant on the outside while expressing fear and agitation within.

Regarding the use of the terms G*reek* and Romios - Rum (in plural Romioi - Rums), which the author considers synonymous with the Greek ethnicity, it is noted that Turkish sources differentiate them, considering Greeks -Yunan as the residents of Greece, and Romioi the Greeks who are nationals of the Ottoman Empire. When referencing Turkish sources in this work, the term Rum of the Ottoman prototype was retained for the rebels, citizens of the Empire. The study alludes also to the war of words waged by the Ottoman side against the rebels.

Finally, regarding the dates used in sources, there may exist a difference of 11 days (in the 18th century) and 12 days (in the 19th century), based on the calendar, Julian or Gregorian utilized, although efforts are spent to utilize primarily the Julian.

OVERVIEW

The Modern Greek nation had already begun to form without a formal or legal frame, essentially in the early 11th century, perhaps even earlier, with the beginning set by some historians at a few centuries after the end of the ancient world. Medieval Hellenism is expressed by means of Byzantium. "There was a Greek nation throughout the Middle Ages", writes in 1853 Stefanos Koumanoudis[2], but "it surrendered to the despotic doctrines of the Roman Empire that had a foreign past that was never renounced".[3]

The Byzantium, or Romanea as it was sometimes referred to, was at its outset a Roman state with regards to its terminology and administrative features. Although it maintained these attributes until the end of its existence, it gradually became a nation of Greek Christians, having as main characteristics the Greek-language and Christian Orthodoxy. Although Byzantium was a multinational state, it became monocultural by the osmosis of its Roman traits with the Hellenistic tradition and the Greek ecclesiastical language, so crucial in Byzantium. Greek became the official language of the state after the reign of Heraclius (610-641), while Byzantine populations inhabited Greek regions. Their language was Greek, the Alexandrian Common. [4] Their faith, progressively after Constantine the Great, was the Christian Orthodoxy. As stated by Eleni Glykatzi-Ahrweiler,[5] "Greek language and Orthodox faith, are the signing elements of Byzantine

---

[2] Greek scholar and archeologist, 19th century.
[3] Dion. A. Zakynthinos: Political History of Modern Greece, Athens 1965, p. 50 (in Greek).
[4] Helene Glykatzi – Ahrweiler: Ibid., p.p. 11,14, 26, 28.
[5] Greek academic, Byzantinologist, Rector of the Academy and Chancellor of the Universities of Paris (1982-1989).

civilization and life. Do I need to underline that these elements define (basically) the current Modern Greek identity?".

Lord Byron wrote that the Byzantine Empire was a fusion of a Roman body, a Greek spirit, and an eastern mystical soul.[6] The Eastern Church found itself confronting Rome to the degree leading to the schism. Moreover, the race for commercial prevalence in the Mediterranean and national movements in Asia Minor - Anatolia, differentiated Greeks from Westerners and other nations in Byzantine territory. The "Empire" of Palaeologus is nothing less than a national Greek state.[7] George Gemistos - Python (1355-1452), born in Constantinople and later following the invitation of Emperor Manuel II Palaeologus settled in Peloponnese in the Despotate of Mystra (Despotate of the Morea), was a defender of the natural and cultural continuity of Hellenism: "Greeks we are, as the language and our education professes". Byzantine intellectuals shed light on ancient Greek literature. Until the Fall of Constantinople, it was the Byzantine monasteries, and no other resources, that rescued the ancient literature through transcribers and intellectuals, without of course overlooking the work of the Arab philosophers such as Averroes and Avicenna.[8]

The word "Hellene", which once was considered synonymous with heathen, began gradually to find its original meaning and sometimes replaced the term Roman. In 1204 crusader Geoffrey de Villehardouin repeatedly wrote that their opponents were the Greeks. The Greek states founded after the Frankish conquest were Greek not only in

---

[6] John Julius Norwich: Histoire de Byzance, Edit. Perrin,1988 p. 434 (in French).
[7] N. Svoronos: Survey of the Modern Greek History, 1981, p. 34 (in Greek).
[8] Helene Glykatzi – Ahrweiler: Ibid., 2016 p.p. 22-23.

the organization but also in name. The Empire of Nice (Anatolia) was called the "Greek Kingdom", while the term Greek was used even for Byzantium itself; the "Emperor of the Romans" began to use the title "King of the Greeks".[9]

During the Fall of Constantinople, the Ottoman Muslims, for the sake of their religion and "nation", did not clash with the Roman Christians but with the Greeks. The conqueror Fatih Sultan Mehmed, probably recognizing this difference, resettled Greeks (and not Romans) in Constantinople and tried to strengthen the Orthodox faith, which he had realized it identified with a distinct nation in contrast to Western Romans. In this context, particularly at that time, religion and nation were one and the same. Fatih appointed a Greek Orthodox Patriarch as an opposing pole to Latin Catholics in an effort to eliminate a likely cause for a future crusade of Europeans against him.

Athanasios Komninos Ypsilantis[10], who lived in the 18th century, in his work "After the Fall", which he wrote during the end of that century, takes for granted from the outset the existence of a Greek nation throughout the period he chronicles. In his work, he refers to "genus" and "Romioi" and not to Greeks, with this designation meaning mainly the Orthodox Greeks and not the whole of the Roman (Orthodox) nation under the Ottomans. Komninos, with regards to Greeks, provides remarks among other "nations" in the Balkan peninsula, primarily only for Maniates,[11] who were destined to be the ones that started the Revolution in Peloponnese (Morea).

---

[9] N. Svoronos: Ibid., p. 28.

[10] Greek-Ottoman doctor and writer.

[11] "Maniates, a small nation in Peloponnese are descendants of Spartans...They are not totally tributary to the Ottomans, only some of them pay taxes...".

15

Classically, the beginning of the history of the Modern Greek nation is placed in the years after the Fall of Constantinople. Several researchers append to it the period between the two Falls, Latin (1204) and Ottoman (1453).[12] However, it is noted that after the Latin Fall, the Byzantine state -Eastern Roman state-retained its essential characteristics and organization. Therefore this classical beginning of the history of the Modern Greek nation, i.e., after the Ottoman Fall, is the prevailing one among historians.[13] As expressed in a letter from I. Kapodistrias to William Horton, Deputy Minister of war and colonies of Britain, in October 1827, "The Greek nation consists of individuals who, after the conquest of Constantinople, did not cease to profess the Orthodox Religion, to speak the language of their Fathers...The boundaries of Greece have been drawn justly for four centuries now and neither time nor suffering, or the conquest could ever erase...".[14]

This designation of the beginning of the Modern Greek nation does not, however, explain adequately the Greek character of the populations that had remained in Anatolia during the earlier years, the approximately four centuries of its conquest by the Turkmens -from the defeat of the Byzantines at Manzikert, 1071- till the Fall of Constantinople, 1453. A question that comes to mind is how Greek populations maintained their Greek identity in Pontus, Cappadocia, and elsewhere in Anatolia under highly unfavorable assimilation conditions for more than eight centuries until 1922 (the reference is made for the indigenous populations and not for Greeks who emigrated later). The Orthodox religion and language are not adequate explanations, as parts of those populations had

---

[12] Among others, Spyridon Zebelios and George Finlay (1854).
[13] Dion. A. Zakynthinos: Ibid., p. 9.
[14] I. Kapodistrias: Texts, 1976 p. 33 (in Greek).

forgotten the Greek language. In contrast, the non-Greek but Orthodox communities of the region remained orthodox but non-Greek. On the contrary, during the exchange of populations,[15] after the First World War, the Greeks, even the Turkish speaking, did not renounce their ethnicity and preferred to abandon their birthplace instead. These prove, without doubt, the Greek character of part of the Byzantine population in Anatolia, without implying generalizations. Moreover, the neo-Greeks generally consider Byzantium to constitute part of the history of the Greek nation.

As far as the origin of the political history of the Greek state -and the end of the Revolution- is concerned, although it is accepted that it did not commence on February 3, 1830, when Greece's independence was recognized by the London Protocol, or by the Ypsilantis "Proclamation" of February 24, 1821, or, perhaps more accurately, with the "Warning" of the Messinian Senate of March 25, 1821, the present story of the Greek Revolution covers the entire revolutionary period, until the drama is resolved.

Geographically, in this study, the term Greece refers to the initial cradle of Hellenism, the Greek peninsula and the islands,[16] including the northern provinces Macedonia, Rumeli (mainly the Balkan peninsula), and the whole of Thrace, areas where compact Greek populations lived at the time of the Revolution.[17]

In this period, Greeks in Anatolia (Asia Minor) inhabited mainly the Aegean coast, Pontus in the

---

[15] The exchange of populations took place in 1923.

[16] Dion. A. Zakynthinos: Ibid., p. 9.

[17] Jacques Ancel in "Peuples et Nations des Balkans (1930)" refers to geographic "Greeces" i.e. Archipelago, Peloponnese, Greece of the Aegean, Regions of North, Greece of the Ionian.

north, and Cappadocia, in the center. However, due to the large majority of Muslims in these regions, there was no chance of any national revolutionary movements surfacing there.

The history of the Ottoman Empire is a history of many peoples under the common rule of the Sultan, of different origins and various religions, who sometimes are bound by common interests, while other times conflicted by antipathies or disputes. The cohesive element of the "Ottoman nation" was the Ottoman dynasty plus the Islamic religion. The Ottoman Empire showed from the outset an aggressive and conquering trait, especially towards the western territories, resulting in the enslavement of the entire Greek nation, as it had already been established in an earlier form.

In a sense, the Greek nation was considered to have "sacrificed its political freedom to preserve its ancestral dogmas",[18] although this theory is not widely accepted today. The role of the Orthodox faith and the Eastern Church was, of course, catalytic in preserving the nation's Greek identity, especially after the Fall, but the assertion that between Catholicism and slavery to the Turks, the Byzantines chose the second, is not valid. Moreover, the Byzantines of Constantinople fought up to the bitter end against the Ottoman invaders.

During the Turkish occupation and before introducing the concept of nation, the terminology of the Roman genus and "genus genesis" (instead of ethnogenesis) was used. Later on, the Patriarchate's Pan-Orthodox sovereign inclination changed (in part) into the sovereign initiative of the Greek nation.[19] The conceptual distinction between the Greek nation and

---

[18] Archimandrite Germanos Afthonidis: Foreword to "Historical Events After the Fall", Ath. Komninos Ypsilantis 1870 (in Greek).
[19] Dion. A. Zakynthinos: Ibid. p. 40.

the genus has only symbolic and historical value. The Great Idea comes to reconcile the opposing tendencies of ecumenism and the nascent nationalism.

The "Christian sector" of the population in the Ottoman Empire suffered for a long time through "abnormal and wretched conditions due to the prevailing intolerance and fanaticism that surrounded Sultan's throne".[20] The primary goal was to preserve the ethnicity achieved through religion. "We have seen deplorable years of prejudice and damage. But we admired the strength of our nation; persecuted openly or covertly, afflicted, escaping dangers from foreigners and our own, laboring and begging, we saved the nation... striving in the last corner of the East... ".[21]

However, the decision to revolt and pursue political freedom and freedom to exercise Orthodox worship was not universal in the enslaved nation. But even where there has been such a resolution, it has not always been possible to realize it. The segment that remained enslaved, along with its church, continued its course independently from the free state of Greece, as it had perceived it feasible from the outset. After the first post-revolutionary years of slaughter and atrocities, the still enslaved part of the nation lived under the Ottoman Empire a period of relative "prosperity and political equality under the scepter of our popular Sultan and the government of its prudent ministers".[22]

As early as the 6th century, the Greek language had prevailed among other indigenous languages of western and central Anatolia, as far as

[20] Archimandrite Germanos Afthonidis: Ibid.
[21] Manouil Gedeon: Chronicles of a Columnist, Athens 1932, p. 315 (in Greek).
[22] Archimandrite Germanos Afthonidis: Ibid.

Cappadocia.[23] The Greek language and scripture were never abandoned, with the Church often being its most important guarantor for its salvation. Apart from the editions of works of ancient Greek literature, mainly in foreign languages, Greek words were gathered and published by Errikos Stephanou in his book "Thesaurus of Graece Linguae", Paris, 1572.[24]

The words used in colloquial and written language were every so often not Greek. The language, depending on the place where it was spoken, not only contained a mixture of words of Turkish, Albanian or Italian, but the Greek words used differed in meaning, usually due to their varying evolution during the centuries from the classical times. The vocalization also varied by location. However, there was no regime of "Babylon",[25] historical references for the difficulty of communication among Greeks in that period are scarce and rather anecdotal. Moreover, these variations exist to some extent at present and are much more widespread not only in Greek but also in many other languages. The Greek language and nationality are not linked in absolute terms. The notion of national conscience transcends the borders of the language, and some of the most heroic national fighters of the Revolution were Albanian or Slavic speaking.

The role of religion and the Church in preserving the national conscience had been crucial throughout the Ottoman occupation. The Church, in particular, had the role of guardian of language and morals. In some Christian enclaves in Cappadocia,

---

[23] Spyros Vryonis: The Decline of the Hellenism of Middle Ages and the procedure of Islamization, Athens 2008, p. 45 (in Greek).
[24] Skarlatos Vyzantios: Dictionary of the Greek Language, Athens, publications of 1839, 1852, Publisher Andreas Koromilas (in Greek).
[25] D.K. Vyzantios Babylonia, play (in Greek).

where the Greek language had vanished, and Turkish had become the vernacular language, the Greek, the language of the Fathers, was preserved through the language of the Church. Occasionally, the Greek alphabet served in the writing also of the Turkish language, given the difficulty of the officially used Arabic script.

One of the reasons that the assimilation of Greeks by the Ottomans proved not feasible, as it might have been expected, and it has indeed happened in many other instances in history between conquerors and conquered, was the religious parameter. Otherwise, according to Ibn Khaldun, the conquered tend to mimic the conquerors and try to integrate into their social and cultural system.[26] However, according to another point of view, this is not the case among distinctly differing cultures. It has been proven, from the depths of eons, and without any intent of assessment of the two religions, that there is an unbridged cultural difference between Christianity and Islam. These were the prevailing history and circumstances of the era.

Indicative of the importance of Christianity was the political legacy of the "Old Man of Morea" Kolokotronis to the young people of Greece through his speech in Pnyka shortly before his death.[27] Further, General Makrigiannis wrote that "without virtue and pain for the fatherland and faith in religion, nations cannot exist". Christian Orthodoxy is, therefore, a cultural component of Modern Greek identity. It is not "Hellenism", but the latter could hardly exist as a modern historical continuance without Christianity. That happens to be

---

[26] Spyros Vryonis: Ibid., p. 360.
[27] "Above all, keep your faith and your homeland in your soul..." A.B Daskalakis, Introduction to the Memories of Kolokotronis, Narration of events of the Greek race, Papyros publ. (in Greek).

one of the multiple links that bound Greeks with Europe and its spirit, regardless of its secularity.

The clash of the Greek nation with the Ottoman Empire was first held in the realm of ideas, and from that point of view, the Empire was defeated even before conflicts on the ground started. The two opposing "camps" had something in common that came about from historical evolution: the same capital, Constantinople. As a result of this, the liberation of the Greek nation did not follow subsequent patterns of the liberation of other Balkan peoples that took place around their historical capitals, but instead, it was realized in a unique manner. Despite the preliminary planning, the armed struggle, instead of starting from the classical and natural for the time capital of Hellenism Constantinople, it commenced from the periphery, initially Moldavia-Wallachia and afterward Peloponnese.

However, Constantinople and the church of the Agia Sophia (Holy Wisdom of the God) remained in the hearts and minds of the enslaved Greeks (but also in later times, until 1922) as the ultimate vision of liberation. Countless folk traditions that spoke about "After years and times, it will become ours again...". After all, the idea that freedom and sovereignty were lost with the Fall was etched in the nation's memory.

Greek schools were being established in all regions of Greece under the leadership also of Church, starting from the 18th century. Philosophers and poets emerged. The Greek language remained, to some extent, lingua franca among the orthodox Christian populations of Balkans. The Greek books issued towards the end of the 18th century were abundant. Although Greek intellectuals came from the bosom of Church, whose schools had attended, they adopted a scientific approach and a secular

22

perception of history, mainly thanks to ancient Greek philosophers.[28] This approach, however, was rejected by Church. But the idea of the nation's freedom and its struggle for it had not yet matured.

The Ecumenical Patriarchate, the center of the administrative institutions of the Greeks of the Ottoman Empire, was based in Constantinople and operated, in collaboration with the civil institutions established meanwhile, as a substantial government body of the nation in chains. A special place is devoted to the history of Patriarchate since the Ecumenical Patriarch was the Head of the nation under the Ottoman administration, the axis around which all the political and social life of the Constantinopolitan Greeks and beyond revolved. However, for political, religious as well as historical reasons, the Patriarchate regarded this institution above the nation, condemning the phenomena of ethnic-racial fundamentalism. The Patriarch was the Head of the Orthodox nation according to the religion-centered administrative system of the Ottoman Empire, which included all the Orthodox Christian nations of the Empire and not only of the Greeks. Thus, he was obliged to act in accordance.

The "lament of Constantinople" had been the guide and consolation of the nation throughout the years of Ottoman domination, but also the impetus to the beginning of the struggle for freedom. National movements were continual but of limited scope and unsuccessful. The Revolution of 1821 was, therefore, the crowning of a long evolutionary journey. The Greek transition of 1821 was a process that began in 1769 with the rushed uprise of Orloff [29] that, even though failed, brought about an increase in the number of Greeks with a revolutionary mindset. It

---

[28] Richard Clogg: The struggle for Greek Independence, 1973.
[29] A failed uprising incited by Russians

also led to the inclusion in the Treaty of Kucuk Kaynarca, after the great Russo-Turkish War (1768 - 1774), of a clause on the protection of Christians by Russia as well as on the freedom of trade for the Greeks and their ensuing enrichment that helped the Revolution. This was followed by the decimation by Kleftes (Greek militias) of the Albanians who had come to Peloponnese at the invitation of the Turks to help suppress the Orloffic revolution but subsequently refused to leave despite Sultan's order, robbing and killing Greeks, signaling the first war action.

The term "revolution" encompasses the aggregate of events that lead or attempt to lead to the disestablishment of the status quo, causing change or redefinition in some or all social, political, legal, economic, or religious structures. A revolution is a turning point in the linear evolution of situations and usually develops in an international environment from which it is influenced and which it affects. Its purpose can be either the enforcement of demands against the government or the state or the overthrow of the regime. The processes leading to a revolution are basically social, while the motives may be predominantly political or religious, but the economic parameter is almost always present. Therefore, the study of the social structure of the ensemble is important for examining the elements that lead to a revolution.

In principle, for a revolution to commence, a general urgency for a change that is widely embraced by a social group that shares one or more of its elements is needed. The demand can be ideological and social (French Revolution), political and economic (American Revolution), ideological and political (Russian Revolution), or even religious (Iranian revolution). It is essential that appropriate conditions must have formed beforehand, as with the

Enlightenment in France or with the Marxist ideology in Russia. The transgression must incite some form of uncontrolled rage in society for the culmination of the outbreak of the uprising. A revolution may be triggered by a coincidental event or a result of a plan, but there are always underlying causes that set it off.

In the case of the Greek Revolution, the common element for the rebels was the nation, and whatever this concept entailed. The social infrastructure of Hellenism was, to some extent, urbanization and the militancy of armed groups. The conditions were shaped both through the French Enlightenment and through the spiritual and cultural revival of the nation, the Modern Greek Enlightenment. The rage that instigated the Revolution sprang from the nation's enslavement. The purpose of the Revolution was freedom, and its planning was carried out by the Friendly Society that acted with secrecy.

In the final years before the Revolution, the leading class of the Greek nation, formed under the domination of the Ottomans, aligned with the ecumenical idea of Byzantium. It was a form of the Great Idea, by which Hellenism would be instigated from within the Ottoman Empire and would transform into a powerful entity making the Greeks co-rulers of this Empire, which would turn it into a multiethnic state, an Ottoman "Greek" state. The concept of a nation with modern perception may not precisely have existed then, but the notions of genus and religion were well-established.

This idea was also expressed by Rigas Fereos, a revolutionary figure, having in mind that such a development would also serve the interests of the European states. This notion was at odds with the idea of autonomy, of a national Greek state, as projected by the French Revolution and the Enlightenment. Hellenism was confronted with these

25

ideas, unable to choose between the two contradictory aspirations, and in 1821 it attempted to carry them both simultaneously, in Moldovlachia and Peloponnese.[30] However, the two movements cannot be separated; they were two phases of the same revolution.[31] Conclusively, the Greek Revolution of 1821 was not a spontaneous reaction like the Serbian revolution, but a well-planned act thought of by the Friendly Society in advance. It is widely accepted that the birthday of the Greek Revolution is February 24, 1821, when Alexander Ypsilantis issued from Iasi his Proclamation to the Greeks.

The beginning of the victorious Revolution in Peloponnese is marked by the entrance of the Greek rebels in Kalamata on March 23, 1821, with the Ottomans of the city surrendering without a fight in the face of a superior force under Petrobey Mavromichalis and the subsequent issuing of the "Warning" of the Messinian Senate on March 25, 1821. It has not been confirmed that there was a special general kickoff ceremony in Agia Lavra or elsewhere.[32] However, local ceremonies were organized in many cities, including Kalamata, for the commencement of their participation in the Revolution.[33]

The onset of the Revolution in Peloponnese was likely planned for a later date, but it was moved up once the Ottomans became aware of the intent of the Greeks. On the contrary, Turkish historian Ali Fuat Orenc argues that the Revolution would have

---

[30] Arnold Toynbee: A study in history, Oxford, 1947.
[31] Dion. A. Zakynthinos: Ibid., p. 59.
[32] According to François Pouqueville but disputed by historians.
[33] May be also at Kalavryta or Lavra Monastery as Archbishop of Patras was there.

started earlier, but it was delayed because of the strict administration of Ali Pasha of Ioannina.[34]

The Friendly Society appears to have planned the start of the revolutionary movements in 1820 on three fronts. The first entailed Constantinople, where the leadership of the Greek nation resided, the second in Peloponnese, with the critical presence of dignitaries (Heads of communities - Proestoi) who were committed to the Friendly Society, of Armatoloi (armed guards) and of Kleftes (covert militia who acted as a national guard). The third front was considered as an invasion from Russia to Moldovlachia by Greek forces.

The operation in Moldovlachia, poorly prepared, at an unfavorable time and place, with Russia opposing it because of the conjunctures of the Laubach Conference, was doomed to fail. Romania's territory was not Greek, and it was Romanian villagers and not Turks attacking local Boyars' estates. At the same time, insurrectionist Tudor Vladimirescu refused to assist Ypsilantis, bearing in mind primarily the interests of Romanian Boyars. There, it became clear that the ecumenical ideal, simply, was not feasible.

Not only the Sultan's powerful army in the capital but also differences of opinion among the various classes of Greeks of Constantinople prevented a revolutionary movement in the Polis. The Great Tribulations [35] that followed in Constantinople stifled any thought of revolutionary activity there.

As for the reasons for the Revolution, reference can be made to the "Warning" issued by the

---

[34] Ali Fuat Orenc: History Magazine Issue No. 46, 2007 (in Turkish).
[35] Violence against Greeks of Constantinople during the Greek Revolution.

Messinian Senate to the European courts on March 25, 1821.[36] The highly apt text, irrespective of its author, answers questions expressed in the past in certain circles that still surface up, that dispute the fact that the oppression of the Turks was the reason for the Revolution or even whether that period was the most appropriate for its launch, while they promote the significance of the social parameter in its success. In any case, the Greeks basically fought for their human rights and human dignity.

The development of literacy, the spread of European education, and the wealth accumulated by trade were the means for the outbreak and success of the Revolution. The finances of the Revolution were secured by private funds, while at times, wealthy Greeks organized and maintained military units.[37] The enlightenment and ideals of the French Revolution, the modern (for that period) European ideas of which Kolokotronis became aware from his contacts in the Ionian Islands, played a relatively minor role, and the Friendly Society while leading - especially in the field of strategic planning- had basically a preparatory role.

The demographic parameter, as often demonstrated in ancient or modern history, is an essential factor of power. The Greeks of the Empire were the largest non-Muslim minority and constituted the majority in Peloponnese. The compact Greek population in Peloponnese and elsewhere contributed to the success of the project along with their devotion to the idea of freedom that a significant portion of Greeks had wholeheartedly adopted. There were, of course, objections by Greeks who were wary

---

[36] "The unbearable yoke of the Ottoman tyranny...drove us to the decision to liberate ourselves or die".
[37] Vasilis Kremmydas: The Greek Revolution of 1821, Athens, 2016, p. 83 (in Greek).

of the uprising and preferred nonactivity. Among the unresolved were some dignitaries of Morea - Peloponnese. Their summoning by the Pasha to Tripolitza (Tripoli of Peloponnese) and the fear of their execution, however, dispelled any hesitation that they might have harbored. But any reticence was partly justified and should not have come as a surprise. The danger was real and imminent. On the other hand, the severity of the aggressiveness of the rebels has been questioned by Modern Greek historians, while the slaughtering of Muslims, especially during the liberation of Tripolitza, is deemed intolerable under any circumstances. One could argue that the Ottomans also slew Greek populations whenever an opportunity arose, typically on a larger scale.

The choice of timing of the outbreak of the Revolution was also disparaged, as should have been expected, by the European powers of the Vienna System, due to the European Order established just a few years ago, in 1815. The Friendly Society may have set constraints on the timing. Still, it was a given that from some point onwards, the situation had escaped control because of the spreading of the knowledge of the plan and the great desire of the Greeks for liberation. Therefore, the Greek Revolution may not have been spontaneous since it was planned, but its eruption was the result of the historical evolution of events. Moreover, Mahmud II was preparing his new army, and although Asakir-i Mensurei Muhammediye had been defeated in its first battle by the Russian military (and in the second by Mehmed Ali of Egypt), no one could predict the outcome if the new army confronted the ill-organized Greeks. It was also considered that the Ottoman administration was facing the rebellion of Ali Pasha of Ioannina. At the same time, the involvement of the Tsar's officer, Alexander Ypsilantis, in the Revolution in Moldovlachia created the expectation that Russia would not remain neutral for long. The Greeks, however, felt that they would prevail without the participation of Europeans, a notion that was confirmed in the first phase, even though Europeans were essentially against them. In any case, the warriors of Mani did not seem to have considered any of these factors when they took up arms against the Ottoman administration of Kalamata on March 23, 1821.

The Revolution generated a dynamic analogous to a fire spreading into an explosive matter. Victories followed it in succession that secured the liberation of Greek cities in Peloponnese and the mainland. The Ottoman administration, not having been caught off-guard, reacted by mobilizing as many forces as it had. But despite its sporadic victories, it was unable to cope with the decisive victory of the Greeks, who fought for their lives in a battle to the end. The Greeks managed to keep the liberated regions, repelling the Ottoman counterattacks.

After the initial phase, the Revolution stabilized; the situation stagnated as neither of the two sides was strong enough to bring about a decisive victory. In this second phase, the Ottomans were forced to retreat to their bases in Thessaly after their defeats or because of adverse weather conditions in winter, while the rebels were not strong enough to counterattack, failing to secure a crucial victory. Also, the uprisings in Sterea, Macedonia, and Epirus delayed the Ottomans in their effort to cope with the situation in Peloponnese. Another cause for the lack of activity was the internal discords of the Greeks. In a broad sense, the political leaders, represented (in this phase and general terms) by the Phanariot Alexandros Mavrokordatos and Hydraen shipowner Georgios Koundouriotis, in an assembly consisting mainly of notables, dignitaries, and wealthy merchants were opposed by soldiers of the small regular army, the irregulars and the former Kleftes, faithful to Theodoros Kolokotronis. The political discord culminated in a civil war in 1824. Along with these conflicts, the interventions of Britain, France, and Russia, which sought to safeguard their strategic political and economic interests in the Ottoman Empire, contributed to the impediment of the revolutionary momentum.[38]

The entrance of Mehmed Ali, Pasha of Egypt, vassal to the Sultan onto the stage characterizes the third phase. Ali sought to overthrow the Sultan or gain independence while he saw fit to join him to secure favors. The Turkish-Egyptian fleet had been moored at Pylos in the Gulf of Navarino, while the Turkish-Egyptian army, which had been reformed according to the French standards, had started to drown the Greek Revolution in blood.

In the meantime, however, there had been a shift in the system of balance in Europe, and the three Great Powers -Britain, France, and Russia- could not remain passive in the face of this rather unexpected development in Greece. They have aspired strategies that did not pursue clashes with the Ottomans either on land or sea. Even though the Admirals of the Allied fleet did not have direct orders, their involvement in the naval Battle of Navarino was not totally "fortuitous". The Great Powers, mainly Britain, could not tolerate Egyptian domination under the sole influence of France in the eastern Mediterranean that would subvert the balance of power. The series of events, as presented from a Turkish viewpoint, indicate that the Allied fleets did not enter the Gulf of Navarino just for overwintering but with an offensive mindset, and that they had initiated the exchange with the pretext that Ibrahim had not abided to what it had been agreed to, i.e., stay inactive. The stated

---

[38] S.W. Sowards: The Balkans, 1996.

goal was, however, to expel the Turkish-Egyptian fleet from Peloponnese or at least to restrain it, which was not possible under the explosive conditions prevailing. It took one (perhaps) unplanned event to set the guns on fire. The Turkish-Egyptian fleet was destroyed. The naval Battle of Navarino was a crucial turning point for the Greek Revolution. The road to independence for the Greeks could hardly be halted after that.

The fourth phase entails the denouement of the drama and concerns the reversal of Western aspirations, now in favor of the Greeks. It also encompasses the arrival of a French expeditionary corps -under Nicolas Joseph Maison- in Greece as well as the Russian -Turkish war, the Ottoman defeat, and the Treaty of Adrianoupolis (Edirne). That was followed by the "London Protocol of February 3, 1830, on the independence of Greece", the Treaty of Constantinople, and finally the Protocol of July 18-20 / August 3, 1832, that established the borders of Greece.[39]

Even from the beginning, the Greeks had tried to establish a democratic polity. They were not a band of thieves trying to seize whatever they could or enforce their laws as pleased, but from the outset, they organized a national movement with a moral and ideological background. Otherwise, it would not have attracted the widespread sympathy of many European nations and the United States in favor of their struggle. Already, according to its first constitution, Greece would provide asylum to all

---

[39] S.T. Laskaris: Diplomatic History of Greece 1821-1914, Athens 1947, p.p. 24-48, (in Greek).
Dion. A. Zakynthinos: Political History of Modern Greece, Athens 1965, p.p. 58-65 (in Greek).

"those who are persecuted for their struggles for freedom".

It was remarkable the way that the personalities of the allies of Greece influenced their policies. The death in 1825 of the reluctant Czar Alexander I and his succession by the more resolute Nicholas I had benefited Greece. Likewise, the suicide of the foreign minister of Great Britain, Robert Stewart, Viscount Castlereagh, in 1822, and his succession by George Canning, later Prime Minister of Britain, also helped Greece. However, this positive sentiment of Britain shifted a little later, when Arthur Wellesley, first Duke of Wellington, became Prime Minister at the end of 1827. Still, by then, the impetus had already been given. The fall of Wellington later facilitated the enhancement of the Greek borders that had been established by the Protocol of February 3, 1830. The views of Britain are worth noting not only because it was a significant Power but because France, which seemed to have initially supported the Ottomans, followed Britain on its "philhellenic" stance.

Despite all kinds of problems that the newly independent state would inevitably have had to face, such as political rivalry, civil strife, hunger, misfortunes and massacres, and all adversities of the war that lasted throughout the long period of the Revolution, Hellenism never second-guessed its ideals of freedom over slavery. That is why the Greek people had courageously endured all the suffering and never compromised, even when they had the leeway to do so.

THE OTTOMAN CAMP

Ottomans are the descendants of the statelet that constituted the vanguard of the Islamic world towards European Christianity. Initially, there was no concept of a nation among the Ottoman Turks, nor was religion the characteristic that prevailed. The first concern of nomad Turkmens was their survival. They managed to dominate because of their bellicose character and their discipline, organization, and orientation towards military conquests. In terms of economic organization, however, they were significantly lagging, in addition to the fact that they considered these tasks inferior to war and administration, which suited them better. The Ottoman state managed to become a coherent political expression for the majority of the Anatolian Turkmens of the 14th century, and from there on it succeeded, by uniting them under a single administration, to instill in them the sense of community that would characterize a nation, if there were such a concept at that time.

In the first centuries since its founding and rule, the personality of the Ottoman state mirrored that of its ruler of the Ottoman dynasty at the time.[40] However, some common features characterize the founding tribe of the state. These features emerge in the evolution of history and distinguish the Ottoman state. The central feature is the temperament for expansion through conquests. The main instruments of the Ottoman Empire's policy were swords and cannons, but without ignoring the benefits of diplomacy.

---

[40] Vasilis Moutsoglou: Turkey: The Evolution of the Personality of the State, Athens, 2016 (in Greek).

The Ottoman state had shown perseverance and patience regarding its objectives. It realized that continuous expansion could ensure the viability of the state at a time when its main adversary, the Byzantine state, but also the other relatively short-lived Muslim "Beyliks"[41] in Anatolia, were not concerned with their territorial integrity.

The Ottoman dynasty organized a state that was considered person-centered but knew how to reward (although not always) values, bravery, credibility, and commitment to duty; most of the time, it was not daunted by occasional defeats. It diplomatically steered whenever it deemed necessary while realizing the interests of the state promptly and followed policies that would secure them. Occasionally, it showed benevolence to the defeated and, in general, displayed tolerance to conquered Christian peoples. In contrast to Christian European states of the time, religion in the Ottomans followed the rule of the state, not explicitly but essentially. The Ottoman state was less successful in developing its economy but later did not hesitate to adopt the European innovations offered, both in administrative and military art and, although less so, in the economy. However, European penetration in its economy with the concessions (capitulations) and exploitation of wealth-producing resources contributed to the regression of the Empire.

The battle of Manzikert (1071) is a milestone in the conquest of Anatolia by the Turkmens. However, the infiltration of Turkmens had begun earlier through migrations, and gradual conquest and violent colonization of Anatolia continued for

---

[41] Anatolian Beyliks, also known as Turkmen Beyliks, were small principalities. The word "Beylik" denotes a territory under the jurisdiction of a Bey, equivalent in other European societies to a "Lord".

centuries after, with ongoing raids and looting, as a result of which, despite the sporadic victories of the Byzantines, the Turkish-nomadic tribes were able to settle on the Anatolian peninsula. The local -mainly Greek- population was subject to Islamization and subsequent Turkification. At the time of the founding of the Ottoman state around Bursa, the Turkmen tribes had long been occupying Anatolia, with the Empire of Seljuk dominating, although under duress from the Mongols.

With the power of arms, the Turkmens achieved in no small extent control of the region. They imposed the primacy of their religion, their language, and any civilization they had imported from the east along with a few Byzantine elements of culture. Starting at the Beylik of Karamanogullari, an early version of the Turkish language was consolidated as the official language (circa 13th century). The most devastating of all for the peoples of the region were the members of the nomadic tribes. Their system of sacking and burning contributed much to the depopulation of the Christians. These acts were supplemented with enslavement and sporadic violent Islamizations, although there were quite a few voluntary islamizations in exchange for a favor. Occasionally there have been massacres of Christian inhabitants, sometimes wiping out entire communities.[42] The success of the Turkmens was since their conquering of territories was not primarily for tax or looting but for finding areas to settle by eradicating or assimilating the ancient inhabitants of the region.

---

[42] Spyros Vryonis: Ibid., p. 311-355.

After the conquest of Anatolia, which meanwhile had largely been Islamized,[43] The Ottoman Empire expanded rapidly to Rumeli, gradually occupying the entire area of Greece. The conquests westward, in Rumeli, against the Byzantines, in Dar al-Kufr (land of infidels) or Dar al-Harb (land of war) usually came about as a result of wars waged, but the first acquisition on European soil was realized through a gift. The Emperor of Byzantium John Kantakouzinos accorded Sultan Orhan a fortress in Gallipoli to thank him for his assistance to the Byzantines during a Balkan War of that time. This was a significant event since the first acquisition of land in Europe was made through concession and not arms, thus without provoking the Christian European states when the Ottoman state was relatively weak.

The Ottoman Empire quickly adapted to changing situations. Sultan Murat focused on developing institutions and moved the capital of his state from Bursa to Edirne in Europe, to demonstrate the shift of the center of gravity of his interest towards the west. Murat founded the unit of the Janissaries (new army) with the Islamization of the children enslaved after the conquest of Edirne. Turkmens had previously applied this tactic during the long process of their conquest of Anatolia. The Sultan was awarded a fifth of the spoils his soldiers were seizing, including captive children. The youngsters after Edirne's conquest were sent to the outskirts of Bursa to grow up with Muslim Turkish families before joining the Janissaries' body. Subsequently, when the conquests and the number of prisoners of war diminished, the Ottomans organized forceful child-gathering among Christians to recruit the Janissaries' body. Later,

---

[43] At the beginning, besides violent Islamizations there have been also several voluntary conversions to Islam in exchange for privileges entailed for the new Muslims.

when Janissaries became an enviable entity, Turkish nationals of the Sultan, mainly for financial reasons, demanded that their sons join the body, which had started gradually falling apart, and not just because of this.

In 1395, after the failed talks with Byzantines in Xanthi, the Ottoman army attacked southern Greece and arrived in Attica. In 1397, raids were organized against Koroni and Methoni, which belonged to Venice, with the intent of plundering. However, the Ottomans did not resettle Turks in those areas, as they had done in other parts of Greece. The lack of colonization of Peloponnese and the Aegean islands with Muslim settlers from Anatolia would prove to be a costly mistake for the Ottomans since it was there where the fateful for them Greek Revolution of 1821 began.

The defeat by Timur

The conflicts of the Ottomans with the other Turkish Beyliks of Anatolia had ended during the time of Bayezid I (1389 – 1402) with their dissolution and accession of their territories to the Ottoman state. Besides, the Ottomans succeeded in occupying the areas of southeastern Anatolia, expanding their borders to the Euphrates.

However, the Turkish Beys of Anatolia, expelled by the Ottomans, fled to the Turkish-Tatar Timur, who aspired to the revival of the Mongolian Empire. During the Battle of Ankara (1402), the administrations and army of these Beys crossed to the side of Timur, who defeated the Ottomans, thereby dissolving the political unity established a short time ago in the 14th century under the Ottoman state. Although the state of Timur could not survive long after his death, the heavy defeat was a severe blow to the Ottoman state, which remained headless

39

during the so-called "Fetret Period" (Sorrow period, 1402 - 1413) and was torn apart by the aspirations to the throne of Bayezid I's four sons. Eventually, Mehmed I (1413-1421) was the one who prevailed and succeeded in restoring the unity of the Ottoman state.

Not only the resilience of the Ottoman state was remarkable, but so was the fact that throughout the defeat by Timur and their internal conflicts, the Byzantines and other Balkan countries failed to take advantage of the existing favorable circumstances to liberate their lands. Turks attribute this indifference to the satisfaction of Balkan peoples with the Ottoman rule and order, and in particular the system of land ownership they introduced, that was more progressive than the pre-existing order in the Balkans. This is, of course, not accurate – the Balkan states and Byzantium were utterly powerless to attempt anything, there was neither the sentiment nor the financial means, while Venetians and Genoese or other Balkan countries shared no common interests to undertake any action against the Ottomans. The promotion of this view, however, demonstrated an aspect of Ottomans' attributes; that their success was not only due to their strength but also to their good administration and organization. Turkish historians, however, believe that Byzantium missed out on a unique opportunity to extend its survival for a few more decades, at least.

On the other hand, at that time, of the sixty-seven Metropolitan Sees that were dependent on the Patriarchate of Constantinople, just eight remained within the confines of possessions of the Emperor of Byzantium, and seven others of the Despotate of Morea. The rest of the Metropolitan Sees not only were in Ottoman territories, but the Greek population there had been decimated through enslavement and Islamizations (often voluntarily) that led to Turkification. The Emperor had lost his power, and the Patriarchate felt that it should be very cautious regarding its jurisdiction in ecclesiastical matters.

The former territories of Byzantium

The gradual predominance of Turkmens, in the three centuries before the Fall of Constantinople, had been disastrous for Hellenism-Christianity in Asia Minor. The Byzantines failed to repel them in time, nor impose any threshold beyond which any new advancement would be intolerable. After all, the homeland of the Turkmens in Central Asia no longer existed; they had come to Anatolia to conquer it and settle there. The Byzantines did not realize the magnitude of the danger that threatened them, and it seems that they did not make a rational assessment of the graveness of the situation.

After the initial looting, the mass slaughter of the residents of the cities that resisted, and the sale of Greeks-Christians as slaves, the Muslim Turks had now asserted their power over the Christian inhabitants of Anatolia. At the same time, as conquerors, they imposed their customs, their language, and sometimes their religion, most often as a result of the historical fact that "the vanquished always wants to imitate the victorious in all its characteristic customs and habits" and that "the nation that has been defeated and found itself under the rule of another nation quickly vanishes".[44] Even though it did not materialize in all cases, nor was it a universal phenomenon, it seems that it occurred quite often in the former Byzantium and particularly in the eastern provinces that remained for many centuries under Turkish Muslim domination.

Although Ottomans did not proceed to mass Islamizations in Anatolia, they did seek to convert

---

[44] Spyros Vryonis: Ibid., p.360.

Christians because Islam regarded proselytism as a virtue. Thus, they converted most churches into mosques and prevented the advent of bishops from Constantinople to their provinces. Thereby, the Christian inhabitants felt isolated, far from the center that could provide them moral support.

Byzantines who possessed a weak national conscience were assimilated mainly by Islamization, followed by Turkification, while many city dwellers that were not immediately Islamized nevertheless changed their everyday language to Turkish.[45] Finally, many Byzantines under Ottoman occupation converted to Islam and embraced the Turkish language. Yet other Greeks in Anatolia, especially in Cappadocia in the center and Pontos in the north (Black Sea), by virtue of their Christian religion, managed for centuries to maintain their Greek conscience, though not always their language.

The proportion of Muslims and Christians in Anatolia was overwhelmingly in favor of the former and only in the 18th and 19th centuries, as a result of migrations mainly from the Greek islands of the Aegean, there was some increase in the number of Greeks there, along with a small reduction of the Turkish population, as Turks chose military life instead of family. However, when the Ottoman state threatened Byzantium, very few Byzantines were left within the former territories of the Empire to warrant a massive pan-European effort to be liberated. The same could also be said with regards to the Greek Revolution at the beginning of the 19th century. That is why no major revolutionary venture had been planned and undertaken in Anatolia.

In the era of Sultan Murad I (1362 - 1389), the image of the Ottoman state was influenced by the fact that its size had quintupled and had become the most

---

[45] Spyros Vryonis: Ibid., p 311-355.

potent power in Southeast Europe. The Ottoman state was transformed into one resembling an empire, and Murad I himself, through his character, personified this change. He fancied grandiosity and etiquette, and he saw himself as an emperor. The ascetic life of the sultans – warriors, was abandoned. Murad was, of course, rigid, even cruel sometimes, but he could also be generous. He always wanted to be fair and was very demanding in matters of discipline. This is how the persona of the Ottoman state had taken shape just before the Fall of Constantinople (1453). The defeat by Timur was quickly forgotten. Mehmed II, the Conqueror (Fatih), felt strong enough to attempt to accomplish what his ancestors could not achieve. Constantinople was not a real obstacle for the Ottoman state, politically it was just a thorn, but in the reverie of the Ottomans, it was an old dream of greatness.

With the Fall of Constantinople in 1453, although little changed at a substantive level, much was transformed in the political and psychological facet. The Fall and the subsequent fleeing of Byzantine scholars to Western Europe signaled the start of the Renaissance. The Ottoman state would now become an empire, heir, to Byzantine only in the geographical sense, of course, despite some Turkish theories on the succession of the two Empires. The Fall would also mark the milestone of the start of the conquest of Greece. The Byzantines could not comprehend that the state was based on their existence and instead gave priority to their political quarreling. They also failed to focus on confronting the common adversary, while certain factions kept their distance from the state. Thus, they were destined to live in slavery. Byzantine Emperor Constantine Paleologos emerged as a heroic personality of medieval Hellenism who, with his bold attitude in defense of Constantinople during the Fall,

43

contributed to the shaping and consolidation of the idea of the Greek nation in its modern form.

Fatih Mehmed presented the Fall as a timeless victory of the Muslim Arabs and Turks, commemorating the Arabs who had died in previous sieges of Constantinople by naming city districts after them. He feared the organization of a crusade by the Catholics for the recapture of Constantinople. Thus, in addition to crediting the victory to Islam in general, he considered it appropriate to restore Constantinople's Orthodox (anti-Latin) character, reinstating Greek inhabitants and the older doctrine of their faith. This also signified his perception that the ancient inhabitants of Constantinople were a different nation, unlike the western Romans, who spoke another language and believed in another religious doctrine. A few years after the Fall of Constantinople, Greece, except for the islands of Rhodes, Crete, and Cyprus, was occupied.

The situation on the western side of the Ottoman Empire was different than the eastern Anatolian side. The Aegean divided the Empire into two regions with different histories. If the Turkish conquest of Anatolia began formally after the defeat in Manzikert in 1071, the conquest of ancient historical Greece was realized in more than three centuries later, in another era. The circumstances of the relocation of Turkmens - Turks in the area were also different. It was no longer the nomads, who were looking to settle anywhere, but it necessitated incentives. Beyond coercion or the provision of command positions and land, the Sultans had no other incentives to offer. Moreover, the Sultan now wanted to collect the increased taxes paid by Christians and did not favor Islamizations. The demographic parameter, essential for the final historical conclusion of sovereignty, worked in favor of the Greeks. From another point of view, the

44

Turkish conquest of the Balkans was not as long-lasting and repetitive as in Asia Minor, and the Christian communities in the Balkans had not been cut off from the church leadership for an extended period. The Patriarchate, which after 1453 was within the territory of the Ottoman State, had much greater power over the conquered than in the previous period when it was in the Byzantine Empire, and the Church at the time was perceived as an enemy by the Turkmen states.[46]

The local administrative institutions of the Ottoman Empire were different on the two sides of the Aegean. On the western side, because of the demographic superiority of the Greeks and the indifference of the Sultan to deal with issues that did not fall within the military or sovereign sphere, the system was somewhat more tolerable. The middle, Constantinople and its surroundings, was a unique case; it was neither Anatolia nor exactly "Greek land", and it was, after all, the capital of the Ottoman state. With Patriarchate having its base there and the prominent and robust presence of the Greeks, along with the tolerance of the sultans, a one-of-a-kind Ottoman capital city took shape, where Christians excelled. By then, shortly after the Fall, Greeks began becoming aware of their ethnicity. In the conscience of the enslaved, the idea of the emancipation of the nation with its central theme of liberating Constantinople took root.

The administration in the Ottoman Empire

The head of the Ottoman administrative system was the Sultan with an advisory and executive body, the Divan-i Humayun, led by the Sadrazam, the European Prime minister's counterpart but with

---

[46] Spyros Vrionis: Ibid., p. 439.

much less authority since the system was authoritarian under the Sultan. The Ulema (wise men) constituted a second instrument of the central administration, exercised the judiciary, controlled the education, and "interpreted" the sacred laws. The Mufti, the religious leader, was responsible for confirming the compatibility of executive orders, including the ones by sultans (Fetva), with the Sharia.

In short, the Ottoman administration and the "Ministry of Foreign Affairs" are being referred to as Sublime Porte (Bab-i Ali, High Gate) or only Gate and in colloquial Greek, just "Porta (door)".

In the second level of administration, civil and military, there was the Sandjak (county), where matters relating to taxes and services were regulated. Subservient to Sandjak were the Kaza and Nahiye. In some instances, there were broader forms of the Sandjak, such as Beylerbeyliks and Eyalets, that incorporated several Sandjaks. The head of administrative units was the Vali (Prefect), while the judiciary was exercised by the Kadi that judged the cases under the Islamic law, although the rule of the Sultan usually prevailed.[47] The administrative system of the Ottoman Empire did not remain the same throughout its existence but changed and evolved, with only a constant, the absolute domination of the Sultan.

The organization of the Ottomans

Any land conquered by the Ottomans was the property of the Sultan, who distributed it to the warriors as compensation for their services, as well to

---

[47] The Muslim Presence in Epirus and Western Greece: (http://earthlab.uoi.gr/escutis/Books/ESCUTIS_Greece_study.pdf) (Last access 03/09/2020) p.p. 288-289

his favored. These concessions, the timars,[48] encompassed all kinds of private or public income. Within the timar system, the state gave timariots, including the cavalryman, the authorization to have control of arable lands cultivated by local villagers in bondage. In return, the timariot had the duty of safeguarding order in his region and collecting taxes. At the same time, the timar system provided the Sultan in the event of war, which often happened, armed horsemen. Also, the Sultan, who was deemed to be the sole owner of all land, had the discretion of selling feudal-timariotic privileges of landowning. At any rate, the timariotic system in the Ottoman Empire was different than the feudal system in Europe, mainly because Turkish timariots' power was limited and less burdensome to the villagers, and only existed to the extent that it was tolerated and allowed by the Sultan.

Thus, in Anatolia and Rumeli, most of the fertile plains passed to the Ottomans, either in the form of full ownership or in the form of timars. Another segment of the land and structures were allocated to religious institutions. Christian farmers worked for the owner or the timariot under a unique serfdom regime. Initially, during the period of conquest, the Ottomans abolished the serfdom regime of the Byzantines, facilitating the subordination to them. Later, they relocated Christian populations, along with some Muslim people, to regions in Rumeli. The Christians that settled in Muslim estates as particular serfs were later freed formally with the Seri law. The petty military timariots were mainly interested in collecting taxes and less in the profitability of their estate. The land left to the Christians was mostly mountainous. On

---

[48] A timar was land granted by the Ottoman Sultans between the fourteenth and sixteenth centuries, with a tax revenue annual value of less than 20 000 akche.

the other hand, the Ottoman administration, for mainly political reasons, did not confiscate the property of the Christian monasteries, which thus could afford to contribute to the development of the Greek nation's education. [49]

The Ottoman economy was based on agricultural production, the work of free farmers, and shepherds. The rural community, within the framework of the Ottoman-era timariotic system, served a crucial operational mission though with limited autonomy and self-government.[50] The roots of the community system of Christians could be traced to the Byzantine era. The Ottomans had no particular interest in changing a socio-economic system that was already operating in a productive way beneficial to them. The independent community was structurally tied to the "oriental way of production" not exclusively within the system of the Turkish feudalism, in contrast to the Christian landowner who operated in the context of a timar type approach.[51] After the 16th century, the timars were transformed into estates, with full ownership, and the ties of the owner with the farmers became feudal. The reason for the concession of decentralized administrative powers was the inability of the central authority to command the vast empire. This system had allowed the creation of a self–governed body for the collection of taxes.[52] Gradually the local Ottoman commanders would gain more power, prompting the central authority to take measures against them.

Already in the Balkans, since the 15th century, there had been resettlements of Christian

---

[49] N. Svoronos: A survey of the history of contemporary Greece (in Greek).

[50] A. Vakalopoulos: History of the new Hellenism, 1964 (in Greek).

[51] V. Filias: Society and power in Greece. 1. The Forged Urbanization 1800-1864, 1974, p. 21 (in Greek).

[52] The Muslim Presence in Epirus and Western Greece, p. 295.

populations among regions of the Empire as well as from the ottoman-occupied areas in the Balkans to areas under the control of European Catholic States. They were sometimes permanent, sometimes temporary, sometimes legal, but usually uncontrolled, and involved many people.[53] Greeks in growing numbers resettled in mountainous areas, and this trend continued within the 17th century. The reason for these movements was the need to move away from the Muslim inhabited centers of cities and also avoid the large taxes imposed on farmers.[54] The percentage of land ownership of Christians in mountainous areas was considerably greater than in the plains dominated by Muslims. Mountainous communities developed a self-sufficient economy with agricultural and craft production. The inaccessibility of regular Ottoman troops to mountainous territory provided them a setting for some autonomy and safeguard of their nationality and traditions.

The Balkans of the time was an impoverished region, and the food produced locally was not adequate. The villagers, however, avoided trading with money and preferred self-sustenance with some bartering, wherever and whenever needed. Economic characteristics of the community were self-sufficiency, self-consumption, low degree of the money economy, and small commercialization.[55] But the non-monetary economy had both social and individual ramifications. Personal moral issues were established as central values. The notion of social solidarity and goodwill, honesty, and trustworthiness were considered not only individual virtues but the

---

[53] The Muslim Presence in Epirus and Western Greece, p.293.
[54] K. Moskof: National and social conscience in Greece, 1972 (in Greek).
[55] V. Filias: Ibid., p. 14.

necessary lubricant for the functioning of the socio-economic mechanism.

Gradually, as time passed, the era of the currency exchange began, an early form of capitalism emerged, as did the organization of a contemporary Ottoman state. The poor Christian villagers were confronted by both the landowners and the central administration of the Ottoman state, which, using new methods, collected taxes more efficiently. From that perspective, one could reason the emergence of mass nationalism in the Balkans in the context of these dramatic economic and social developments.[56] Nevertheless, the driving force here could not be attributed to a spontaneous class consciousness but to the desire to liberate the oppressed nations against an authoritarian Ottoman administration.

The Rums - Greeks according to the Turks

The Byzantines at the time of their confrontation with the Turkmens mostly considered themselves Romans and Christians. The schism and the crusade against them, but also the prevalence of the Greek language over Latin, distinguished them from the Western Christians. After all, the Catholics considered them as heretics at a time when religion meant almost everything. With today's standards, Byzantine Greeks would be characterized as Greeks who belonged in the same present-day nation while considering themselves different from ancient Greeks. At the time, they did not think that they constituted their continuity and did not in any way want to be affiliated with the name "Greek" that they associated with paganism. The retrogression of the word Rum and Rumeli, used by the Turks to name various regions in Anatolia and Greece together with the

---

[56] Mark Mazower: The Balkans, 2000, p. 39.

Byzantine Roman, resulted in the coinage of Rum in Turkish and Romios in Greek for the Greeks under the Ottoman Empire.

Rums, according to Turks, are remnants of the ancient civilizations of Anatolia, who adopted the Greek language and the Orthodox religion during the period of Byzantine rule, namely the Eastern Roman Empire. The inaccuracy, among others, of this Turkish perception, lies in the word "adopted", as these ancient civilizations of Anatolia were almost in their entirety already Greek from a previous era that dated back even before the classical period of ancient Greek civilization, to its creation of which they had contributed.

According to another Turkish historical point of view, the idea of Hellenism began with the idea of being Romios. In relation to the Hellenism of northern Greece and Peloponnese, Rums constituted a broader community covering western Anatolia, the Greek islands, and various places of Roumeli (i.e., in Thrace and the Balkans), while both were completely lacking racial unity and the whole community of the Rums-Greeks was a unity exclusively of language and religion (sic). The theory could have been enhanced if they had made references to the common culture, morals, and religious traditions as well as the perception of the common sharing of their fate. The concept of the nation here does not insinuate any racist – racial overtones and bears no association with the birthplace of the people who constitute it. According to the Turkish viewpoint, Byzantium was not an exclusively Greek state but consisted of tribes of Anatolia, which were integrated into the context of Christendom. It, therefore, expressed the culture of Anatolia. Nevertheless, the West considered that, at least during the last centuries of its existence, Byzantium was a Greek country.

On the other hand, the long coexistence of Turkmens with Islamized Greeks, quasi barbarians and Balkan peoples as well as remnants of ancient Anatolian civilizations, led to the creation of a "new race", the modern Turkish nation, with features rather European and Balkan than central-Asian. According to Jacques Ancel, the term Ottoman or Turkish refers to individuals whose only common characteristic is Islam.[57] Eugène Pittard, on the other hand, points out that even ancient Greeks had no ethnic homogeneity. However, any discussion of racial characteristics is devoid of any substantive content that could produce results. Nations are determined by their common language, common culture, and history, often their shared religion and their inherited historical character, but primarily by their awareness of a community of fate. In this sense, the personality of the Ottoman-Turkish state was not altered but simply evolved.

The period of regression

The long period of expansion of the Ottoman Empire was followed by a period of stagnation that eventually wound up with a period of regression. The period of retrogression is considered, to begin with, the Karlowitz Agreement (1699) signed between the Ottoman Empire and the "Holy Alliance" (in this case, Austria, Venice, Poland, and Russia) after the defeat suffered by the forces of the Ottoman Empire in Zenta. It ended with the agreement of Yash signed between the Ottomans and Russia in January of 1792, which established the borders between the two empires.

After many years of decline and regression, the Ottoman Empire during Selim III (1789 – 1807)

---

[57] Though not all Muslims in the Ottoman Empire were Turks.

initiated a notable effort to modernize the scientific, political and military sectors, having Europe and especially Austria as a model. Based on the organization of the Austrian Army, its military academies, the training of officers, etc., a new army corps was created, which was called Nizam-i Cedid (New Order). The backlash from regressive politicians and Janissaries who rebelled in 1808 resulted in the abdication of Selim. The throne was seized by Mustafa IV (1807 – 1808). The new army corps was disbanded, and progressive politicians were punished. The victory of the conservatives lasted only a few months. In 1808, Mahmud II (1808 – 1839) came to the throne and responded with ferocity to a series of uprisings and revolutions in the Balkans.

Despite the period of regression, the Ottoman Empire was not a weak state. More or less, it succeeded in impeding the Russian aspirations militarily and suppressing revolutions such as that of the Serbs, of Ali Pasha of Ioannina, or even the Revolution of Ypsilantis in the Balkan Principalities. It was this Ottoman Empire, with some weaknesses, yet vast and powerful that the Greek Revolution had to face. The Revolution did not take place against a state powerless to react.

Kavalalı Mehmet Ali

The political rise of Mehmet Ali is a consequence of the Ottoman decline. When French troops withdrew from Egypt in 1798, Khurshid Ahmet Pasha took over an official post in Alexandria. With the support of Kavalalı Mehmet Ali, a man of significant influence in Egypt, Khurshid was appointed Prefect of the Province of Egypt. But Khurshid was seeking extraordinary powers in Egypt, and Mehmet Ali was in his way. To oust him along with the Albanian Janissaries who were loyal to

Mehmed Ali, he made arrangements with the representative of Britain in Egypt and brought from Syria mercenary corps, the so-called "Deli". However, Mehmet Ali succeeded in joining forces with them, and with the help of the Oulemas, traders and trade unions, declared himself Prefect of Egypt in May of 1805, in Cairo. Khurshid, isolated, was compelled to withdraw to Cairo fort. The Sublime Porte acknowledged with a decree the fait accompli of Mehmet Ali and Khurshid was forced to leave Egypt. He would re-appear later in the Balkans.

Mehmed Ali, as Egypt's ruler, although formally under the authority of the Sultan, was virtually autonomous. After consolidating his power, Mehmet Ali embarked on a series of administrative, agricultural, industrial, and above all, military reforms, attempting to create a modern western type state, an "empire" that would overshadow and perhaps conquer the staggering Ottoman Empire. At the end of the Napoleonic Wars, peace in Europe allowed the Egyptian commander to purchase many surplus weapons and order several ships from British shipyards at a bargain price. These purchases came from a ruthless and rigid tax policy that impoverished the poor, furthermore compelling farmers to become soldiers.

For the organization of his army, Mehmet Ali employed European officers as trainers. Officers of different nationalities, mostly French veterans of the "Great Army of Napoleon", but also Italians and Spaniards, sought military work in Egypt of Mehmet Ali. The social origins and the motives for the enlistment of these officers displayed a great variety, from fanatical Bonapartists with an uncertain future in monarchical France to simple adventurers. In 1824, France of Bourbons, trying to secure a dynamic new ally in the eastern Mediterranean and restore its prestige as a great power, formally joined forces with

54

Egypt. A regular French military unit was integrated with the French officers that had earlier joined the Ottoman – Egyptian army. And all these took place when Mehmet Ali's army was already in Peloponnese and was fighting against the revolting Greeks.

The Turkish narrative on the Revolution

The official Turkish historiography traditionally tended to downplay the significance of the Greek Revolution in contributing to the subsequent developments with which the Ottoman Empire lost territories in the Balkan Peninsula. This course of events was not attributed to the Greek Revolution but more broad foreign elements. However, the contemporary academic approach of Turkish historians regarding the reasons and the international context of the Greek Revolution has taken a turn towards an analysis more consistent with the objective consideration of historical events, reflecting to a large extent the relative reduction of the influence of the nationalist political parameter of the Kemalist period.

According to the contemporary Turkish historiography, the turn of the 18th to the 19th century was important for both Europe and the Ottoman Empire. The reclassification influenced the old European empires and ushered the process for founding nation-states. Most notably, it affected the Austro-Hungarian, Russian and Ottoman Empires, which suffered not only territorial losses but also constitutional and identity changes. [58]

---

[58] Mehmet Seyitdanlıoglu: The Greek Revolution and the politics of Mahmud II, University of Hacettepe. (in Turkish).
http://journals.manas.edu.kg/mjsr/oldarchives/Vol06_Issue12_20 04/396.pdf (Last access 03/09/2020) (in Turkish).

Among the first empires impacted was the Ottoman. The Ottoman Empire, with a territorial extension from North Africa to the Caucasus and from the Balkans to the Middle East, and with a multinational population of perhaps around 30 million, had realized its vulnerabilities, but international developments prevented its reform efforts. Sultan Selim III (1789 - 1807) had planned a reform process (Nizam-ı Cedid, new order), which was halted after the uprising against him. Mahmud II (1808 - 1839), who ascended to the throne after a year of unrest, was confronted with both the need for comprehensive reform of the state and external challenges that were not only territorial but also political. In dealing with them, he had neither proper state machinery nor a dependable organized army.

From the point of view of the Turks, the agreement of Kaynarca of 1774, signed with Russia following the Turkish defeat, had a crucial role regarding the launch of the independence movements of the Christian minorities under the Ottoman domination, starting with the Greeks. This agreement marks the beginning of the dissolution of the Empire, with Russia taking on the role of guardian of the Orthodox populations and leading the process for the independence of Greece.[59] As a result, still according to Turkish sources, the Greeks were instrumental in introducing the European values of enlightenment to the Ottoman territories, and to its integration, to a certain degree, in the social life of various parts of the Empire. The clause in the Kaynarca agreement with which the Rums were enabled to trade in the Black Sea under the Russian flag created a strong Rum urban class. The distinctions that prevailed in the Ottoman Empire allowed the rich Rums to have direct

---

[59] Oral Sander: History of the Ottoman Diplomacy (in Turkish).

exposure to the European currents that promoted national independence.

During the Ottoman domination, the cultural and economic center of Rums was Constantinople (renamed Istanbul in the 20th century). In the opinion of the Turks, Rums, given the rights accorded to them by the Ottoman State, were the nation least inclined to rebel. This was because of the unique socio-political structure that the Rums enjoyed over other nationalities, as the "nation" of the Orthodox Rums had always held a special place in the internal system of the Ottoman Empire. Thus, even though only Muslims were allowed to take up duties in the administration of the Ottoman state, the Sublime Porte assigned political tasks to Rums, such as the interpreter of the Court and the Voivode of Wallachia and Moldavia. Among other privileges, Rums also enjoyed economic prosperity.

The Rum Patriarch represented all the Christian Orthodox communities of the Empire, while Phanariotes took up the positions of Great Interpreter, in Divan-i Humayun, and of the fleet as well as ruler in Moldavia and Wallachia, acceding to the Ottoman Political elite, without having to change their religion. In any case, Phanariotes were members of the Ottoman bureaucracy, along with whatever this notion entailed.

The Rums, the largest nation after the Muslims in the Ottoman Empire, lived in western Anatolia, the capital Constantinople, the islands of the Aegean, and Morea, the southernmost part of the Balkans and prevailed over the other Christian nations of the Empire. Their main occupation was agriculture and maritime trade. The wealthy Rums sent their children to study in Europe, and through them, France disseminated the principles of nationalism to the Rums of the Ottoman Empire, who enjoyed the freedom of language, religion, and trade.

57

Rums were also supported by Russia, which harbored aspirations of reinstating the Byzantine Empire.

Rums contributed significantly to the development of the Ottoman economy. In particular, during the 18th century, they held the reins of the Ottoman maritime trade in Europe, southern Russia, and the Mediterranean. They sold agricultural products and raw materials to Europe and imported processed products for the Empire. Consequently, a wealthy class of Rums that possessed significant capital was created. Meanwhile, Rum villagers held small areas where they cultivated traditional Mediterranean agricultural products, but their economic situation, like most of the people in the Empire, was not adequate. In addition, they were also oppressed by local Ottoman officials and crushed under heavy taxation. Because of these, theft was widespread among them, while in the islands, there were Rums that resorted to piracy. These social thieves "Kleftes" were among the first to join the revolutionary forces.

As such, the Greek-Rum population of the Empire consisted of three classes: Phanariotes, interpreters, constituents of Patriarchate in general; wealthy Rum merchants, shipowners, and landowners; city dwellers, members of various trade unions, and the relatively poor villagers who dealt with agriculture as well as the ordinary seamen.

The Ottoman Empire did not grasp in time the significance of the French Revolution of 1789, interpreting it as a European internal affair.[60] It never crossed the minds of the reformists but authoritarian Sultans Selim III and Mahmud II that its

---

[60] A.K Ypsilantis, who was part of the Ottoman bureaucracy, in his book "After the Fall" does not recount a single sentence on French Revolution even though he narrates seven pages for the year 1789.

repercussions could impact the Empire, as they were also preoccupied with the internal affairs of the state. This apathy helped the Balkan countries to pursue their goals.[61] The first (sic) solid strike came from Peloponnese as the nationalistic currents and independence movements of Balkan nations, inspired by the French Revolution, began to shake the foundations of the Empire.

Poets, writers, and intellectuals such as Rigas and Korais communicated the desire for an independent and constitutional Greece. Rums, whose model was also followed later by the Young Turks, founded secret associations that triggered the spark of the Revolution. Among these, the Friendly Society, founded in Odessa in 1814, was the most important. Its aspirations stretched beyond the independence of Rums to the rest of the Balkan nations.[62] The Friendly Society, from 1814 to 1821, succeeded in creating a strong independence movement among Kleftes, Greek peasants, merchants, priests, and intellectuals.

As the French Revolution was the work of the bourgeoisie born after social and economic developments, thus the revolutionary movements in Greece were, in part, the work of Rum traders and intellectuals who early in the 19th century had made significant progress. In particular, the uprising in Peloponnese that was far from the administrative center of Constantinople succeeded because of the support and assistance provided by the European states in the fields of diplomacy, military, and finance.

---

[61] The moniker of the Friendly Society for the Sultan, as the "indifferent", was obviously no coincidence.
[62] This Turkish historiography misleads, perhaps intentionally, by alleging that the Society's honorary head was Czar Alexander A´, either believing in what the Friendly Society was then propagating deliberately, or it was using history as a prop in contemporary politics.

59

The European Order of 1814, which ultimately also included the Ottoman Empire, with the political, diplomatic, and intellectual terms it introduced, contributed to creating the settings for the emergence of the Greek revolutionary propensities. The Concert of Europe (Concert Européen), with main supporters Austria-Hungary and Russia, viewed the idea of traditional multinational empires as dominant and opposed the views emanating from the French Revolution on national statehood and nationalism. Britain and France, while respecting the emerging European order, participated in the European balance of power as rather liberal forces. Concerning the Ottoman Empire, the Eastern Question had been resolved in favor of maintaining its territorial integrity at the time, with main supporters of this position being Britain and Austria-Hungary.

However, the viewpoints of the European public opinion and intellectuals differed. The roots of European civilization were attributed to ancient Greece, and their admiration for it was reflected in their support for the Greek Revolution. In various European countries, therefore, committees were established for funding the Revolution, while volunteer groups were heading to Peloponnese to join the fighting. Public opinion in Britain, France, Russia, and Prussia was ready to accept the idea and supported the independence of a Greek state. The framework for the commencement of not just a rebellion but a real revolution had been laid down.

Collectively, the causes of the Greek Revolution according to contemporary Turkish historians are the nationalistic ideas born in the French Revolution; the Panslavistic Balkan policy of Russia that sought to descend "to warm seas"; the void created by the abolition of the Order of the Janissaries (although this occurred after the initial outbreak of the Revolution); the efforts toward the organization of the Revolution by the Friendly Society; the will of the Greeks to implement the Great Idea;[63] the resolve of the European States to yield to the descendants of ancient Greece their independence;[64] and finally, the upheaval caused by the rebellion of the Prefect of Ioannina, Tepedelenli Ali Pasha.[65]

Despite the failure of the Revolutionary movements in Moldavia, the Revolution in Morea spread quickly with the help of Europeans. From the Turkish point of view, the Greeks had emerged as the spoiled child of Europe. They were seen as the "children of the Ancient Greeks", with the Revolution being welcomed with great interest by Europe. When the initial maneuvers for independence in Peloponnese began, the Ottoman administration of Constantinople saw the event as a matter of internal public order which could be settled by military means. Possibly, the failure of the revolutionary movement of Alexander Ypsilantis that preceded the Revolution in Peloponnese contributed to this conviction. Mahmud II and the high bureaucracy of the Sublime Porte initially regarded the events as a mere insurrection and called it "Rum's Unrest" (Rum fessadı). Yet, this was not an ordinary uprising, but an innovative nationalistic movement reflecting the change in the social, economic, and political balances of the Balkans, that was under the command of an

---

[63] That is the rebirth of the Byzantine Empire.

[64] Perhaps by specific individuals but certainly not by states.

[65] It could be discerned that these same causes that the Turks are referring to, led the modern Turkish state of the 20th century, in taking stark measures against the religious freedom of Greeks of Constantinople, with restrictions on construction and repair of churches, in the field of education with restrictions of the Greek curriculum and strict controls in Greek schools, in the use of language with the campaign "compatriot speak Turkish", and with restrictions in owning property (including the property tax during WWII).

authoritarian state. After the growth of the movement and the interventions of Europeans, Ottomans began to refer to it as the "Greek issue" (Mes'ele-i Yunaniyye) and "Greek Revolution".

The Ottoman administration, from 1821 to 1829, had set the Greek Revolution as the first item on its agenda. However, at the same time, Mahmud II, in the context of his reform process, perceived as the main issue the strengthening of the central authority along with his own, by way of neutralizing the various local leaders in the Empire who harbored leadership ambitions. This program of "reforms" concluded with the execution of the Prefect of Ioannina Tepedelenli Ali Pasha. Sultan Mahmud initially had not realized the magnitude of Tepedelenli Ali's influence on the region's administration and preservation of the Ottoman order there, as well as the degree of threat of the Greek Revolution to the Empire. He resorted to traditional military methods such as the execution of rebel leaders, thinking that in this way he could suppress the uprising. Among the measures he considered appropriate was the hostage-taking of a member from the children and relatives of eminent Greek families in the rebel areas and their transfer to Constantinople for one year. The measure was applied between 1821 and 1827, and 22 persons were detained in Constantinople's Bostancıbası neighborhood. The measure failed to produce any results and was withdrawn by Sultan's decree.

The "Revolution of Rums" was not led exclusively by Ottoman ordinary subjects but also sometimes by Phanariotes appointed to the Ottoman administration. This angered the Ottoman Muslims who, besides persecuting the Rums of Constantinople they massacred many Rums, especially in the Greek islands, as well as hierarchs in Constantinople. Persecutions against Rums also took place in

Anatolia, but they ceased after the hanging of the Patriarch (according to Turkish sources).

Based on Turkish narratives, after the eruption of the Revolution, the only power that clearly supported the Ottoman Empire was Austria. Prussia, Britain, and Spain were neutral, while Russia and France favored the independence of the Greeks (sic). The Greeks, under the command of the British Generals Lord Cochrane and Sir Richard Church, were defeated by the Egyptian army of Mehmet Ali Pasha, who had been promised to take over the prefectures of Peloponnese and Crete. The Ottoman – Egyptian victories ended abruptly on October 20, 1827, with the "tragedy of Navarino". The Allied fleet of Britain – France – Russia entered the port of Navarino, where the Ottoman fleet was moored, and without raising a war flag, opened fire and destroyed it (sic). In response to the Ottoman request for compensation, the three allies countered with the demand for Greece's independence. When the Ottomans rejected this request, France and Britain answered through "diplomatic means" while Russia declared war on the Ottomans. Russia handily defeated the Ottomans, reaching as far as Edirne. At the same time, Mahmud II was deprived of his fleet, and the new army he had organized after the decimation of the Janissaries was not ready for war.

Nevertheless, the naval Battle of Navarino caused by a random event did not suffice for the liberation of Greece. The defeat by the Russians of the new Ottoman military corps that had just been created along with the agreement of Edirne in 1829, ultimately forced the Ottomans to acquiesce to Greece's independence.

The views of the Sultan and the executives of the Ottoman administration for the Phanariotes and the Patriarchate changed radically after the Revolution. The Muslim public opinion of

63

Constantinople also turned against the Patriarchate. The Phanariotes who served in Ottoman bureaucracy were accused of being traitors, including those who did not participate either in the Revolution or as members of the Friendly Society. Most of them were fired from the government, and those who were considered guilty were executed.

The Turkish historiography admits that these were political executions. After that, no administrative posts were assigned to Rums save for a few exceptions.[66] Mahmud II established at the Ministry of Foreign Affairs a translation office and set up a diplomatic service that he could trust.[67] This service is the one that drafted the reforms of the Tanzimat (Reform) period. After 1829, the Rums of Anatolia and Constantinople evaded attacks against them but were kept away from the Ottoman bureaucracy and engaged mainly with commerce.

Patriarch Gregory V was judged guilty because of the letters of Alexandros Ypsilantis that (supposedly) had been found in his office (sic), despite the ex-communications he had issued against all those who had participated in the Revolution. According to the historian Ahmet Cevdet Pasha, Ottomans maintained the view that the act of ex-communication was issued to disguise his betrayal. In any case, Sultan Mahmud concluded that the Patriarch, who was the leader and shepherd of the Rums, was responsible for the fact that the Rums had rebelled. From there on, although the Patriarchate continued to maintain its influence upon its orthodox

---

[66] In essence, they did not concede only the governor positions to Moldavia and Vlachia and the Interpreter of the court.
[67] Therefore, the employment of Greek Phanariotes was no longer required.

flock, it had lost the trust and esteem it had in the Palace court.[68]

According to Turkish historians, feelings of sympathy and support for the Revolution from the Patriarchate and Phanariotes should be considered logical. But it could also be said that because of their fears that this situation could have an impact on their administrative, economic, and social positions in Constantinople, to a certain degree, they had kept their distance from the Revolution. On the other hand, the radical decisions of Mahmud II, such as the execution of Tepedelenli Ali Pasha of Ioannina are criticized from a diplomatic point of view, has led to a greater resolution for both the rebels as well as the public opinion in Europe for the necessity of the creation of a Greek kingdom, independent from the Ottoman Empire. Indeed, the truth, according to the Turkish historians themselves, is that the Sultan, with the help of his vassal in Egypt, Kavalalı Mehmed Ali Pasha, had previously been successful in suppressing the Revolution to a large extent.

Finally, after the "raid" of the Navarino in 1827 and the crushing defeat of the Ottoman army in the war with Russia 1828 - 1829, Sultan Mahmud was forced to grant independence to the Greek kingdom. Thus, began the dissolution of the Ottoman Empire; a nation became a state due to the ideas of the French Revolution, and soon after, the conquest of Algeria by France resulted in part of the Empire becoming a colony of a European state. The situation with Egypt, due to the Greek Revolution and the aspirations of Mehmed Ali, created a significant problem that

---

[68] With regards to this Turkish historical observation, it could be argued that, if the (wretched) behavior of the Turks up to then reflected the "trust" of the Sultan to the Patriarchs, then the Patriarchate, with all the persecutions it had suffered, must not have given up much with that "loss".

65

troubled Mahmud II for a long time. At any rate, the Greek Revolution was one of the events that shaped the personality of the Turkish state, which regarded Greece as a hostile entity from the outset, not without reciprocity of feelings.

The period of reforms

The Ottoman state exploited to a large extent the differences among the European States and, in particular, the rivalry of the West with Russia by following a policy of balances to ensure the continuity of the Empire. From the Europeans' point of view, adversaries or not, the Empire was referred to as the Great Patient, a moniker attributed by the Czar. Nevertheless, it was a patient too big to fail. The introduction of the reforms addressed the modernization of the Empire, but in so far as it concerned the rights of Christian minorities, they were imposed by Europeans, usually, not for the benefit of the Rums but as a way to eliminate the need for protection by Russia, that was of the same faith.

By the 17th century, the Ottoman Empire had realized that it had begun to weaken and that the great European States had surpassed it in all areas. In response to a series of defeats, the Ottoman leadership attempted to introduce some reforms. One of the most important among them, during the reign of Mahmud II, was the abolition of the Janissaries' body. This military branch, over time, had lost its status and turned into a hotbed of constant uprisings. It had become a state in its own right. They dethroned sultans, subverted politicians, and proceeded to killings of their opponents. Inebriated Janissaries terrorized the population of Constantinople by killing and seizing their belongings. People started abhorring them. Their constant attacks against intellectuals and scientists,

66

who were held in high regard, resulted in Janissaries being viewed as enemies of the people.

In the face of the Sultan's intention of establishing a new tactical corps of the army with a European education, the division of "Eskinci", the Janissaries rebelled considerable times. On June 15, 1826, they began demonstrations at the Byzantine hippodrome and attacked the Sublime Porte, seizing a significant amount of money. But the time was ripe. Sadrazam Selim Pasha brought together politicians and religious leaders, soldiers who were not part of the Janissaries as well as sailors, and announced that he would take on the Janissaries. State officials took to the streets, gathering people for this encounter. The Janissaries on their side warned their friends about the events with heralds. Sadrazam made the Sultanahmet mosque his headquarters and gave weapons to the people. The Janissaries, who held Bayezid Square when the conflict started, were forced to withdraw to the Hippodrome and closed the doors. The Sadrazam did not hesitate to open fire on them with cannons, breaking the doors. The mob swooped in, and the Janissaries fled to their camp. The batteries demolished the camp, and the leaders of the Janissaries corps were executed. Those who survived were sent to exile. In the Ottoman Empire, the enforcement of reforms usually entailed bloody clashes.

After the events ended, Mahmud II announced the dissolution of the Janissaries unit through a ferman.[69] With this, the source of several evils for the empire was eliminated. Prussian officers, working in the framework of the still lasting Turkish-German friendship, organized the new army named Asakir-I Mensurei Muhammediye. The new army, however,

---

[69] Written order of the Sultan

did not prove so effective on the battlefield when confronted with strong armies.

About a month after the massacre of the Janissaries, the religious order of the Bektashi that was guided by the same principles as Janissaries was outlawed. It was well known that the dervish Bektashis battalion was the one that had influenced the organization and style of the Janissaries. The significance of this double blow against a section of the army and its religious representatives in a state with a peculiar texture as the Ottoman signifies the determination of the Sultan to proceed to important reforms aiming at transforming the Empire into a modern state. The trials and tribulations of the Ottoman Empire in going through this reformation process demonstrate that the top-down approach to modernization is complicated. Nevertheless, the method was pursued persistently and systematically ever since. These events were taking place at a time when the Empire was confronting the Greek revolution, and during the period that Ibrahim was succeeding in Peloponnese and the Ottoman army dominated central Greece.

The reform in the Empire continued in 1829 with the imposition of the European suit and the European military uniform. The Fez replaced the chariques.[70] It was mandated for Muslims to wear red Fez and for Christians' black. However, women and priests were permitted to wear their traditional costumes. The westernization of Constantinople spread rapidly, starting in the district of Pera, a renowned Rum neighborhood and headquarters of many European embassies. In 1836, the Ottoman Empire established a Ministry of Foreign Affairs, in the western sense of the term. It was followed by the issuance of the reforms of Tanzimat at the Garden of

---

[70] Kind of head cover

Roses in 1839, guaranteeing the right to life for non-Muslim nationals of the Empire.

It could be argued that the founding of the Greek State allowed the Ottoman Empire to rid itself of the Greek burden. This empowered the Empire to take steps towards progress, to cooperate with the Western states and, by allowing the Rums in Constantinople, Rumeli, and Anatolia to develop their social, cultural, and economic affairs, it benefited itself. The Turkish historiography avoids highlighting this aspect of the revolution.

THE STATUS OF THE ENSLAVED GENUS

The status of the Greeks in the Ottoman Empire, in the early 19th century, was set both by the theocratic character of the Ottoman State and by the historical evolution of the presence of Greeks in the area. In this sense, the term "Rums" and not Greeks (Yunan) was coined, consistent with the terminology that was formed by the Ottomans in the region. Apart from these, the relationship between the subdued Christians and the sovereign Ottoman state was shaped, to a certain degree, by the very nature of the hawkish and invading character, and in that respect, the particular fabric of the Ottoman society.

The theocratic nature of the Ottoman Empire derives from Islam in which the Islamic way of life represents the spiritual life, culture, and social status of Arabs during the period of the birth of this religion. At the time of the inception of Islam in the periphery of the then known world where Arabs, who had just emerged from their nomadic stage lived, it was not possible to distinguish between state and religion. This was because of the coercive way Islam was generally imposed as well as because of the influence Islam exerted on neophytes that were stronger than any other existing political or social force.[71] According to Islam, as interpreted in early Ottoman times, religion and state were one and the same. Religion was the moral principle and strength, while the state could be interpreted as the administrative mechanism for its enforcement. The laws of the state were institutionalized according to the foundations of the holy book, the Quran, and were generally called Sharia. According to Muslim jurists, the state had no legislative capacity. God and only God could legislate,

---

[71] Bernard Lewis: The Arabs in History, Hutchinson University Library, 1968, p.40.

and his laws could be found in the Quran and the sermons of the Prophet that formed the Islamic political tradition.[72]

The Ottoman Empire, from its founding to almost its demise, had been an Islamic State, devoted to the task of advancing and spreading Islam at the outset, and defending it against non-believers, later on. The head of the Ottoman Empire was the head of Islam; its army was the army of Islam; its laws were the laws of Islam.[73] In such a theocratic state, the position of non-Muslims was problematic from the very start; the situation was made even worse because of the intolerance of the Islamic religion for non-Muslims. Indeed, the right to citizenship, according to Islam, was only reserved for Muslims, while non-Muslims should either not live there or, if this was politically not feasible, should not enjoy this right. However, Islam, according to its teachings, did not replace but supplemented Christianity and Judaism. Therefore, the faithful of these religions should be distinguished from the sheer infidels and pagans. Whereas against the latter two, a war till their extinction was imposed, the faithful of the religions of the Bible were allowed to live in a Muslim state as subjects, but under restrictive and degrading conditions.

This parallel coexistence of Muslims and non-Muslims in the theocratic Ottoman state posed a problem, concerning mainly the rules governing family law, but also a set of other laws. Sharia, the Holy Mohammedan Law, and at the same time, the civil and administrative rule, could not be applied to non-Muslims. Yet, once coexisting with Christians could not be avoided, it was necessary to recognize a

---

[72] Bernard Lewis: Istanbul and the civilization of the Ottoman Empire, Norman 1963.
[73] Paul Wittek: The birth of the Ottoman Empire.

72

specific civil and administrative framework to concede some limited, so to speak, autonomy. This way, several administrative and tax-collection problems were also resolved.

The Muslim Turks, during the Ottoman period, considered work to produce goods as an inferior occupation. Their primary mission -a task they considered not only noble but consistent with their religious imperatives- had always been the art of war. A consequence of this mentality, eventually leading to the economic and politico-military decline of the Ottoman Empire, was the need to rely on the work of the conquered to satisfy the financial requirements of the Empire. For the enslaved Greeks, compulsory unpaid labor, looting, and bribery (which was standard practice), should also be included in the notion of "taxation". These benefits of the rulers were the reason for the cessation of Islamizations, including the voluntary ones, in order not to reduce the source of "taxpayers".

In the medieval theocratic Ottoman state, where religion meant everything, it was natural that the main distinguishing feature of ethnic groups was their faith. Later on, the introduction of the "European concept of the nation" in the Ottoman Empire was bound to bring about a general reclassification in the underlying forces. But it should not be presumed that the concept of nation was utterly foreign to the Ottoman Empire. The Fall of Constantinople was realized by Muslims who had defeated not just Christians but also the Byzantine Greeks. The continuation of a "Greek nation", through their presence within the Ottoman Empire, was unacceptable to the Ottomans. Byzantine noblemen did not fare well as the Patriarchate; after being conned to get officially documented in a royalty book by the conqueror, Turks massacred them soon

73

after.[74] The message delivered with this act by the conqueror was clear. Tolerance existed for Christians under Ottoman rule, but not for a Greek nation and any political connotation pertaining to it. The supranational policy of the Patriarchate of Constantinople was not exclusively the choice of the clergy, but it was imposed by the conqueror.

In the early 19th century, the "state" of the religious community of Orthodox Christians, the nation (millet) of Rums, was represented by the Ecumenical Patriarch. This religious community encompassed not only Greeks but also Bulgarians, Serbs, Albanians in national conscience and language, as well as the Slavic, Vlachian, or Albanian-speaking Greeks, with a fluid or firm ethnic conscience. Multiculturalism was ingrained in the Ottoman Empire as the "heir" of the Eastern Roman territories. All in all, in the early 20th century, approximately 17 separate nations (millet) could be documented. Gradually though, the designation "Romios - Rum" ended up being used exclusively for the descendants of the Greek Orthodox Christianity, with the decisive attribute of "genus".

The totality of Islamic laws, the Fıkıh, was created for the faithful of the religion and sought to organize the Muslim nationals exclusively in the Muslim Ottoman state. For non-Muslims, it was not applicable, or it was applied in a discreet manner against them, resulting in the absence of any political and human rights for this class of Sultan's subjects. Thus, the non-slave nationals of the Sultan were classified into two categories, according to religion. The Muslims themselves were also categorized as the privileged and the deprived, with the former (ruling class, timariots, military men, bureaucrats,

---

[74] Eleni E. Koukou: Institutions and Privileges of Hellenism after the Fall, Publ. Sakkoula, Athens, Komotini, 1988, p. 141.

administrators, and priests) oppressing the lower classes. Considering that the lower Muslim classes themselves enjoyed more entitlements than the non-Muslims, one could sense the plight of Christians under the yoke of the Sultan.

Above all, the life and property of non-Muslims were not guaranteed by the state to any extent. Although non-Muslims were to some degree free to practice their religious affairs in churches, construction of new temples, even the repair of existing ones as well as the liturgy in the countryside following the orthodox tradition, were subject to many constraints. They endured a series of humiliating discriminations, such as their exclusion from testifying in Ottoman courts regarding their disputes with Muslims. The right to own property for non-Muslims was limited while the inequality in taxation was visible. For their taxation, Ottoman authorities offered nothing, neither education, health, justice, nor any other social consideration. The Ottoman taxes were not uniform, nor were they stable for long periods. Added to this was the obligation for bribery, not only to carry out any daily occurrence with the Ottoman authorities but in many instances, just to save their property or even their lives from situations that were deliberately orchestrated by Ottoman officers. Non-Muslims were forced to silently succumb to any request for drudgery by both the Sultan and the central government and the last Aga and last Muslim, even of a subordinate caste.

Non-Muslims were not allowed to join the army or serve in public offices. Even the Greeks, who immediately after the Fall, were assigned to lower financial-accounting and diplomatic services, or later from the 17th century on, were appointed as interpreters and secretaries or rulers of the Danube provinces, did not possess an official position or status among the Muslim ministers of the state.

Although these notables, the so-called Phanariotes, enjoyed great prestige and influence both among the Greeks and the Muslims, they did not have the right to carry weapons, ride a horse, or dress in the same way as Muslims.

Despite all this, Constantinople at the beginning of the 19th century was an exception. By then, it had become the administrative and political center of the Ottoman Empire. Consequently, the non-Muslims of Constantinople enjoyed some distinct freedoms and privileges. They were better off in terms of security and socioeconomic status than non-Muslims in provinces. The imperious way of administration of the Ottoman authorities, widely prevalent in Ottoman provinces, did not apply in Constantinople, because of the proximity to the Ottoman government and Sultan's Court, as any high-handed act would quickly attract the attention of Sultan as well as that of the international emissaries that had their headquarters in Constantinople, in the 18th and 19th centuries. Finally, Constantinople enjoyed a special preferential tax regime that contributed to the economic development of Greeks active in urban professions.

Despite the sporadic Islamizations, the assimilation of Muslims and Christians and especially Turks and Greeks, did not materialize. For the Greeks, what made that not viable was primarily the religion, but also culture and language. Not only were there no intermarriages, but the participation of both Muslims and Christians in social events was relatively rare. Within this framework, in the early 19th century, Hellenism was mainly on the rise, with Constantinople emerging as the center of expression of an awakened and spirited Greek nation.[75]

---

[75] Delphi Conference 1988: Greek civilizations of the East. N. Sarris, G. Kamarados-Vyzantios, D. Theodoridis (in Greek).

The Patriarchate

As a consequence of his decision to allow cohabitation with the Christian - Orthodox element in Constantinople, the victorious Sultan Fatih Mehmet gave Christians the right to perform their religious customs, conferring some privileges freely. These concessions were not bestowed to the Ecumenical Patriarch because of Sultan's generosity, but for political reasons, most important was dismissing one of the premises for a new crusade by European countries. With time and practice, the privileges given to Patriarch, Church, and clergy were passed on to the Orthodox Christians. At the same time, the Patriarch himself evolved into an institution representing all Christian Orthodox subjects of the Ottoman Empire in matters with the Sultan. Religious contexts were surpassed, and under the existing state of affairs, a political and national concept came into being.

The privileges were conventional and primarily not of juristic character. They were held up and violated by the rulers at their discretion.[76] As for their content, they were of religious, administrative, and judicial nature. Religious privileges included religious freedom, ecclesiastical authority, tax-exemption of ecclesiastical property, the sanctity of temples, and charitable foundations. Administrative privileges included the institutionalization of administrative bodies such as Patriarchs, Holy Synod, clergy-laity assemblies as well as legislative bodies on issues of Greek communities, educational and charitable institutions. Judicial privileges concerned the family law. The Patriarch had high supervision over the Metropolitans, Archbishops, and Bishops, as well as the churches, monasteries, and

---

[76] K. Paparrigopoulos: History of the Greek Nation (in Greek).

their estates. In return, the Patriarch had not only the duty, but he was responsible for ensuring the allegiance of all members of the Orthodox community to the Sultan. This was the fundamental reason for maintaining the status of privileges for so long after the Fall, even after the motivations behind their original implementation had dissipated.

Ultimately, the powers conferred on to the Ecumenical Patriarch by the conqueror resulted in the reinforcement and expansion of the ascendancy of Hellenism. Due to the administrative and judicial authority vested to the Patriarchate and because of the title of the leader of the nation-religion awarded by the Conqueror, the Patriarch was considered by the enslaved Orthodox Christians not only as of the supreme ecclesiastical official but also as their political leader.[77]

The Ottomans abstained as much as possible from meddling in the administrative affairs of the Greeks. They left them to their works, with the only condition to remain loyal subjects and slaves, and to pay their multi-faceted taxes. The Ottomans were neither seriously concerned in administering justice nor for the safety of life and property of the Greeks, and of course, not at all for their education nor any other civil or social issues.[78] In this context, the privileges were instead an instrument of the Ottoman policy to resolve the administrative handling of the Greeks and were not intended to create a legal setting that favored Christians.

The privileges, like everything else in the Ottoman governance, should not be regarded as being firmly administered. They should be perceived under the dynamic form of instability that existed at the

---

[77] V. Moutsoglou: The Greeks of Constantinople 1821-1922, Athens, 1998 (in Greek).
[78] K. Paparrigopoulos: Ibid.

time and their arbitrary implementation by the Ottomans as they saw fit. But most importantly, it was their gradual degradation with the passage of time that contributed to the weakening of the Patriarch's status.

To the demise of the Patriarchate's position contributed to a significant degree the Greeks themselves. Many chose to take advantage of the weaknesses of the Ottoman administrative system in promoting their own interests by using bribery. Bribery, which started as a deliberate act, ended up as an obligation for the Patriarch to make payments not only for the acceptance of his election by the Sublime Porte but also as a special "tax". This was in addition to other expenses incurred in favor of various Ottoman officials, as well as the "gifts" he had to offer in resolving the affairs of the Patriarchate. Inevitably, all these expenses were borne by the Orthodox Christians through the archbishops, bishops, and priests.

The Greek society of Constantinople

The pyramid of Greek society undoubtedly had the Patriarch at its peak. The ecclesiastical organization, moreover, held a dominant position in the "nation" of Rums, as a consequence of the political conditions and particular circumstances that were unfolding. The Patriarchate, as a result of the privileges conferred upon it by the Sublime Porte, had become the leading spiritual and administrative center of all Orthodox Christians of the Ottoman Empire. The leadership of the Patriarch and the rallying of the Greeks around him created a unique situation, where politics and religion had molded into a mixed entity, that, although formally remained strictly religious, practically created a novel notion, that of "Head of the nation", Ethnarch.[79]

The Greek "noble" class of the era was primarily engaged in liberal professions such as medicine or trade, in addition to being employed, at times, by the Ottoman administration in the financial and accounting sectors. Greeks of the Empire benefited from the economic development and expansion of trade with Western Europe and Russia, facilitated by the "Ottoman peace" that had settled in the region. The innate aversion of the Turks for occupations not related to political, military, or administrative branches, together with the activity of the Greeks, who managed to excel in these fields, led to their economic prosperity. Economic growth and the expansion of economic activities in many sectors had led to the gradual formation of a sort of Greek urban class that started to display the Greek facet of the Ottoman Empire.

The Ottoman system favored the creation of trade unions, recognized even by the Ottoman government. These guilds consisted of a large number of workers from all provinces of the Ottoman Empire and were viewed by both the genus and the government as legal representatives of the Rum nation to the Sultan.[80]

Phanariotes held a special place in the politico-social organization of the Hellenism of Constantinople. Their name was derived from the district where the Patriarchate was based. In 1601, the Patriarchate, after having been forced to roam for 150 years in various districts of the City, was finally relocated to the Church of St. George (also convent at

[79] D. Tsakonas: Sociology of the Modern Greek Spirit, Athens 1969, p.38 (in Greek).
[80] Manouil I. Gedeon: References of events before my time, 1800-1863-1913, Athens 1934 p.181 (in Greek).

the time) in Diplophanaro or Phanari that retained this name from the era before the Fall. Over time, powerful families that constituted Patriarchate's court came and settled in Phanari, building majestic mansions in the till then poor and inconspicuous district.

The name "Phanariotes" eventually characterized the Greeks who were actively involved in the administration of the Ottoman state or as luminaries of the Patriarchate, in political or administrative matters of Greeks. Phanariotes should be regarded as a distinct social-aristocratic class consisting of several families who had earned the trust of the Ottoman dynasty. The members of these families, usually of exceptional education, populated the Ottoman administrative positions that customarily were assigned to Greeks.[81] The Phanariotes lived in a manner that did not have much to envy from the grandeur of the European nobility. Phanari became the national, spiritual, and social center of the enslaved Hellenism.

The Greeks benefited financially from the expansion of the Ottoman Empire, comparatively more than any other ethnic group under the Ottomans.[82] From the early start, with the prohibition of navigation in the Black Sea imposed on European states, but also gradually, with the consolidation of Ottoman domination in the Balkans, trade passed into the hands of the Greeks. The same group, through Islamized Christians, benefited from the Ottoman leasing system of state taxes, buying out the rights that gave them even greater wealth and power. Maintaining good relations with the Greco-

---

[81] Eleni Koukou: Ibid., p 171. K. Paparrigopoulos: Ibid., p.p. 406-412.
[82] Nikos Svoronos: Overview of the Modern Greek history, Athens, 1981 p.p.51-57 (in Greek).

Ottoman rulers of the Danube principalities, they infiltrated the economic life of these rich regions. Moreover, business entities started to be established in Constantinople, cooperating with the Greek communities abroad, especially Italy. The economic prosperity resulting from these activities, combined with the relations developed in the West, allowed the children of the members of the wealthy class to study in Europe and to learn foreign languages. This qualification was essential for the occupation of a public position in the Ottoman administration, since Muslims, because of the religious perceptions of that era, abstained from learning foreign languages. At the same time, these young people were messengers of the innovative tendencies and enlightenment that had started to make its appearance in Europe.

About two centuries after the Fall, the Ottoman administration began employing with increasing frequency literate Greeks, mainly in diplomatic tasks. The emergence of complexities in Europe's evolving international relations and the increased trust of the Ottoman dynasty in the Greeks due to their loyal service in the past contributed to this eventuality. The long-standing lack of confidence of the Ottomans in Greeks, heirs of the Greek Byzantine Empire, had started to dissipate as a result of the centuries that had elapsed since then. Moreover, several Islamized Europeans that had been used in such positions had failed and sometimes betrayed their mission. An important factor for the shift of the Ottoman attitude towards Greeks was the stagnation of the growth of the Ottoman Empire, in contrast to the scientific and intellectual progress and development of Europe.

Phanariotes began to appear on the political scene, initially as interpreters of the embassies in Constantinople and the Sublime Porte. Their successes, mainly in diplomatic affairs, led gradually to the awarding to Phanariotes three of the most important posts: The Great Interpreter of the Porte or Dragoman, the Interpreter of the Ottoman fleet, and the Ruler of Moldavia and Wallachia. This was followed later by the assignment of several important ambassadorial posts to Greeks. By consolidating their position in the Ottoman administration and drawing on the trust confided by the dynasty, inspired by their long-standing and faithful service, the Phanariotes evolved into a closed hereditary caste.[83] The Phanariot constituent appeared perfectly integrated into the Ottoman economic and political structure. The differentiation was in their social-national identity that remained irreconcilable. It was not only the difference of religion that carved a deep chasm but also the disparity in the level of intellect and lifestyle. Phanariotes, although part of the Ottoman administrative apparatus, appeared to be fully conscious of the nation they belonged to, which they even embodied sometimes politically. Even though Phanariotes managed to combine these qualities by virtue of the stand of Patriarchate, the pursuits and aspirations of these two leading poles of the Greek society failed to conform fully.[84]

Phanariotes were not bourgeois in the European sense of the word. On the contrary, they sought to overcome the level of this order from the onset and penetrate directly into the existing state apparatus, although without the intent of transforming it. Despite being aware of the sentiments of liberalism and renewed ideas of nationalism spread by the French Revolution, Phanariotes remained affixed to a supranational ideology of evolution of the Byzantine cultural tradition under the Ottoman domination. They did not seem to favor the dissolution of the Ottoman

---

[83] Eleni Koukou: Ibid. Vas. I. Filias: Ibid., p. 30-31.
[84] D. Tsakonas, Ibid., p. 36-50.

Empire or its exclusion from the West, but they envisioned reshaping it to a state, organized according to the European standards of the time, in the governance of which they would have the dominant role. The metamorphosis of the Ottoman state to some type of Turkish-Greek empire, an eastern federal state that would respect the rights of various nationalities, became a constant political goal of Phanariotes.[85] Under this scheme, they anticipated reserving the political and intellectual hegemony of Balkans to themselves, while the Patriarchate would be confined to the pursuit of religious supremacy. As a result of this, those who embraced these views sided up, albeit not openly, with Rigas Fereos, an intellectual revolutionary who echoed a form of this approach, while at the same time, some among them, because of this very same notion, opposed the Revolution.

The Patriarchate appeared more conservative in its policy regarding the future of the Ottoman Empire and its affiliation with Hellenism. Basically, it also followed a form of supranational policy concerning the Christian nations under its spiritual leadership. It did not attempt to Hellenize the Orthodox Christians; instead, it allowed the free expression of the various ethnicities, as long as the pious Christians remained in his flock. However, apart from the purely political issue on the future of the nation, the dispute between Phanariotes and Patriarchate also focused on matters such as the rapid progress in science as well as the modernization of the language that the Patriarchate opposed.

---

[85] Otherwise formulated by a foreign observer: "The general policy of the Phanariotes was concentrated in the establishment of an eastern federal state, which would respect the rights of the different ethnicities." D. Tsakonas refers to Ellisen Anelechten V. III, p. IV.

The administrative regime in Constantinople

The administrative regime of the Greeks formed gradually, ever since the Fall of Constantinople. At the beginning of the 19th century, the administration of the enslaved nation was jointly held by clergy and laymen, sometimes with clergy-laity assemblies, with clergy being the prevailing partner. It was a complex and ambiguous system, derived from the combination of traditional practice and the occasionally released verats (forms of Sultan's orders). It regulated the relations among Greeks as well as with the Ottoman administration.

The head of the genus, the supreme spiritual leader of the Church and the Orthodox Christians of the Empire, was the Ecumenical Patriarch. He was assisted by the Holy Synod, while the Committee of the Public along with the Council of the Elders, which was comprised of senior Metropolitans, helped considerably in its governance. Guilds and trade unions (Esnafia), together with luminaries of the Patriarchate and the notables (logades), also exercised substantial influence. The election of the Patriarch was held by a general assembly of clergy and people, where the Metropolitans who were present in Constantinople, the luminaries of the Patriarchate, the commissioners of the public, the representatives (Kapukehaya) of the Danube rulers, as well as the chiefs (protomagistores) of the "blessed guilds" participated. Before 1821, the Great Interpreter of the Sublime Porte, the Interpreter of the Fleet, and those who have been senior officials of the Rulers of Wallachia and Moldavia, as well as the former Rulers of these provinces also used to attend as members of the assembly.

The Holy Synod has consisted initially of the Metropolitans who were present, residing in

85

Constantinople or those whose seats were near the City. The Holy Synod was the supreme core of the Church. It constituted the preeminent advisory and executive assembly and possessed even the power to depose the Patriarch. The Synod, chaired by the Patriarch, presided over many matters concerning administrative or judicial affairs of family law. Regarding the secular administration, after the Patriarch and the Synod, the third major executive group was the luminaries of the Patriarchate. These notable officials of the court of the Patriarchate were either clergy or laymen.

The notables of the nation were the chosen laymen, personages who stood out because of their intelligence, experience, and knowledge, but most of all because of their economic status. The "aristocratic" ancestry had always played an important role and, consequently, names were taken on, and myths were created, typically ascribed to the Byzantine era. The notables were also acting behind the scenes with various tacit actions and influence they were exerting at an interpersonal level.

An additional administrative unit set up by the mid-17th century was the Committee of the Public responsible for managing the Patriarchate's financial affairs. This committee consisted mainly of laypeople, ten or more notables of the nation, and two or three Archbishops.

The participation of the folk element in the administration of the nation took place through trade unions. The trade unions (Esnafia), with their representative function granted by the Ottoman government, at times had gained considerable clout, to the extent that they even partook in the election of Patriarchs. The trade unions also participated in the general assemblies convened at the Patriarchate for matters of common concern. At the same time, they had a say in Patriarchate's finances, along with the

86

Council of Elders. The trade unions also represented the Orthodox nation at the level of the Ottoman state and, usually, jointly, 70 or 80 together, had the right to submit to the Ottoman Government petitions and memoranda on their requests. The Greek guilds constituted, in some way, a kind of parliament for the Greek nation.

Various factions criticized this administrative system with increasing intensity. Notwithstanding many brilliant exceptions, the caprices, the bribery, the gradual moral decay, and corruption, but mainly the authoritarianism and lack of democracy that generally characterized the behavior of the social and administrative pyramid of the genus, created resentment and disgust. That was particularly evident in circles that had the discretion to come into contact with Europe and weigh things up with the moral and ethical values introduced by the reformist currents that prevailed in the developed European countries. In particular, the clergy and the Phanariot aristocracy were accused of non-observance of criteria of merit in selecting executives of the upper clergy or luminaries. They were also criticized for unauthorized involvement in various matters, for ulterior motives and clandestine objectives of policies followed, and for wasteful spending and lavish living. The anticlerical movement was initially limited to a conceptual level and in accord with similar intellectual, reformist propensities of European enlightenment. Of the two opposing perspectives, the conservative was championed by the Church, and the progressive by the Constantinopolitan bourgeoisie of the time, the merchants, and the intellectuals. This controversy was not confined only to Constantinople but encompassed the whole area of the Ottoman Empire, wherever Greeks resided.

The administration in Greek territories

In addition to the "central administration of the genus" from Constantinople through the Patriarchate and priests dispatched to provinces, parallel islets with some jurisdictions were created at local communities of Greeks, depending on the peculiarity of each region. An interesting feature of these was their system of "democracy",[86] with its limited political sovereignty emanating from its own communities, as opposed to the undemocratic and somewhat authoritarian formation of the Greek society under the Ottoman administration. Sources of attributes of the ruling power were its assets, heredity, as well as the natural virtues of its leadership. In islands and trade centers, the ruling group encompassed shipowners and merchants, whereas, in rural areas, it consisted of landowners - dignitaries affiliated to some degree with the "bourgeoisie". The common trait of these quasi sovereignties, excluding the Kleftes[87] and often the Armatoloi,[88] was their "good" relations with the Ottoman leaders of each region, until the eruption of the Revolution.

---

[86] The concept is relative as is the notion of democracy of all political systems. Authoritarianism is discerned more clearly.

[87] Kleftes were rebels who, in order to avoid the oppression of the Ottomans, had gone to the mountains and formed armed groups. They were characterized by dignity, pride, hospitality, simple morals and bravery but also seen as profiteering and vindictive. They regularly fought the Ottomans, while in the interim, they imposed forceful "taxation», mainly on the Ottoman villagers but also on Greek landowners and villagers, in order to meet their needs. For the Ottoman administration, they were thieves and were hounded.

[88] Armatoli, was a martial order in the pre-revolutionary Peloponnese associated with the Venetian rule.

The "Community" institution appeared in the 16th century as a proper regional administrative entity organized by Sultan's decrees. Each village not belonging to a manor had its local self-government, charged with collecting taxes, resolving civil disputes as well as regional security, among other matters. Communities in cities in other regions, along with the partnership of Church and trade unions, appeared as adequately developed robust forms of self-government. Secondary structures of self-government under the type of a federal organization also started to appear.

Community institutions in mountainous regions of mainland Greece were interwoven with the institution of Armatoloi. In western Greece, this entity enhanced the spirit of self-government and promoted it to a degree of semi-autonomy.[89] Occasionally, the Sublime Porte recognized local rulers as in Mani, although, after the Orloffics in 1770, their election was subject to the approval of the Sultan. Mani did not participate in the revolutionary movement of Katsonis (1790), while Kleftes had even helped the Ottoman administration in the decimation of the Albanians who were ravaging Peloponnese after the Orloffics. The formidable leader of Mani, Petrobey Mavromichalis, was the one who prompted the onset of the revolt in Peloponnese. Mavromichalis was a well-respected and quite influential chieftain. When asked by the Pasha of Tripoli to deliver the revolutionary army leader Theodoros Kolokotronis who had just arrived at Kardamili, in Mani, he could plead ignorance of his whereabouts and suffer no consequences.

The system of the Community Heads - dignitaries (Kocabash in Turkish), a form of nobility that in some fashion had functioned during the

---

[89] Ap. Vakalopoulos: Ibid., Vol. II, p. 364.

Venetian and Byzantine era, envisaged the sharing of jurisdictions of the state concerning the interior of provinces, particularly about the collection of taxes. Since the Community Heads were selected among wealthy manor holders, their title, Kocabash, ended up being identified with a negative connotation. The Greek population did not always like both manor holders and Community Heads during the Turkish occupation. In provinces, they also functioned as judges, along with local Ottoman authorities Voivode and Kadi. Assembled in the capitals of areas, they constituted the representative body of the Greek people, by whom occasionally they were elected. They tried as much as possible to shield the Greeks from the innumerable ills of Ottoman vagaries, sometimes by begging, at times, through persuasion for the righteousness of the case, while others via issuing implicit threats but most of all by bribing. This way, the Greeks, primarily in Peloponnese, had managed to attain a particular political representation and clout while facing the central Ottoman authority. In continental Greece, however, the authoritarian administration of Ali Pasha prevented any similar operation of the Community institution. The Community Heads of these regions were merely instruments of Ali Pasha and represented him rather than the Greek people as they were supposed to.

The system of the Senate of community Elders was common in all provinces of Greece without, however, being uniform neither in its composition nor in its performance. In the broader region of Peloponnese and continental Greece, the senates were municipal and relatively weak, unlike Mani and the islands, where they almost bore the attributes of an oligarchy. In Peloponnese, the senates were influenced directly by the Community Heads, but not as much in continental Greece. In Mani, they were under the sway of the captains of Kleftes and Armatoloi. The senates worked along with Ottoman authorities and the Community Heads to collect taxes and functioned as a small-claims court in civil matters. The single-term members of these senates, who were referred to as Lords, as well as the Community Heads of continental Greece, enjoyed a variety of privileges with regards to the internal administration of their region.

The administrative system, as described above, was a form of organization of the Greek nation that was more or less associated with the Ottoman administration and displayed the spirit of adaptation to the conditions of enslavement.[90] Outside this system, Kleftes and Armatoloi, who had not been subservient to the Venetians or the Ottomans, had an active role and say.

Revolution-era writer I. Philemon in his historical essay about Friendly Society (Nafplio, 1834), referring to the administrative system of the enslaved Greeks, did not seem to find the conditions of Greeks under the Ottoman rule particularly harsh. Yet, in a different entry, he mentioned that the notion for the revolution was brought forth because of the tyranny of the Turks. He affirmed that under the Ottoman yoke, Greeks did not possess any civil or political rights and lacked security for even their own lives. The views of Philemon are of particular significance as they were expressed only about ten years after the start of the Revolution.

The Aegean nobility

In the Aegean islands, the Community Assembly differed from that on the mainland. The Sublime Porte recognized various privileges to address the de facto regime of local sovereignty and tackle piracy. The islands were under the command

---

[90] N. Svoronos, Ibid. p. 47.

of Kaptan Pasha. The situation there was described as better, with fewer taxes and with an arbitrator for critical cases, the Interpreter of the Ottoman fleet of the Mediterranean, who was often of Greek origin.[91] Sometimes the islanders had representatives also in the Ottoman central administration. Mainly, Aegean Cycladic islands had the right to some form of self-administration and collection of taxes.[92]

Moreover, the distinctiveness of the Aegean islands was due to the delay of their conquest by the Ottomans, their lengthy occupation by Franks, and their relative isolation due to geographical conditions. Above all, the Turks were mainland inhabitants who avoided dwelling in islands. These peculiarities of the islands culminated in the birth of a class of landowners almost exclusively Christian, in a western character of a landowning system, along with the preservation of European-style administrative mechanisms and the seamless evolution of the Community institution.[93] The existing circumstances formed near the end of the 18th century with the Napoleonic Wars and the need to transport goods by non- belligerent fleets facilitated trade and shipping and the islander ruling class rushed to take advantage by undertaking a shipowner role. However, prevailing conditions for the establishment of merchant-shipping businesses were not comparable to those of the West. Nevertheless, as the shipping business grew, it created employment opportunities in other sectors of economic life.[94] It also proved extremely valuable when during the Revolution,

---

[91] Ioannis Philemon: Historical essay on the Friendly Society, Nafplio, 1834 p. 29 (in Greek).

[92] Dalegre, Joelle : Grecs et Ottomans, 1453-1953 : De la chute de Constantinople a la disparition de l'Empire Ottoman, 2000.

[93] Vas. I. Filias: Ibid., p. 30-31.

[94] Vasilis Kremmydas: Ibid., p. 25-27.

cannons were placed on merchant ships converting them into warships, which intimidated even the regular Ottoman navy.

After the end of the Napoleonic Wars, the period that offered advantages to Greek captains, with their taking over of the trade in the Eastern Mediterranean, ceased. European states, once again, gained control of trade and shipping. This change of the role of Greeks in these affairs led to an economic crisis, particularly for islanders. However, the notion of the Revolution was already etched in their minds and could no longer be overturned.[95]

The Community Heads of the islands appeared to adopt a conservative view and were not particularly willing to jeopardize their position with an uprising. After all, the precedent of Orloffics and the memory of persecutions and damages suffered were relatively recent. The participation of the islanders in the Revolution, albeit swift, materialized only after the strong impetus provided by sailors, captains, and small shipowners, who were more urbanized and prone to the acceptance of the notions set forth by the European enlightenment.[96]

Hellenism of the Diaspora

The Greeks, who started migrating abroad even before the Fall, mainly to Western Europe and Russia, and continued afterward, became not only cultural sources for the host societies but also channels transferring the new ideas of enlightenment to -under the Ottoman Empire- Greeks. They maintained and rescued Hellenism and functioned as links between the under Islamic domination genus and Christian Europe. The Greeks of the diaspora

---

[95] V. Kremmydas: Ibid., p. 38.
[96] Vas. I. Filias: Ibid., p. 35.

played a vital role in the rejuvenation of the nation's education, which was mostly due to the Greek community in Venice that had progressed, on account of capabilities provided by this country, with efforts in establishing schools having started as early as 17th century. This precedent was later followed by other Greek communities abroad.[97]

The Greeks of the diaspora were in constant contact with communities in Greece. However, their stance varied based on the duration that they had established themselves abroad, as well as the economic, political, and social ties that they had created there, and their occupations, especially for those with careers within the administration of the countries that hosted them. In addition, many among them were cut-off and unaware of the developments of Hellenism in the Empire and thus did not reflect the Greek reality.[98] The most decisive role in the preparation of the Revolution was undertaken by students who planned to return to their homelands after the end of their studies, intellectuals, as well as small and medium-scale traders who had national rather than cosmopolitan propensity and functioned as conveyors of the ideas that forged the French Revolution.

The ideas of the enlightenment contributed to the creation of a militant Greek consciousness in the communities abroad and passed on to Greece mainly through Greeks of diaspora. The role of the communities for the Neo-Hellenic enlightenment and the shaping of the framework of ideas and conditions that led to the Revolution were crucial, despite all social variations that were discerned within the Greek communities abroad.[99]

---

[97] K. Paparrigopoulos: Ibid.
[98] Vas. I. Filias: Ibid., p. 43.
[99] Vas. I. Filias Ibid., p. 43.

When the time for the Revolution arrived, members of the Greek communities abroad were the first who organized the nuclei of philhellenism and philhellenic organizations and who afterward played an active role during the struggle for independence, both in the political and military sectors.

The Greek Revolution of 1821

THE CULTURAL REVIVAL OF THE NATION

The period of stagnation and regression of the Ottoman Empire led to the partial liberalization of its politics and economy. The rise of the bourgeoisie in Europe at the same time did not leave the Ottoman territory unaffected; ideas circulated, not hindered by borders. Moreover, the willingness for reforms that would keep the Empire among the top nations was not amiss from Sultan's court. An additional factor was Russia's strategy for geopolitical reasons, to be seen as the protector of Christians' rights in the Empire. The Ottomans' ally, Britain, who feared any southern Russian excursion, also supported the Christians' rights in order to keep Russia at bay. Moreover, Sultan did not believe that Greek education and schools posed a danger to the Empire. All of these circumstances worked out in favor of the Greeks, who tried to make the most of it. However, none of these resulted in the rescinding of their status of slavery. History may not evolve linearly, but sometimes rationality prevails.

National identity is not always firm but is shaped according to historical developments under the dynamics of internal and external interventions, through a continuous interchange of a variety of factors. However, the edifice of national identity is based on the foundations of its constituent elements. Among these, Dimaratos, the former king of Sparta who had fled to the Persian court, enumerated language, religion, morals, and "race", without all of them bearing the same significance.[100] Particularly "race", in essence, and practice, has lost some of its

---

[100] Helene Glykatzi – Ahrweiler: How much Greek is Byzantium, Athens, 2016 p. 52 (in Greek).

sways in the modern age. However, under the Ottoman Empire, the "genus" designated the "national" identity in accordance with these four components. Nevertheless, cultural identity evolved gradually with education playing the leading role.

The educated Greeks of the time came from the Phanariot families, the Hellenes of diaspora, the middle affluent urban classes in the Ottoman Empire, and the clergy. Since the 17th century, a growing number of Greeks had started migrating from the Ottoman Empire and settling in Europe's major trading centers. A Greek merchant fleet of considerable size was established. Seafarers from the Aegean islands, who traversed the Mediterranean while trading, have come in direct contact with the European culture of the time. Greeks of the diaspora, having Vienna as their basis, spread their activity throughout the Austro-Hungarian Empire. In Moldovlachia, Phanariot Princes created an enlightened aristocracy around them.[101]

The Greeks of the European diaspora were not only pursuing economic gains but also trying and succeeding to evolve intellectually and socially. In the process, they considered their duty to assist their brethren who remained in their birthplace with their enlightenment as the first step towards their liberation. With the financial support of the wealthier, many Greek schools were established in various centers of the Ottoman Empire. Children of the urban class in the Empire continued their studies at European universities, especially in Padua. As early as in the 16th century, along with the continuing migration to Europe, several Greeks born and studied in Europe had started returning to the places from where their parents had departed. There, they created

---

[101] Linos Politis: History of the New Greek Literature, Athens 1979, p.123 (in Greek).

small academic circles and intellectual movements that contributed to enhancing the educational tradition of Greeks.[102]

From the mid-18th century and on, the political, economic, and social conditions of the enslaved and torn apart nation were radically changing, improving, and leading to a new setting that strengthened the middle class. The relative urban ascent, the Phanariot tradition not only with the occupation of government posts but also with the accumulation of wealth, the engagement with trade and subsequent affiliations with Europe as well as with the ideas born there, and lastly, the significant accomplishments of Greeks in education, led the genus to an intellectual reawakening, forging a distinct Modern Greek cultural identity. The development of civil conscience in urban areas was consistent with and contributed to the strengthening of the national identity.[103] Nevertheless, some writers raise objections regarding the urbanization in Greece of that time as spurious.[104]

Social, as well as the cultural tradition, was expressed in a variety of forms and actions. Secular education opposed that of the Church. As early as the 18th century, schools were differentiated as schools of "religious letters" and "schools of Greek,"[105] with the latter referring to secular education. Popular literary production, domestic or foreign, contended with the scholarly one. Trends in Greek Christian Orthodoxy, classical antiquity, and European

---

[102] N. G. Svoronos: Overview of the New Greek History, Athens 1981 p. 51-64 (in Greek).
V. I. Filias: Society and power in Greece. 1. The Forged Urbanization 1800-1864, 1974, p. 35-44.
[103] V. Kremmydas: Ibid., p.32.
[104] Vas. I Filias: Ibid.
[105] Manouil Gedeon: Chronicles of a Columnist, Athens 1932, p. 315 (in Greek).

intellect met, collided, or reconciled. The variety of literary events and pluralism were not divisive, at least during this period, but tended towards synthesis and harmony. The art, both ecclesiastical and secular, was proof of the cultural community of the Greek world as well as of the richness of its diversity.[106]

The revolutionary and liberal ideas that permeated from abroad had both social and economic implications. In the 20th century, Konstantinos Dimaras coined the term "Neohellenic Enlightenment" in describing the osmosis of the European enlightenment values with Hellenism during the pre-revolutionary period.[107] To others, the term was attributed to the intellectual movement for the much-aspired education of enslaved Greeks. Although some historians consider excessive the role of Greek enlightenment to the inception of the Greek Revolution, the contribution of Greek education in the direction of the liberation of the nation and in creating a Greek State was of decisive significance.

In Rumeli, Agios Kosmas Aitolos (Patrokosmas), who lived in the 18th century (Aitolia, Greece 1714, extrajudicial execution by Turks, Albania, 1779), preached that only the return to the simple life of the first Christians could lead to a Modern Greek renaissance. He was against trade and enrichment. He was in favor of social justice, but at the lowest possible common denominator. The communal idea of Christian Orthodoxy ignored social classes and economic interests while abstaining from historical reality and political methodology. Patrokosmas believed that Hellenism and Christianity were one and the same thing, and of

---

[106] Dion. A. Zakynthinos: Ibid., p. 54.
[107] K. Th. Dimaras: Neohellenic Enlightenment, 1974 (in Greek).

course, at that time, within a fanatical Muslim environment, this was a tangible reality.

Patrokosmas possessed a clear anti-Western view, while his actions were perceived as an expression of Russian propaganda. Nevertheless, his hopes for support from Russia vanished after the Orloffics. He advocated that national liberation could materialize through cooperation with the Ottomans, a notion supported by the Patriarchate at the time. The contribution of Kosmas Aitolos was significant in the awareness of the concept of national unity in addition to his teachings, as well as through the establishment of approximately two hundred Greek schools. But the Revolution moved in a direction opposite to the tenets of Agios Kosmas and succeeded by adhering to the principles of Enlightenment, judiciousness, and liberalism that constituted the bedrock upon which the Modern Greek state tried to lay its foundations. Patrokosmas was declared a saint by the Patriarchate of Constantinople on April 20, 1961.

From Balkans and Vienna, Rigas Velestinlis, "Rigas Feraios" (Velestino 1757 – extrajudicial execution by Turks, Belgrade 1798) captured the idea of Greek freedom. Yet he perceived it in a multi-national context, in a state that would include all the peoples of the Balkans, an ideology parallel to the one expressed by the Jacobins, "friends of freedom and equality". He urged all enslaved peoples to join in a fight against Ottoman domination, an idea that resembled the Phanariot approach for resolving the national issue. But he pushed ahead enticed by hopes he had entrusted to Napoleon and French promises that could not be truly realized, even if the will had existed. On the other hand, Phanariotes were looking ahead to a peaceful and rather gradual transition towards a free state, an idea that did not seem unreasonable at the time.

In 1797, Rigas published a draft constitution for the Ottoman Empire, inspired by the Constitution of the French Jacobins of 1793, that pertained to a republican state and foresaw the ousting of the monarchy. The Ottoman Empire would be renamed "The Hellenic Republic," with all its inhabitants, regardless of religion and language, enjoying a sovereign status. Rigas was primarily interested in the political and social uprising of the urban class, with the Greek language selected, rather for practical reasons, as the primary language of the new state. Given the vital role of the Church among Greeks, it was odd that Rigas had chosen to leave out any referencing to it. However, it was consistent with the general secular spirit of his Constitution and the ideas of the French Revolution. Objections to his multi-national model arose from the premise that a single cultural identity could not be formed without differentiation from the already existing powerful ethnic identities. Thereby attesting to the notion that no single mixed society consisted of factions entrenched in incompatible political, religious, and cultural identities could be forged. This, of course, was affirmed in the Ottoman Empire, where Muslims and Christians could not live peacefully, on equal terms.

The radicalism of Rigas alienated both Muslims and Christians because of the secularism and equality of all he had advocated, while the principles of the French Revolution that had been included in the draft constitution led to the hostility of both Austria, that arrested him when he was found within its territory, as well as the Ottomans that carried out his extrajudicial execution after he was delivered to them by the Austrians. The Patriarchate was also forced to condemn the ideas of freedom and rebellion against the Ottoman Empire, which in its view, "had replaced the Byzantine, as the will of

God".[108] Yet, the Ecumenical Patriarchate should be regarded as an internationalist and should be judged in this context.

By the beginning of the 19th century, Hellenism had attained a robust stature, which soon manifested its force. This was a consequence of having succeeded in safeguarding its national status and building a Modern Greek cultural identity, shaped and mixed with elements of the Greek tradition of freedom and democracy, enriched with European liberal ideas along with some Ottoman traits -as in the art of war-. This process took place throughout Greece as well as in the Greek communities of Europe. Constantinople was not the main focus of the shaping of the national idea -at least the one with the armed revolutionary character- but surely, as the national center of Hellenism (and the Empire), anything that took place there had a special significance because of the publicity it came with, as this were where the eyes of all Greeks were tuned in to.

Constantinople had become the real capital of Rums. The Greeks reigned intellectually all Christian peoples who were subjugated to the Ottomans. They constituted the link between them and the European way of thinking. Thus, they acted as a catalyst for the national awakening of the rest of Christian ethnic groups. Moreover, the Greeks, who were recruited at the service of the Sublime Porte, acquired great power as they were entrusted with the Ottoman government's secrets and gradually became its real advisors on matters pertaining to external relations of the Empire. The senior clergy that depended on Ecumenical Patriarchate had Greek education and guided the entire flock of Orthodox Christians.

---

[108] D. Kitsikis: History of the Ottoman Empire, Estia, 1988, p.158 (in Greek)

The struggle that had already commenced between progressives and conservatives, focusing not only on the linguistic issue but also on the overall criticism of clergy and Phanariotes, shifted to more substantial levels. Nevertheless, the liberation of the nation that was paramount compelled the Greeks. Russia, despite the failure of the Orloffics, had always been the power to which the eyes of the enslaved turned to with hope. It was a fortunate coincidence that, just before the Revolution, Ioannis Kapodistrias was among the leading advisors of the Czar.[109] Even when he was Secretary of the Territory of the Ionian Islands (quasi-prime minister, 1803), he had entrusted his hopes to improve the fate of the nation to Russia. Kapodistrias, who participated at the Congress of Vienna as a member of the Russian delegation, found the opportunity to bring to the attention of the participants the grievous conditions the Greeks lived under the Ottoman Empire, thus indirectly drawing international attention to the Greek issue.

Many Phanariotes, together with senior clerics, did not endorse the ideas of the enlightenment. Besides, the situation that arose in France after the French Revolution could not have been regarded as enticing. The clergy opposed the new "troubling" political ideas and the teachings of science, which it considered clashing with the religion. Moreover, Phanariotes and senior clerics were satisfied with their modus vivendi in the Empire and would not want to risk it with a general revolution.

---

[109] Vas. I. Filias: Society and power in Greece. 1. The Forged Urbanization 1800-1864, 1974, p.p. 44-52.
D. Tsakonas: Sociology of the Modern Greek Spirit, Athens 1969, p.p. 83-98. (in Greek)

The National Awakening

The national idea had been developing progressively since the Byzantine years. At the outset, Greeks abandoned their "Roman" identity not so much because of differences in languages (both populace and ruling class) but disparities in religious doctrines and especially relating to the ecclesiastical administration. The Fourth Crusade (1204) marked the definitive end of the Eastern Roman Empire with its Roman character. The Byzantium of Palaeologus could be regarded as a Greek state, but its people did not fully realize its Hellenic character. Confusion concerning the ethnicity ensued immediately after the enslavement by Ottomans, as the conqueror was not tolerant of the Greco – Byzantine ethnicity. Diversity within the Ottoman Empire was underscored primarily in the context of religion. The nation was referred to as genus, without regard to race but to religious and cultural features, resulting in the smooth integration of foreign ethnological entities (Slavs, Vlachs, Albanians) into the "national" Orthodox Christian core. Gradually, the parameter of religion was abandoned as the primary identifier of ethnicity, while the idea of reviving the Byzantine Empire changed content reflecting European developments.[110] Along with these, the subhuman treatment of the Greek subjects by the Ottoman master, and senseless discriminations against them, could only provoke an adverse reaction to the enslaved people. This reaction was a crucial feature in the emergence of awareness for national identity. The particular ethnicity of Greeks was further reinforced through their rivalry with the Ottoman administration and Muslim religion.

---

[110] N. Svoronos: Survey of the Modern Greek History, 1981, p.58 (in Greek)

The awareness for national identity was fortified in the 18th century by the Russian parameter that sought to exploit the national aspirations of the Greeks for its own political objectives. The transition from the stage of the theoretical conception of the national idea to putting it to action was undoubtedly linked to the international developments in the region, and in particular to the Russo-Turkish competition, a result of the weakening of the Ottoman Empire and the yearning of Russia to extend to the south. Russia's Balkan policy encompassed not only the control of the Black Sea and the Balkans but also aimed in the replacement of the Ottoman Empire by a Rum "Balkan Empire" under the Russian dynasty. In justifying these ambitions, the Russian emperors also invoked the fact that Sophia Paleologina, niece of the last Byzantine emperor, had married the ruler of Moscow Ivan III, in Rome, in 1472. Czars later used this Byzantine lineage as a pretext to appear in the eyes of the Orthodox Christians as direct successors of glorious ancestors.

Russia looked to the continuation of the Byzantine Empire and the political benefits that could arise from an alliance with the Greek coreligionists, and as such, took the initiative to aid the Greeks. Russian envoys took action in Greek territories to create conditions favorable in extending the Czar's power to the south and contributed to the eruption of several unsuccessful insurgencies. The first actions of Greeks at the end of the 18th century functioned as diversions to Russia in its historic conflict with the Ottoman Empire. However, despite their failure, these uprisings prepared the Greeks for the path to follow.

The French Revolution, also, with its resonance and ramifications in Europe, could not have left the Greeks -who foresaw in its principles the foundation of their own liberation- indifferent. Napoleon's victorious campaigns and the conquest of the Ionian Islands by France nurtured hopes, which were refuted not too long after. However, the proximity of the Ionian Islands with the enslaved Greeks in the mainland facilitated the communication of the principles of the French Revolution with Greeks.

The intellectual rebirth of the 18th century modern Greeks did not take long to lead to the national resurgence of the genus with its primordial constituents that had evolved over centuries. The Greek national idea was formed under the influence of the renewed currents of the European spirit, the Enlightenment, and the emerging principle of nationality. The national idea, now devoid of parameters that blurred its expression, transformed at the beginning of the 19th century into a radical expression, a set of constituent elements that embodied Hellenism from antiquity and throughout centuries to the contemporary era.

In France, Adamantios Korais (Smyrna 1748 – Paris 1833 in self-exile), who interacted directly with European thinking, focused his attention on secular education. His pedagogical programs, inspired by the Greek antiquity and reflecting the spirit of enlightenment, attempting to reconnect the modern Hellenism with Europe, brought him in confrontation with the conservative Patriarchate and the authoritarian Ottoman state. Korais fostered the need to create an all-embracing Greek constitutional state.

According to Korais, there was an irreconcilable social-psychological gap between Greeks and Ottomans, while any contact with the culture of the latter hindered Greek advancement. Korais rejected anything that was Ottoman. In this context, he dismissed the designation Romios - Rum and advocated the term "Greco",[111] which, on the grounds of not being authentic, failed to prevail in Greece. Thus, Korais asserted that the ideas of cooperation with the Ottomans, promoted by Phanariotes, or political affiliation with the Ottoman peoples, promoted by Rigas influenced by the French Enlightenment, should both be rejected.[112] Korais was in favor of the separation of state and Church and opposed the recognition of Christian Orthodoxy as the national Church. Because of this, he clashed with Phanariotes, who were appointed luminaries by the patriarchal court, whom he called "Turkish-ordained slave-princes", echoing perhaps in this way his opposition to the "ecumenical" idea.

Phanariotes, however, had also been a conduit of liberal spirit conveyance and an institution for the intellectual advancement in Constantinople. However, together with the senior clergy, their mindset in general -but not in their entirety- was conservative, particularly in their stratagem of action, as their aspirations had not coalesced in the direction of national redemption. On the other hand, the main leverage for the national awakening and the perception of commencing a national movement was a small pioneering middle class with a relatively advanced degree of urban awareness and a fairly high level of education. This class was staffed in cities by middle social layers, which, despite their heterogeneity and incongruity, were the breeding ground for the development of progressive ideas and action.

---

[111] Among the arguments for the adoption of the term Greco was, that the term had been used in the past by the Europeans for the Greeks. In contemporary times, the European Union uses the term "Hellas" as Greeks call their country (and Hellen for themselves). In the UN the term used is Greece.

[112] D. Tsakonas: The Sociology of the Neohellenic Spirit, 1969, p.p. 95-98 (in Greek).

The demographic element and the relationship between Christians and Muslims in each region shaped the national consciousness and highlighted its strength. In his book "References of events before my time,"[113] Manuel Gedeon noted that the Greek population had increased during the past century, and the Greek (historical) conscience had survived with all its diverse influences. He underlined that even three centuries ago, the Byzantine Greek ancestry was alive.

In addition to internal factors, external elements also had a role in shaping the national awareness of Greeks. In Europe, several intellectuals viewed the contemporary Greeks regarding language and geographical place, as the continuance of the ancient Greeks whose culture they considered as a source of their own. A second aspect was the common Christian faith, although Christian Orthodoxy was regarded discretely by Catholics.

Nevertheless, the yearning for national liberation through a revolution, in line with other revolutionary movements in Europe and elsewhere,[114] began to take shape mainly by endogenous factors. Various social groups defined their attitudes and objectives they sought in light of their ethnicity, as it was understood at the time. The resolution of the nation's uprising using its own powers and not depending on others was considered earnestly by the pioneering urban class that held a stature between the Phanariotes and the middle class. It should be

---

[113] Manuel I. Gedeon: References of events before my time, 1800-1863-1913, Athens 1934 (in Greek).

[114] Philemon in his historical essay about Friendly Society (Nafplio, 1834) mentions the "Swiss who shook the yoke of the Austrians, the Spaniards against the Arabs in the past but also their fight against Napoleon, the Dutch and Portuguese against Spaniards, the British colonies of America against the Metropolis and the struggle for the freedom of the blacks of St. Dominic." p 40-41.

noted, however, that the messengers of these ideas were not confined to a place or a social circle alone. After all, the aspirations of each group did not coincide on all aspects but only in one common denominator: changing the existing status quo.

The social diversification that began to appear was, in fact, a manifestation of progress and evidence of an evolving society. Apart from national liberation, relevant opinions and views were expressed everywhere, especially in the Ionian islands and other places outside the Ottoman Empire. They not only were directed against Turks but against any kind of social or economic oppression, expressed either through the clergy or through administrative bodies, heads of communities, etc. The emblematic pamphlet "Greek Nomarchia" ("nomarchia" referring to "sovereignty of the laws"), by "Anonymous the Greek" was published in Italy in 1806.[115] It is a work of literary and historical value, devoted to Riga, attacking with a strong language the clergy and various heads of administration, the rich and the merchants, "who think only about their profit". "Anonymous the Greek" considered that "the ignorant priesthood and lack of outstanding fellow citizens were the causes that continued to keep the nation chained in tyranny." It is a text that rivals the Korais spirit and an adversary to the preaching of enlightenment.[116] Despite its excesses, the book certainly showcases a trend in Greek society, which has since maintained its course while solely changing the means of expression via constant modernization. The authorship of the work remains unresolved, but the contribution of Athanasios Psallidas to the

---

[115] Modern Greek registry, Pelekanos Publications, Athens 2009 (in Greek).
[116] V. Kremmydas: Ibid., p. 34.

creation of a similar revolutionary spirit in Epirus is underlined in this setting.[117]

The French Revolution, on the other hand, inspired the Kleftes and the middle classes of merchants, while the ideas of enlightenment infused the national movement with a liberal disposition. Together with the revival of the national idea, the democratic French state was perceived as the model for the organization of the new state, a notion ingrained in the national idea, in planning the future of Hellenism. Within the framework of community self-government, democratic parties in Kozani, as well in islands such as Kea, and Samos stepped up, with their followers calling themselves "Carmagnoles" in a direct reference to revolutionary France. The first political contrasts based on economic and social statures made their appearance in the Ionian state, created by the Constantinople Convention in 1800.

Bourgeois class ideas existed, but their content differed from those developed in Europe, as it was influenced by the social, economic, and political environment of a more ancient order. For Hellenism, the Bourgeois class consciousness did not develop in a way parallel to that of the national conscience, as was the case in Europe, but it was formed in the context of the antithesis of the conquered versus the conqueror, and of Christianity versus Islam. The call for freedom for the subdued Greeks was primarily of national context and only secondarily socio-political.[118]

The Ottomans, for their part, believed that the Greeks were thoroughly content with their welfare, and at any rate, they considered that this was the "natural" order of things. As far as they were

---

[117] Chr. Frangos: Athanasios Psallidas and the Greek prefecture, 1972 (in Greek).
[118] Vas. Filias: Ibid., p. 49.

111

concerned, the clergy performed their religious duties "freely", the upper class and Phanariotes had secured privileges, the farmers had security, and the taxation, in their opinion, was not intolerable, at least as compared to the serfs in Europe. They thought that Rums, like many other peoples, both in the Ottoman Empire and in Europe, had accepted that they would live under the sovereignty of the mighty and that this was after all "the Will of God". The Muslim supremacy over Christianity was considered given, and this, in their view, had been acknowledged by the Christians of the Empire. They thought that the local revolts were coincidental phenomena without much resonance and would always be suppressed. Therefore, for the Ottomans, there was nothing too serious to worry about.

However, this was not the case as far as Rums were concerned. The groundwork had been laid by the Friendly Society (Filiki Etaireia), the necessity for the Revolution had become the conscience of the populace, the conditions had ripened, and they all anticipated the go-ahead signal. The flammable material awaited the spark, and the explosion would follow. How could the Sultan and the Ottoman ruling class miss all the telltale signs? Peoples are not irresolute beings, but principles, faith, and ideals possess them. Greek people were aware that they were entitled to equal rights, and they did not want to be second-class subjects exposed to the whimsicalities of any Muslim. They desired change and hoped it would provide them a better life or at least one for their children, both socially and economically, with the latter not being the primary motive.

The Community Heads – landowners were, as might be expected, reluctant, and hesitant. They did not fancy losing what they had secured, but on the other hand, sensed that they should not be left out of the developments. Otherwise, they knew that circumstances could draw them through unknown and dangerous paths. In the pre-revolutionary fever that dominated Greeks, they understood that history would have shunted them. The members of the Friendly Society were apprehensive, yet they felt obliged to approach them, too. In doing that, their main concern was not to endanger their undertaking by disclosing it, not so much because of their safety as to safeguard their project. At any rate, the reaction was generally positive.

Many of the Community Heads, embedded in the idea of freedom, were motivated by high ideals. In contrast, others succumbed to lower motives, recognizing the small likelihood of success of the movement, but at the same time understanding that they could not be alienated from their surroundings. The rest would be persuaded through the fear of the Ottomans, who would most certainly not discriminate between "culprits" and "innocents". Eventually, the most prominent of the Heads of Communities, Petrobey Mavromichalis, the one who stood to lose the most, was the first to organize an army and attack the local Ottoman administration in Peloponnese, giving by his initiative the go-ahead signal for the launch of the Revolution.

Despite the showdown between the Community Heads and Kleftes in 1806, the latter once again took up arms, and after the launch of the Revolution, they assumed its military leadership. Greeks participated wholeheartedly, each one from his own post. Social reasons and opposing interests persisted and constituted a reason for the underlying deplorable internal conflict that pervaded throughout the Revolution.[119]

---

[119] Vas. I. Filias: Ibid., p. 58.

The driving force of the Revolution was neither the base of society nor its head. The urban middle class was the one that processed the idea most effectively by molding a mixture of Riga's ideals of spontaneous patriotism as inspired by the French Enlightenment, the yearning for freedom, the dynamism of Kleftes, the will of higher classes to take part in the developments, and the ever-present underlying Russian policy against the existence of the Ottoman Empire. Its idea emanating in this context, the Friendly Society used as a weapon the secrecy and exclusively personified communication and succeeded in recruiting almost all active Greeks into the national idea, persuading them through its network, one by one.

PRE-REVOLUTIONARY MOVEMENTS

Commencing from the period of the Ottoman occupation of the territories of Byzantium and Greece and the time of "the mourning for Constantinople", a popular poem written shortly after the Fall, the Greeks sought to oppose the Ottomans, either through autonomous movements or by alliances with the Venetians and later on, with Russians. The Greeks did not miss a chance to join forces with any Europeans taking on some form of warfare against the Ottomans. The Naval Battle of Naupactus (1571) found Greeks forced to enlist in the Ottoman fleet against Greeks who fought voluntarily for the Western Alliance (Spain, the Pope, and Venice). Despite the victory of the Alliance, the Greeks of Galaxidi, motivated by the allies to rebel, were defeated by the Ottoman army, and many were slaughtered. At the same time, revolutions in Mani, in Macedonia, and the Aegean islands found no sympathy from the Admiral of the Allied fleet, John the Austrian, and were suppressed. As a result, many Greeks went to exile while others were enslaved or slaughtered by the Ottomans.

The continuous -yet failed- revolutionary movements of the Greeks urged the Venetians to assign privileges to Greeks and employ Armatoloi in their services. The Ottomans followed suit and recognized various orders of Armatoloi to whom they entrusted the guarding of some areas in Greek territories. The uprisings, though, continued. Nevertheless, both in Cyprus and Crete, as well as in Peloponnese, many Greeks who had experienced the

115

strict Venetian rule preferred to align in some instances with the Ottomans rather than the Latins in the battles between them.

When Venetians acquired Peloponnese from the Ottomans by the Treaty of Karlowitz, the peninsula had already been pillaged and depopulated (1690). The fair governance of the Venetians contributed to the increase of the population with migrations from continental Greece. Somehow, the people of the region seemed to prefer the Ottoman anarchy than the order imposed by Venetians, and this may explain its easy recapturing by the Ottomans in 1715. Despite that, the Ottomans, after regaining the peninsula, took on enslaving and massacring the Christians.

The ideological currents developed in the 18th century quickly coalesced in the idea of Greek independence. For the Greeks of the Empire, fighting for the freedom of their homeland had taken over the will to join warfare with European Christian Powers with the sole goal of having them replace the Ottomans as their rulers. They felt that they had found an ally in the face of coreligionist Russia, the "blond genus", even though Russia intended to place them under its sovereignty. As early as the time of Peter the Great[120], expectations had been raised in Rumeli, as conveyed in the popular song expressing the expectance for the Russian saviors: "Still this spring, Rayades, Rayades[121]... until the Moscovos arrives...".[122]

---

[120] Peter the Great, Peter I (Pyotr Alexeyevich Romanov).
[121] Raya was a member of the tax-paying lower class of Ottoman society. Eventually meant non-Muslim subjects of the Sultan (derogatory). Rayades, plural in Greek
[122] K. Paparrigopoulos: Ibid., p. 214.

The Orloffics

Czarina Catherine II (the Great) rose to the throne in 1762 with the support of the army, as well as of the public opinion, following a coup d'état against her husband Peter III, and reigned until 1796. Peter III was considered as "mentally immature", and a friend of Prussia, and therefore was unpopular. The German-born Czarina had the vision to raise Russia to the level of the great European Powers. During her reign, she succeeded in increasing the territory of Russia and reorganizing its administration and legislation. She was a fan of the Enlightenment and a personal friend of Voltaire and Diderot. In the period before the reign of Elizabeth Petrovna (1741 - 1762), daughter of Peter the Great (1672 –1725), Russia had defeated the Prussian King Frederick II during the Seven-year War (1756 - 1763), and the Russian-British relations had improved. Thus, the conditions for turning the interest of the state southwards were considered ripe.

The pursuit of Catherine the Great for the conquest of Constantinople and the rebirth of the Byzantine Empire with her as its head, led her first to the commission of George Papazolis, of Greek descent, who was sent from St. Petersburg to Greece (1766) to stir up the Greeks. Yet, before anything commenced, Turks beheaded the Metropolitan of Peloponnese Ananias Lambardis (1767) and slaughtered Greeks they suspected or just for exemplification. In 1768, the Ottoman administration, because of the war with Russia, seized all the weapons that Greeks possessed. Even with the faintest suspicion of the uprising, Patriarch Meletios II was tortured and exiled to Tenedos. The ruler of Moldovlachia, Ioannis Kalimachis, and the Great Interpreter Nikolaos Soutsos were beheaded in 1769. The Ottoman administration also tightened its control over Mani in Peloponnese.

117

Subsequently, Catherine assigned (her lover) Count Grigori Alexei Grigoryevich Orlov with the mission of inciting the Greeks against the Sublime Porte. The Russian fleet under the command of Count's brother, Admiral Theodore Orlov (Fiodor Orlov), entered the Mediterranean at the beginning of 1770 and anchored in Itilo (Mani). The promises of the spontaneous uprising of thousands of Greeks, however, did not materialize. Maniates, even though quickly realized that Admiral Th. Orlov's plans were difficult to succeed, responded to the call, although not in the numbers expected. Besides, the weaponry that the fleet of Orlov brought along was insufficient to arm a substantial rebel force. Despite all that, several Greeks in Peloponnese and Crete enthusiastically joined the calling. The Maniates formed small bodies referred to as Eastern and Western Legions of Sparta. The Eastern Legion seized Mystra and increased its force, but it resorted to looting and, worse of all, to slaughter all the Muslims surrendered under the agreement of not being harmed. In the meantime, another naval squadron had arrived under Admiral Alexei Orlov (Count Alexei Grigoryevich Orlov, nephew of Count Grigori) that besieged Koroni. Although the siege initially failed, A. Orlov eventually succeeded in seizing Koroni and Pylos, turning next to Methoni. However, the victories were inflated by rumors, instigating many cities in Peloponnese, Greek Mainland, and Epirus to raise the flag of revolution.

After its initial successes, the movement was crushed by the Porte with relative ease due to the lack of adequate help from the Russians, resulting in the slaughter and exile of tens of thousands of Christians, rebels, or not, throughout Greece and the Balkans. The Albanian commander Hatzi Osman, with the Sultan's mandate, attacked Messinia with fury where the revolution was still going on. G. Orlov ignored the call of the Greeks and departed without making a stand against the Ottoman troops that marched on Methoni and Pylos. After the failure of the revolutionary commander Psaros to capture Tripolitza, the Ottomans slaughtered thousands of Greek residents of Tripolitza while in the mainland, in Trikala, a significant number of revolutionaries met the same fate. Clergymen were put to death, while Greek dignitaries in Constantinople endured the wrath of the Ottomans against them.[123]

In his book "After the Fall", Athanasios Komninos Ypsilantis, who lived the events and narrated them from the Ottoman point of view, attached minimal significance to the contribution of Greeks in the operations of Orlov; on the contrary, he argued that Russians perceived that the Greeks of Mani had betrayed them. After the defeat of the 1770 revolution, the decree of the High Divan (Divan-ı-Humayun) on the general massacre of the Greeks in Peloponnese was not carried out; Captain Pasha, Algerian Gazi Hasan Pasha, argued that "if we kill all the Rums, who would then pay the taxes?" However, Albanians recruited by the Ottomans to suppress the revolution continued their savagery against both Christians and Muslims and refused to leave Peloponnese even after the Ottoman order. Captain Pasha Hasan took action, and with the cooperation of Kleftes, the help of whom he had sought, succeeded in their decimation. Nonetheless, he imposed heavier taxes on Maniates, though without much success, and pursued the Kleftes, who did not declare allegiance, including Petmezas and the Kolokotronis family, which he slew except for infant Theodoros Kolokotronis.[124]

---

[123] The numbers referred in historical books of the time should be taken under consideration with caution, as they are based on descriptions and impressions and not on written records.
[124] Theodoros Kolokotronis: Narration of events of the Greek race, Papyrus p. 29 (in Greek).

Revolutionary movements, albeit small in size, continued and usually resulted in disasters. The islanders, for their part, carried on attacking Ottoman ships while concealing their identity. In the meantime, Russia provided support only if it served its interests.

With Catherine's incitement, the always eager for freedom Greeks planned a new ambitious campaign in 1788. Even though Russia ultimately backed off due to diplomatic maneuvering, Souliotes and Armatoloi collided with Ali Pasha of Ioannina. Further, around the same time, Lambros Katsonis, a Greek colonel of the Russian Imperial Army, arrived at the Aegean with a flotilla. However, the 1770's mishap was still fresh in the memories to enable the movement to have a broader response from the Greek population. Katsonis found only a few comrade-in-arms, while not even Mani agreed to join in. For two years, Katsonis blocked the naval trade of the Ottomans and attacked whenever and wherever he found an opportunity. In 1790, in cape Kafirea, he was confronted, in a mighty naval battle, with the united Ottoman and Algerian Navy, twice the strength of his. The Ottomans, with the cooperation of French ships, as France wanted safe navigation in the region, defeated him. Katsonis survived, but many Greek sailors perished. The Ottomans thanked Mani for not participating in the movement, although the Mavromichalis family refused to respond to the Ottoman request to hand over Katsonis, who had fled there.

Despite the period of regression of the Ottoman Empire and its significant weakening, the Balkan peoples were too feeble to launch liberation campaigns. But during the Napoleonic Wars, the local Muslim Beys in the Balkans, with the power they had accumulated, represented an internal threat to the Ottoman administration. It was purely a struggle for

120

power and the advantages it entailed. The constant uprisings in the area made the Sultan start thinking of the need to "reconquer" Rumeli (Balkans).

The Ionian Islands (Eptanissos)

The Ottomans had never enslaved the Greeks of the seven Ionian Islands. However, the introduction of the Western feudal system by the Venetians led to social confrontations. The regime of landowning raised oppositions, to varying degrees, between landowners and tenant farmers. Furthermore, the Greeks of the Ionians had to struggle earnestly to preserve their identity, particularly at the religious and linguistic facets, as they were subjected to the influence of Catholicism and the Italian language.

With the Treaty of Campo Formio of October 17, 1797, and the dissolution of the Republic of Venice by Napoleon Bonaparte, the Ionian Islands were ceded to France. The people of Corfu welcomed the French troops, and many Greeks laid their hopes for the liberation of their homeland on Napoleon. In May 1799, however, after a Russo-Turkish fleet expelled French forces from the Ionian Islands, Russia convinced the Ottoman Empire to set up an independent state, tax-vassal to the Sultan, the Septinsular Republic.The Septinsular Republic (Ionian state) lasted from March 21, 1800, to July 8, 1807, under Russian and Ottoman domination. This state was the first semi-autonomous state in Greek territory after the abolition of the Byzantine Empire by the Ottomans. In 1806, Ali Pasha of Ioannina surmised that the Russian-Turkish war had allowed him to occupy the recently formed Republic. The Ionian Senate commissioned the defense of Lefkada (1807) to Ioannis Kapodistrias, who agreed with the Souliotes as well as the Kleftes and Armatoloi, who had fled to the Ionian Islands to escape the tyranny of Ali. These warriors joined the military formations

121

and contributed decisively to the defense of the islands. Regarding the Armatoloi, the Extraordinary Commissioner of the Republic of the Ionian state[125] I. Kapodistrias, in a memorandum to the administration of Lefkada, pointed out that during the war, the Armatoloi had offered significant services, whereby their daring raids expelled the powerful forces of the Sultan from locations of Lefkada.[126]

In 1807 with the Treaty of Tilsit, the Russian Empire ceded control of the islands to Napoleonic France, which seized them without altering the constitutional form of the state. Britain waged a military campaign to conquer the islands that lasted from 1809 (Kythira) in the south to 1814 (Corfu) in the north. The British intervention resulted in the formation of the autonomous united state of the Ionian Islands, in 1815, under the exclusive "protection" of Great Britain. The British were allies of the Ottoman Empire, but by no means acted like the Turks, although they sometimes ruled with cruelty. Particular attention is drawn to the authoritarian and cruel administration of the British High Commissioner Thomas Maitland.

The Ionian Islands were part of the West and therefore participated to some degree in the rapid developments in the Western world. Thus they constituted a contact area for Greeks with the new European modernistic currents. In this manner, they contributed to disseminating the principles of Enlightenment and the revolutionary idea in the framework of national independence.[127]

The Greeks of the Ionian Islands offered hospitality and protection to persecuted Greeks ever

---

[125] A.G. Protopsaltis: Political History of modern Greece, Issue B΄, Athens, 1973, p. 67 (in Greek).
[126] I. Kapodistrias: Texts, Athens, 1976 p. 15 (in Greek).
[127] Magazine Ardin (in Greek).

since the Fall of Constantinople, including the refugees from Parga who fled to Corfu in their effort to escape Ali Pasha's wrath after the surrender of their city. Also, chieftains and rebels, such as Theodoros Kolokotronis, that fled from the Ottomans, found refuge in the Ionian Islands. The national poet Dionysios Solomos "watched" from Zakynthos the Siege of Messolonghi", and the Philhellene poet Lord Byron resided in Kefalonia for six months before leaving for Messolonghi.

The Serbs

Following the failure of the movement of Kitsos Votsaris and Samuel Kalogirou in Epirus (1802), the Greeks turned their attention to Serbia. The Serbian movement of 1804, however, did not intend to root out the Ottoman domination. When Napoleon invaded Egypt in 1798, the Sultan was forced to withdraw his army from the Balkans, which resulted in the Sublime Porte losing its influence there. Renegade Janissaries invaded Belgrade in 1801, assassinated the legal authority Haji Mustafa Pasha and installed a brutal administration. When at the beginning of 1804, the Janissaries murdered dozens of dignitaries and priests, Serb knezes (local rulers) staged an army of thirty thousand peasants that sieged Belgrade. But this uprising was not an organized Revolution akin to that of the Greeks that followed; Serbs were simply seeking to restore the status quo ante.

The leader of the Serb rebels, Djordje Petrovic (Karayorgis), was just a shepherd. The Serbs took up arms in the name of the Sultan, but the latter hesitated in supporting them, as he could not come to terms with the idea of supporting Christians against Muslims. The Serbs refused to lay down their weapons before the order was restored and drove away Sultan's troops that had been dispatched to impose it unilaterally against them. The Russo-Turkish War that followed (1806 - 1812), gave the opportunity in 1806 to Serb knezes to turn to the Russians, transforming a local uprising into a quasi-liberation struggle. Serb rebels led by Karayorgis and, with the help of Russia, seized Belgrade in December 1806. In 1808, Karayorgis was elected "King of Serbs" Gospodar, while Russia persuaded Serbs to reject any offered compromise. Russia, for its part, might have wanted to help its coreligionists further but was afraid that a split of the Ottoman Empire would throw the region into Napoleon's hands, whereas ongoing Serb unrest served its interests. Meanwhile, the Ottoman state was in turmoil by the revolt of Kabakchı Mustafa with the Sultan having been replaced twice. Sultan Selim III had been assassinated because of his intent to replace the Janissaries with a new army corps, and his successor was in no position to make any compromises. In March 1809, Khurshid Ahmet Pasha, who had left Egypt after the prevalence of Mehmed Ali, was entrusted with suppressing the rebellion. In 1809, when Czar Alexander agreed with Napoleon, the Ottomans regained control of Belgrade. With that, Serbs got first-hand knowledge of the intricacies of international politics regarding the interests of powerful nations.[128]

The circumstances of the imposition of peace in Serbia favored neither the Greek hopes nor Serbian aspirations. During the Russo-Turkish War of 1807, Konstantinos Ypsilantis, the former ruler of Wallachia, who had fought on the side of Russians in the past, formed a Greek military division under an officer of Greek origin, N. Pangalos. Konstantinos Ypsilantis was the son of Phanariot Alexander Ypsilantis -Great Interpreter of the Sublime Porte and ruler of Wallachia- and father of the leader of the

---

[128] Steven W. Sowards: The Balkans, 2000.

Friendly Society Alexandros Ypsilantis. When after the defeat of Serbs, Konstantinos fled to Russia, the Sultan beheaded his father in Constantinople and confiscated the family's property. Because of these events, there were claims that Alexandros Ypsilantis, apart from his patriotism, had acted in haste regarding the failed campaign in Iasi because of his grudge against the Turks. However, historical development proved that this was not the case.

In the meantime, the Serbian campaign went on. Eventually, when Napoleon invaded Russia in 1812, and the Russo-Turkish War of 1809 - 1813 ended, Serbs were once again abandoned by Russia. With the Bucharest Treaty of May 28, 1812, some form of autonomy was granted to Serbs. Still, the Serbs under Karayorgis insisted on independence, a claim that was immediately rejected by the Ottomans. On September 5, 1812, Khurshid was appointed Sadrazam at Sublime Porte but did not leave Serbia to go to Constantinople to take up the post. Instead, he continued the war against the Serbs and defeated them in 1813. Serbian leader Karayorgis fled to Austria, as did tens of thousands of Serbs. The administration of Serbia was undertaken by the rebel Milos Obrenovic, who sought mere autonomy (and not independence). Two years later, Karayorgis was murdered by Obrenovic when he returned from Austria to carry on with the revolution against the Ottomans. Obrenovic pledged allegiance to the Sultan and was appointed as Great Knez. The Serbian uprising failed, but it exposed the weaknesses of the Ottoman administration as it took the Porte nine years to neutralize it. It was only in 1838 that the Sublime Porte ceded to Serbia a special charter of protected sovereignty.[129]

---

[129] Mark Mazower: The Balkans, 2000, p. 80.

In 1814 Khurshid suppressed another Serb revolution under Haji Prodan. He was replaced by Mehmed Emin Rauf Pasha in the position of Sadrazam on April 1, 1815, and was appointed Prefect of Bosnia, pursuing his involvement with Serbia's issues. Later he was appointed Prefect (Vali) in Peloponnese.

Prior to the eruption of the 1821 Greek revolutionary movement in Moldovlachia, Milos Obrenovic reportedly had contacts with the Friendly Society and had become a member. Three prominent Greek military leaders of Vlachia, S. Kaminaris, G. Farmakis, and G. Olympios, had tried in earnest since 1820 to strike a military alliance between Greeks and Serbs. Milos Obrenovic, however, sought to enhance his status, not through conflict but deliberations with the Sublime Porte. Thus, he pursued an opportunistic tactic, avoiding a coalition with the Greeks, but without discouraging the Friendly Society. By the end of December 1820, Ypsilantis drafted an alliance treaty with Serbs, but the bearer of the request, a member of the Friendly Society Aristides Pappas, fell into the hands of Turks and was murdered. At any rate, Obrenovic was not truly going to help the movement of Ypsilantis. Nevertheless, when the Greek uprising in Moldovlachia broke out (and afterward in Peloponnese), he did not renounce the Revolution and did not prevent Serb fighters from participating.

Ali Pasha of Ioannina

The Albanian-born Tepedelenli Ali Pasha took advantage of the absence of the Pasha of Ioannina Ali Zot, who was participating in a military excursion and proclaimed himself Pasha of Ioannina in 1788. The deed was eventually approved by the Sultan, who further extended his jurisdiction to the mainland of

Greece. From the position of Governor of the Sandjak of Ioannina, Ali gradually set the foundations for the creation of a quasi-autonomous state in the region of Epirus and continental Greece. During his authoritarian hegemony, Ioannina became an important spiritual, cultural, political, and economic center. In his efforts to achieve his goals, Ali consorted in various ways with the religious and ethnic groups of his territory. The separatism of Ali Pasha was indicative of the institutional corruption and disruptive movements that prevailed during that period in the area.

Ali showed particular favor and tolerance towards the Greek element of the region but did not hesitate to crush any rival forcefully and was ruthless with those who questioned his authority. The rebellious, brave Souliotes and the Cheimariotes were pursued with great ferocity. The memory of the nation has recorded the self-sacrifice of monk Samuel and the Souliotes as well as the blowing up in Kungi.[130] Ali managed to subdue Cheimara and the villages of the coast of Epirus in 1798. As Souliotes valiantly resisted, Ali unleashed three campaigns against them, in 1790, 1792, and 1800. The pursuit of Kleftes by arms or treachery lasted throughout Ali's reign. Many of them were eliminated, including Katsantonis, while others were expelled. After the surrender of Parga (1819) under the British auspices, Pargians suffered Ali's wrath.[131]

Meanwhile, some of the most prominent warriors of the 1821 Revolution, such as Androutsos, Athanasios Diakos, Markos Botsaris, were all trained

---

[130] On December 13, 1803 Souli was under siege by the army of Ali. After many days of heroic defense, Souliotes were obliged to surrender. Monk Samuel however did not and preferred to blow himself together with five of his companions and a magazine filled with munitions so that the Turks would not get hold of them.
[131] Nikos G. Svoronos Ibid., p. 60.

in Ali's guard and the military school he had founded. Ali Pasha had gathered in his palace several Greek scholars and scientists such as his doctor G. Sakellarios, the politician Ioannis Kolettis, the poet Ioannis Vilaras and others, while the common language of his court was Greek. Greeks were also managers of his property and finances of his state.

In 1820, Sultan Mahmud II, alarmed by Ali's activities, which he perceived them to be a danger for the cohesion of the Empire, ordered his removal from the administration of Ioannina to confine him in his birthplace, Tepedelen, Albania. Modern Turkish historians note the Sultan's mistake to banish Ali and claim that the Greeks of Constantinople were the ones who defamed him because they regarded him as an obstacle to their plans for the revolution. Ali sought to appease the Sultan and asked for the mediation of Russia and Britain with which he maintained relations through their representatives in the region. However, in 1820, the Porte declared him guilty of treason and invited him to appear in Constantinople to apologize. He refused, of course, understanding where that would lead. Mahmud II mobilized an army in the summer of 1820 against Ali, initially under Ismail Pasobey, followed by Khurshid Ahmet Pasha, the prefect of Peloponnese. Ali found himself in a dire situation as he faced significant desertion of his troops, while Souliotes changed camp allying with him (in the context, perhaps that "the enemy of my enemy, is my friend"), especially after his promise that he would let them re-settle in Souli. Despite the involvement of Khurshid Pasha with the Greek Revolution that, in the meantime, had erupted in Peloponnese, Ali was defeated near the end of November of 1821 and was confined along with a few men in his palace. Nevertheless, this internal conflict between the Sultan and Ali proved beneficial to the Greek rebels in launching their Revolution.

128

In January 1822, after hard negotiations, Ali agreed to surrender on the condition that he would be pardoned and fled to the island of Lake Ioannina. In the same month, and after a brief scuffle, he was murdered and beheaded by order of the Sultan.

THE PREPARATION OF THE REVOLUTION

The Friendly Society

The idea of establishing a secret organization for preserving the national conscience of the Greeks and preparing the nation for a general uprising was conceived way before the Revolution. Before the founding of the Friendly Society, several precursors had preceded it in Europe. Greeks, as well as Vlachs, participated in the "Society of Friends" that was established in Bucharest in 1780.[132] In 1787, the Phanariot ruler of Moldovlachia Alexandros Mavrokordatos, founded the "Phoenix Society" in Russia, after fleeing from Moldova. In the early 19th century, other similar associations were established following the model of the secret societies that acted in Europe at the time, in relevance to Masonic lodges. Under the pretext of Greek cultural edification, they tried to lay the groundwork for some form of national rehabilitation of Greeks. Among them, the "Greek-language Hotel" (Paris 1809) and the "Music-lovers Society" (Athens 1812), with its branch in Vienna later on, were noteworthy associations. They were all founded and operated in cities where Greeks were active. Constantinople was naturally exempted, under the presumption that being the capital of the Ottoman Empire, the administration could quickly repress any subversive activity there. The developments later would reverse this tenet.

---

[132] A.G. Protopsaltis: Ibid., Issue A' p. 50 (in Greek).

The Friendly Society, founded in Odessa in 1814 by three friends from the middle-class, Athanasios Tsakalov, Nikolaos Skoufas, and Emmanuel Xanthos,[133] would have a decisive role in the preparation of the Revolution. The Society's goal was to prepare a nationwide insurrection for the emancipation of the genus from the Ottoman yoke. The founding members of the Friendly Society took into account, according to Xanthos, "the character of the Greek people, the sources of its strength, the victories of the insurgents of Souli and Parga over the tyrant of Ioannina Ali Pasha, the political and moral status of the Turk oppressors, Riga's arguments, the action of Kleftes and the victories at the naval battles of Lambros Katsonis, the hatred of the diaspora against Turks and the moods of the European States".[134] Xanthos was a member of the Masonic Lodge and introduced some elements of it in the Friendly Society regarding its organization and closed hierarchical system.

The Governing Authority of the Society grew later with the addition of other members. The position of its leader remained vacant, but this fact was kept secret to the members of the Society, who could envision whomever they fancied in that post. Besides, secrecy was a principle embedded in the Society. In the indoctrination of its members, apart from the idea of freedom cultivated by Rigas Fereos and Adamantios Korais, the liberal enlightenment of the French Revolution was incorporated. The liberal and

---

[133] I. Philemon in the "Essays on the Friendly Society" mistakenly mentions Anagnostopoulos instead of Xanthos among the founders of the Society. He later admitted his mistake. However, the secrecy with which the Friendly Society was founded and operated, combined with the retrospective narratives of some of its members that have blurred the issues even further, hinder historical research. Thus, the accurate presentation of the actions of the Society is not possible.

[134] Emm. Xanthos: Memoirs of the Friendly Society (in Greek).

constitutional views of the British became known to the Greeks through their respective occupation of the Ionian Islands and the Greeks of the diaspora who had European education. However, the notion of the potential assistance of Russia was always the implied mainstay principle in deliberations of the Friendly Society. Its general policy against the Ottoman Empire and the presence of Count John Kapodistrias in the service of Czar, a well-known person in the Ionian Islands, as well as of Alexander Ypsilantis, who was born in Constantinople in a Phanariot family, strengthened this conviction. Although he was not initially a member, Ypsilantis, later on, assumed its leadership when conditions were ripe for the eruption of the Revolution.

The initial lack of success in Friendly Society's aspirations in Russia, along with the dangers its Authority members were facing, led them to consider the transfer of its headquarters outside Russia and within the territory of the Ottoman Empire. Xanthos, who worked in a commercial establishment in Constantinople, settled first in the city, in Mega Revma on the west coast of Bosporus. Tsakalov and Skoufas went from Moscow to Odessa in July 1817, and from there they decided to go to Constantinople where Xanthos had settled. Meanwhile, Anthimos Gazis, already a member of the Friendly Society, came to Odessa from Vienna and met with the Authority. Gazis then went to Constantinople, where he met Xanthos and then departed for Pelion, where he had established a school in the village of Milies. In December 1817, Tsakalov came to Constantinople and left shortly afterward for Pelion to assess the shift of the Society's headquarters there. Gazis, fearing treason, instead suggested Mani as the base of the Authority. With the plan falling through, Tsakalov departed in April 1817 for Smyrna having as final destination Constantinople. Skoufas, Anagnostopoulos, and others also arrived in

Constantinople in the same month. Their main concern was the decision on the headquarters of the Authority.

After considering several options, Constantinople was finally chosen as the base. They were led to this decision because of the large number of Greeks there and the true patriotism they possessed, as well as the inability, as they reckoned, of the Ottoman police to act effectively in the cosmopolitan environment of the city. Moreover, although Constantinople was the capital of the Ottoman state, it constituted historically and in practice the actual capital of Hellenism. From there, the Society could supervise the political situation effectively, stay on top of the Ottoman and Greek issues, and quickly face any problems that might spring up at any instant. The idea proved correct, and the decision turned out to be a success.

The intention of the Society was not to move immediately in a drastic way but to first observe the situation within the Ottoman state to find out how Greeks felt about the idea of freedom and if indeed their assessments regarding a revolt were correct. To make decisions on further actions of the Society, Tsakalov was asked to come from Smyrna to Constantinople, but he delayed his departure. By the end of May 1818, several Peloponnesian chieftains had arrived in Constantinople. A joint meeting took place, and some decisions were taken about the final phase of the big operation. Tsakalov finally arrived in Constantinople only six days before Skoufas died on July 31, 1818, at 40 of heart disease. Skoufas was buried in Bosporus by the Church of Taxiarches in Mega Revma. The Society was thus deprived of its visionary, who seemed to have been its principal founder and practically perhaps its leader until then. Despite this severe setback, the Society continued its work. Chieftain Anagnostaras was sent to Hydra,

Spetses, and Peloponnese to indoctrinate those deemed "suitable". The Society sent off a member to Zakynthos to recruit Theodoros Kolokotronis, while it sent others to Mani to enlist its ruler, Petrobey Mavromichalis. The latter, as it was reported, enthusiastically accepted to contribute to the struggle. Archimandrite Gregory Dikaios (Papaflessas) was sent to Moldovlachia.

But the Society's financial situation was in dire straits. Xanthos, Tsakalov, and Anagnostopoulos, who in the meantime had joined the Society's Authority, were at a standstill, and the grand plan of the campaign to send envoys aiming at the general indoctrination to the Society, seemed impossible. The leaders' efforts then turned to the wealthy and powerful Greeks, who lived or temporarily resided in Constantinople.

Ultimately, the member of the Society P. Sekeris and wealthy patriot Constantinopolitans pulled the organization out of its challenging financial troubles. The very favorable reception by the Greeks of Constantinople had revitalized the Society both economically and morally. The outpouring response shown by the progressive middle class of the Greeks of Constantinople, which was basically represented by merchants and their employees, their willingness to contribute in support of the objectives of the Society and the bravery they had shown was far more remarkable than that of the Greeks in Russia, from whom the Society expected more. By way of the solidarity of the Constantinopolitans, the Society was strengthened even more as Greek merchants, especially those who had the center of their operations in Europe, felt obliged to assist the Society seeing that even those who lived in the home base of the "tyrant" dared to engage in revolutionary operations.[135]

The institution of the boards of the Society, assisted substantially in the systematic organization of the members of the Society in the founding of which Anagnostopoulos contributed largely. A central coordinating role was played by the General Board of Constantinople, which corresponded with all boards of provinces. Papaflessas established the board of Athens with the help of reputable merchants of the city.

Arrangements among members of the Society were made either by correspondence or by frequent travels throughout the Balkans, Russia, and the wider region where Greeks lived. But disputes did ensue; many were created by antagonisms while some from the inquisitiveness of members who were trying to figure out the identity of the Authority. Those Society members in order to find out if Kapodistrias was the leader of the Authority, sent him a letter informing him about the Friendly Society and asking if they could be of any help. The letter was somehow misplaced and came to the Czar's attention. Russia's Ambassador to Constantinople Stroganov proceeded to a demarche to the Sublime Porte, informing the Ottoman authorities about the action of a subversive organization, in connection with the obligations of the Ottoman Empire to preserve the order in its territory. The Russian Ambassador also advised the Greeks of Constantinople to confine themselves to their duties as Sultan's faithful subjects. The Ottoman government, however, acted with its usual passivity, which was further coerced by influential Greeks. The Society thus managed to overcome this problem, as did with other issues that arose. Only in very few

---

[135] Apost. E. Vakalopoulos: History of the New Hellenism, Thessaloniki 1980, Volume V p. 75 (in Greek).

instances had to resort to assassinations of Society members that were traitors and extortionists.[136]

One of the means used by the Friendly Society to bolster its publicity was to conceal its leader (that did not exist until 1820), insinuating that it may have been Kapodistrias or even the Czar. However, as the time for the Revolution approached, it became imperative to appoint the highest authority. At the beginning of January 1820, Xanthos went from Moscow to St. Petersburg, where he visited Count John Kapodistrias, revealing him the Society's system, and asking him to lead the nation's movement. Kapodistrias rejected the offer citing as an excuse the fact of being Czar's Minister and underlining that he considered the move as hasty. Kapodistrias belonged to those who believed that the time was not ripe for the revolution and that the conditions for the liberation of Greeks had not yet matured. In despair, Xanthos turned his interest to another personage, equally brilliant and more capable than the Count in the military sector, Prince Alexander Ypsilantis, who indeed proved to be an excellent choice. He accepted with willingness and enthusiasm to be devoted to the service of Greeks and declared ready to sacrifice himself for the great cause.

Ypsilantis asked Kapodistrias to inform the Czar about obtaining assistance, if not military, at least financial. Kapodistrias not only refused again, but when Ypsilantis proceeded to declare the Revolution, he accused him that his "foolish declarations" boosted the accusations of Jacobinism[137] launched by Austrian Chancellor Metternich and his associates. It is, of course, always

---

[136] E.G. Protopsalti: p. 46-122, Emm. Xanthos: Memoirs of the Friendly Society (in Greek).
    Ap. E. Vakalopoulos: Ibid., p. 75-103 (in Greek).
[137] A revolutionary political movement during the French Revolution (1789–99).

tricky to figure out the "way to Tipperary".[138] Ypsilanti, being Czar's aide, asked for a two-year leave and began preparations, touring the cities of the region and meeting with members of the Society.[139]

The preparations in Constantinople

All perceptions embodied in the social composition of Constantinople were represented inside the circles of the Friendly Society. These notions sometimes took a disruptive character, as in the case of radical Elias Chrysospathis. He, in 1818, seceded along with like-minded Greeks from the Friendly Society and created a new secret association focusing on social objectives in addition to national liberation. With the drastic intervention of Tsakalov, the members who had departed rejoined the Friendly Society.

Eventually, it was decided to sacrifice the secrecy of the Society for the benefit of its broader promotion. Following the nomination of Ypsilanti as General Commissioner and Curator of the Authority on June 15, 1820, the enthusiasm of the Constantinopolitans for the anticipated liberation of the nation reached its peak. The secret of the Friendly Society became known to all Greeks of Constantinople, including women, something unusual for the times. The houses of Xanthos and Dikaios (Papaflessas), like those of other Greeks, were transformed into venues of assemblies of the Friendly

---

[138] From the book: "Defending Europe", 2016: It is an old story with a man who asks someone in the Irish countryside the way to Tipperary to receive the answer "If I were you, I would not start from here". "Here" is where we are. Kapodistrias did not believe that attaining the ultimate goal was possible with where they were at that time frame. Otherwise, undoubtedly, Kapodistrias wanted also to reach "Tipperary".

[139] Emm. Xanthos: Memoirs of the Friendly Society.

Society. The most important councils of the members of the Society were held at Pera, under the pretext of organizing dances.

The more enthusiastic among Greeks believed and started spreading rumors that Russia intended to help militarily the revolt of Greeks. Despite the resistance of the wiser, the local board of the Friendly Society asked Ypsilanti to send Constantinople an experienced army leader along with military supplies for launching the revolution. The proposed reckless plans foresaw the elimination of the Sultan and his court; arson of buildings of the city; burning the fleet, navy quarters, armory and ammunition depot, and seizing the vault! Another plan contemplated, with the secret arrangement of members of the Society, Greek sailors boarding Ottoman warships and cargo ships that would carry ammunition to the naval squadron of the Aegean, with the ultimate objective to apprehend or destroy them! These strategies aimed at "conquering" the state rather than the secession of territories in the framework of the "ecumenical solution".[140]

The various schemes for a move in Constantinople were eventually rejected, and no action took place. This inactivity of the city's board was later criticized. It was speculated that if by various efforts the operation were successful in paralyzing the administration of the state and burn the fleet, the Ottoman Empire would have been unable to promptly muster significant resistance to the martial operations of the Greeks. At least, if Greek sailors were to take over the ships carrying supplies to the Ottoman fleet, they would have helped the struggle of Greece considerably. Lastly, according to

---

[140] The ecumenical idea is a form of the Great Idea, according to which Hellenism would be imposed internally in the Ottoman Empire i.e. take over the state.

this viewpoint, the Turks would have perceived very late the real source of these actions, and the blame would have been, at least initially, ascribed to Russians. It could be asserted that considering the plight of the Greeks of Constantinople, which in one way or another could not have been avoided, and that the immense hardships of the revolutionary Greeks might have been diminished if Greeks of Constantinople had taken action, their inactivity should be considered reprehensible. As it turned out, the progression of military undertakings made it clear that any revolutionary movement in the capital of the Empire would have had no chance of success. In contrast, the total slaughter of Greeks of Constantinople would have been almost a certainty.[141]

The Patriarchate of Constantinople

Following the invitation received in Mount Athos on December 14, 1818, to take over the Patriarchate for the third time, Gregory V arrived in Constantinople on January 19, 1819. It was Gregory's lot to be Patriarch during the great uprising. He must have had known, in general terms, the whereabouts of the Friendly Society due to its significant expansion in Constantinople. He was also informed about it in more detail by a member of the Society, the Macedonian chieftain Yiannis Farmakis, during his visit to Mount Athos in 1818. Still, Gregory refused the oath to join in on the grounds that he was a clergyman.

---

[141] Most importantly, it would have not been possible to prolong the presence of Greeks in Constantinople for another 150 years. The Greeks of Constantinople were expelled or forced to leave eventually in 1960 – 1970 under the indifferent eyes of Europeans and Americans.

Patriarch Gregory must have harbored mixed feelings about the prospect of a revolution like everyone who held any spiritual or social status or had significant property. On the one hand, he undoubtedly yearned for liberation, but on the other, he must have pondered the dire consequences that an uprising could have resulted in. Would all Christian land be liberated? Which regions would remain under Ottoman rule? In Anatolia, there were many scattered Metropolis – islands of Christianity in a Muslim sea. What would happen to Christianity there? Thus, while he did not suppress those who promoted the idea of national independence, on the other hand, was relaying to Turks that the existence of the Empire and its sovereignty over the Christian congregation was God's will. The continuation of the residency of Greek Christians in the unliberated regions of the Ottoman Empire for another hundred years that later allowed their liberation, such as in Epirus, Macedonia, and part of Thrace, was in part due to Patriarchate's policy during the Revolution.

Among the actions of the Patriarch in favor of the national idea that should be attributed to him include his reference letter given to the active member of the Friendly Society and its envoy D. Themelis and his appointment of Gregory Dikaios (Papaflessas) as patriarchal Exarch. By this, he provided him the ability to roam Greece and disseminate the principles of the Friendly Society. To these, it should be added that his secretary and Chief Secretary of the Holy Synod C. Afthonidis was a member of the Society, as well as his letter of July 30, 1819, sent to Petrobey Mavromichalis and other chieftains in Peloponnese for establishing a joint school. However, the probative outcomes of these acts are not as obvious.

There should be no doubt that almost all of the clergy in Constantinople were aware of the Friendly Society, as it wouldn't have been possible for the spiritual leadership of the Christian folk to be in the dark of what thousands of Greeks already knew. As a matter of fact, according to existing testimonies, several high-ranking priests, among them Metropolitan of Derkon Gregory, were members of the Friendly Society.[142]

The situation in Peloponnese

The decision of the Friendly Society for the uprising in Mani seems to have been taken as early as 1820. The member of the Friendly Society Gregory Dikaios, surnamed Papaflessas, had been appointed by Alexander Ypsilantis as a proxy to form the board of Constantinople area. Alexander Ypsilantis, in the terminology of the Friendly Society, referred in his correspondence to the Revolution in Peloponnese as the "School of Peloponnese". Moreover, the members of the Society visiting various areas were hosted as "pupils". In a letter addressed to the "Greek patriots of Peloponnese" on October 8, 1820, A. Ypsilantis wrote that the time for the noble struggle was approaching and that "we must show to all nations of Europe, who are accusing us ruthlessly, that indeed we are the true descendants of the ancient Greeks and heirs of their virtues". In many other areas of Greece, Ypsilantis had sent similar letters.

The Ottomans, although not able to know the extent of the planned movement, had become aware of it for quite a while and tried to take some preventive measures. Mostly, however, they feared the joined attack of the British army based in the Ionian Islands. Their fears were intensified by false information of Russian ships bringing munitions to the ruler of Mani Petrobey Mavromichalis. To avoid any revolutionary

---

[142] P. A. Giorkatzis: The "Aphorism" of Alexandre Ypsilanti, Kavala, 1988 p.168 (in Greek).

actions, they contemplated killing all dignitaries in Peloponnese. Meanwhile, repressive measures were being taken against the Greeks of Epirus who had fallen prey to Ali's cunning. The Sultan, facing both the actions of Greeks and the aspirations of Ali Pasha, compounded with conflicting information regarding the latter from European embassies, seemed unable to decide how to react. Ultimately, he prioritized taking up arms against Ali while imposing policing measures on both land and coasts of Greece.

Khurshid Ahmet Pasha, of Georgian origin, was appointed, after Bosnia, Prefect of Peloponnese (Mora Valisi) in November 1820, and had settled with his harem and staff in Tripolitza (Tripoli of Peloponnese). There, he promptly became aware that Greeks were preparing a rebellion against the state. On November 8, 1820, Khurshid gathered the region's dignitaries to be questioned on the subject, but Greeks denied any such claims. Despite this blatant lie, when instructed to suppress the movement of Tepedelenli Ali Pasha of Ioannina, he departed Tripolitza, leaving behind only a small branch of his army under his deputy, Mehmet Salih.

The focus of the attention of the Friendly Society in Moldovlachia did not allow the drafting of a regulation of the Society in Peloponnese, which would have laid down matters of hierarchy. The situation that arose, with several members of the Society claiming to be "central" executive agents with a license to initiate new members and act at will, resulted in confusion and disagreements that curtailed the preparations for war. The Heads of Communities wanted to preserve their political status based on which they had the primacy. In contrast, various revolutionary elements sought to overthrow the established sociopolitical order. Alexander Ypsilantis, in his address from Odessa, on August 23, 1820, urged Peloponnesians to uphold unity and togetherness as the basis of the operation. The envoys of the Friendly Society, in collaboration with the local priesthood, were more organized in their conceived duty of preparing the revolution. To this end, they sent a document to the Authority for the systematization of the actions that was signed by the Greeks of the region, headed by the Metropolitan of Patras.[143]

On December 24, 1820, Papaflessas sent instructions to the Greeks of Peloponnese, before departing from Constantinople for Kidonies (Ayvalik, western Anatolia), Hydra and Spetses with a ship loaded, as he claimed, with ammunition for Mani as a way to underscore the leadership of the "Anticipated", Alexander Ypsilantis. With these, he called upon all dignitaries to come together, consent, and confer on the means to realize the sacred cause and resolve the issue of hierarchy. Also, he instructed them to organize the military, which, according to the General Curator (A. Ypsilantis), should be confined to only 25 thousand ready-to-fight soldiers to avoid irregular troops.

The Peloponnesians, following the instructions relayed by Papaflessas, agreed to come together to discuss the issues raised and invited him to come to Patras from Spetses. In the Assembly of Vostitza (Aigio), convened between January 26-29, 1821, with the participation of Metropolitans of Patras and Arcadia and members of the Friendly Society, two opposing views emerged. Papaflessas, as representative of the Society, presented the mandate of Alexander Ypsilantis regarding commencing the Revolution in Peloponnese. It called for direct action with the thought that the Sublime Porte was already aware of the plot, and any further delay would endanger the outcome. He assured the delegates that

---

[143]Ioannis Philemon: Ibid., p.214.

ammunition was sent to Hydra, but he was treated with mistrust, apprehension, and open hostility.[144] The Metropolitan of "Old Patras" Germanos brought forth the need to display prudence as neither the preparations were complete nor Russia's position was clear, and further suggested that Peloponnese should not be left to revolt alone. It was agreed that Papaflessas had to cease his actions and leave Peloponnese to avoid provoking the Ottomans, ask other provinces of Greece to be armed, collect the pledged financial donations, and send a mission to Russia to find out its intentions. It was also decided that if it were not possible to divert the suspicions of the Ottomans, and if the latter asked for the gathering of dignitaries in Tripolitza, to disobey and instead flee to the Cyclades to resolve the quandary.[145]

In the meantime, a representative was sent to Hydra to check out the truth about Papaflessas' claim on the dispatched ammunition. Although the Turks had placed the coasts of Peloponnese under police surveillance, the envoy managed to reach the island of Hydra to find out that there was no ammunition, nor a war spirit prevailed among the dignitaries of Hydra. The Metropolitan of Patras was convinced that the war would be harmful if it started in Peloponnese, particularly without the participation of other provinces. Still, not all the dignitaries in Vostitza were of the same opinion. Nevertheless, the views on inaction prevailed.[146]

The Vostitza assembly resulted in raising the suspicions of the Ottoman administration, and the

---

[144] Dionysios Tzakis: E-Historically, Achaia p. 35-42, "The timid, the infamous and the vulgar". The "competent" Papaflessas, according to the Friendly Society, was the "infamous" according to Germanos (in Greek).
[145] Ioannis Philemon: Historical Essay on Friendly Society, 1834 p. 238 (in Greek).
[146] Ioannis Philemon: Ibid., p. 237.

excuses given were not very convincing. The Ottomans began to perceive, from indiscretions and various misguided actions of Greeks, that there was a plan for the revolutionary movement and decided to slaughter dignitaries and senior priests. This plan of the Ottomans remained secret, and it was known only to very few; even Turkish notables of the region were not informed, as some of them had Greek contacts. For the implementation of this project or at any rate for the isolation of Greek leaders, the acting prefect of Peloponnese, Mehmet Salih, invited them to Tripolitza in January 1821. A regular assembly of them took place every March and September on matters of tax collection, but their extraordinary invitation in January that included the senior priests could only arouse suspicions, although not perhaps to the point of suspecting an imminent slaughter. What was sure was that they were going to be held hostages. The low-profile dignitaries and senior priests hesitated to go to Tripolitza. Mehmet Salih, who had been informed about the arrival of Kolokotronis in Mani, fearing movement of the Kleftes and Armatoloi, repeated the invitation more urgently, while at the same time requesting military assistance from the Sublime Porte.

Papaflessas, after he failed in Vostitza, roamed around Peloponnese and was received with ambivalence in several cities and villages. Some of the dignitaries saw in him a representative of a lower social class, seeking in addition to the expulsion of Turks and liberation of Greeks, the overthrowing of the pre-revolutionary social and political hierarchical pyramid.[147] However, Papaflessas also had some successes in his efforts, initiating to the Society several Greeks from lower classes.[148] He met with Petrobey Mavromichalis in Kytries, and as he wrote,

---

[147] View of St. Papageorgiou
[148] D. Tzakis: Ibid.

to overcome his hesitations, he promised him the dominion of Peloponnese after its liberation.[149]

The reopening of Dimitsana's gunpowder mills reinforced the suspicions of Turks, but an Ottoman search force sent there to investigate returned empty-handed. Nevertheless, an order was issued to demolish the mills. Meanwhile, the Ottoman mob of Peloponnese had become furious upon hearing the news about the movement in Moldovlachia and called for the slaughter of Greeks. Metropolitan Germanos departed from Patra on February 27, 1821, supposedly to go to Tripolitza, but instead, he went to Kalavryta and stayed there under the pretense of illness. But several senior priests, either believing that they could no further mislead the Ottoman authority, or because of the dreadful despair induced by the events, or believing that they could appease the Ottomans with their presence, or perhaps because they did not believe in the Revolution, went to Tripolitza early March hoping that they could depart soon with the excuse of the approaching Easter. There were nine senior priests and twelve secular dignitaries that traveled to Tripolitza. Although Mani did not fall under the authority of the prefect of Peloponnese, Petrobey was also invited to ensure with his presence the abiding by the law of the southeastern Peloponnese. Petrobey did not go to Tripolitza himself, citing health reasons, and instead sent one of his sons on February 12, 1821. The arrival of the latter calmed somewhat the Ottomans.[150]

However, the secret of the Friendly Society had been exposed, and the extent of the movement in Moldovlachia had been perceived. The Ottomans once

---

[149] Efi Alamanis: The action of Papaflessas after the meeting of Vostitza, history of the Greek nation, Ekdotiki Athinon, Vol. L, (1975) (in Greek)
[150] I. Philemon: Ibid., p.245

147

again urged other senior priests who had not arrived in Tripolitza to obey a new order on March 19, 1821. Meanwhile, on March 16, 1821, Greek revolutionaries set up an ambush to a squad of Turkish soldiers near Patras, killing them. Senior priests and elders, after consultations in Lavra, agreed not to go to Tripolitza because the Turkish mob seemed to have persuaded the government to kill them. Instead, they decided to stay inactive until it would become more evident where the situation was heading.

THE MOVEMENT IN MOLDOVLACHIA

The stances of the European states

The political attitudes of the European Powers regarding the developments in the Balkans were determined by the historical evolutions of the period following the Napoleonic Wars and the Vienna Treaty. Already with the Chaumont pact in March 1814, the allies Austria, Britain, Prussia, and Russia had guaranteed, collectively and individually, the future of the "territorial and political status" of Europe that would result from a future agreement.

The wars against Napoleon, called "liberating wars", culminated with the establishment of authoritarian regimes in almost all of Europe. After the Vienna Conference (1815), which attempted to establish the order in Europe following the previous wars, the major European conservative Powers formed a dispute settlement system to safeguard their powers, confront revolutionary movements, weaken nationalist forces, and secure the balance of power. The "Vienna System" established by the victorious Powers (against Napoleon), the Kingdom of Prussia, the Empires of Austria, Russia, and Britain, functioned for only a few years and was expressed in two forms, the Holy Alliance and the Quadruple Alliance. The Ottoman Empire was not invited to participate at the Vienna Conference, nor in the subsequent Vienna System regarding the European order, although it had territories in Balkans as it had not participated in the Napoleonic Wars. Besides, it was a Muslim State and, therefore, a "non-European

Power". Consequently, it was thought that it could not be part of the solution in Europe.[151]

The Holy Alliance was founded on September 26, 1815, by Russia, Prussia, and Austria at the initiative of the Czar to protect the Christian social values and the traditional monarchy. In fact, it had no political value, and it was merely an expression of noble aspirations. Nevertheless, in the coming years, the expression of the Holy Alliance embodied the odious European system of the Chancellor of Austria Metternich - with the ulterior motive of conspiring against the freedom of peoples. Britain did not participate in the Holy Alliance, while British foreign minister Lord Castlereagh described this alliance as an act of supreme mysticism and foolishness.[152] Nevertheless, Britain joined the Quadruple Alliance, which later evolved into a quintuple with the addition of France in 1818, and became politically more influential. Meetings within the Vienna system took place during the controversial period of the Greek transition in Aix-la-Chapelle (1818), Carlsbad (1819), Troppau (1820), Laubach (1821), and Verona (1822).

On the contrary, the Concert of Europe that followed the Vienna Conference did not result from contractual arrangements but was formulated with international practice through the power of the states of the European "Directorate". The most critical decision-making criterion in foreign policy, namely, to ensure that leaders continue to hold on to their power, prevailed. The "principle of legality" that was sanctioned at the conference in Vienna (1815), was the application of this criterion in conjunction with the maintenance of the territorial status quo in the context of the balance of power. The ethnic principle

---

[151] S.Th. Laskari: The diplomatic history of Greece 1821-1914 Athens 1947, p.7 (in Greek)
[152] S.Th. Laskari, Ibid., p.7

was not only ignored but was systematically spurned.[153]

During the Napoleonic Wars, the principles of enlightenment, that had acquired a political sway with the French Revolution, were broadly disseminated, and the national conscience of European peoples began to develop. The path towards the creation of independent states by nations that had a commonality of language, cultural, and racial characteristics, in most respects also of religion, was now inevitable. Soon, a diversification of interests together with an awareness of the national community, the common fate of a nation, started to appear. This came about through the common struggle for independence of each different people, but also through the statehood in instances where revolutions prevailed, and states were established, although no proper definition of "nation" yet existed.[154]

The Revolution in Iasi

The most feared among the disobedient local, regional commanders of the Sultan was Ali Pasha of Ioannina, who had extended his influence from the Vardar to Corinth. Ali, in his lengthy conflict with the Sultan, intended to establish his power in Epirus and beyond, exploiting the revolutionary frame of mind of Greeks. The Greeks of the region, for their part, thought that Ali could help their case, as his tolerant administration turned his capital Ioannina into a noteworthy center of Greek learning. In 1821, while the Porte had organized a campaign and had sent an

---

[153] Vasilis Moutsoglou: The criteria in international politics, Athens, 2015, p. 31 (in Greek)

[154] G. Zotiadis: Political and diplomatic history of the New Era, 1973 p. 81 (in Greek)

army against him, the revolutionary movement of the Greeks in Moldovlachia broke out.

Alexander Ypsilantis had been warned that Russia could not support him because of the positions conveyed regarding European order and that in Iasi, there were not adequate military preparations for the movement of the Greeks to succeed. Meanwhile, news from Constantinople arrived, informing that the secret of the Friendly Society had been revealed and that Ypsilantis would have to move as soon as possible. Ypsilantis hoped, based on promises, that the local population would support him in his movement.

From there on, the Revolution got rolling. Having contemplated all pertinent facts, and after consultations with fellow members of the Friendly Society, Ypsilantis resolved to proceed with his movement and, on February 18, 1821, dispatched a relevant document to Greek military leaders of Iasi asking them to get prepared. Subsequently, on February 21, 1821, Ypsilantis departed from Bessarabia, passed Prut river, and entering Iasi (Moldova) two days later on February 24, raised the flag of Revolution. There, he issued a revolutionary proclamation titled "Fight for Faith and the Fatherland"[155] – to a greater extent for Fatherland. At the same time, he sent a letter to members of the Friendly Society, pointing out that the movement was the outcome of many years of efforts and hopes of the Greek nation. Ypsilantis believed until the very last moment that Russia would come to the aid of Greeks: "Rise my friends, and you will see a great power defending our rights".[156] Ultimately, the Russian government kept a negative stance toward the

---

[155] Vasilis Kremmydas characterizes it as the "Manifesto of the Revolution", To Vima 19.3.2017 (in Greek).
[156] Vasilis Kremmydas: Ibid., p. 63.

endeavor of Ypsilantis from the beginning to the end.[157]

The reasons for the choice of Moldovlachia were the fact that the Ottoman army was prohibited from setting camp in these areas and that the ruler of Moldova, Michael Soutsos, as well as the acting ruler at Vlachia Konstantinos Negris, were Greek. Both supported Ypsilantis, resulting in their subsequent deposition by the Sultan. However, the action took place in an area where Greeks did not constitute the majority; at the start, his army was meager, and it often required replenishments of food supplies from local populations, provoking negative sentiments in Romanian villagers.[158] Moreover, Romanians, in general, harbored ill feelings against the Greek rulers of the region, whom they considered surrogates of the Sultan. Regarding Serbia, from which Ypsilantis expected assistance, the messenger with the said request never reached his destination, as he was murdered on his way.

Volunteers from all over Europe arrived in Moldova to join the military corps of Ypsilantis and organized the artillery. The "Sacred Company", consisting of a few hundred students, was formed to assist the Greek revolutionary army. On March 4, Greek sailors took over and equipped 15 ships, while on March 17, Ypsilantis raised the flag of freedom in Bucharest, facing at the outset the army of the Pashas from the area. The Greek army was divided into two regiments under George and Nikolaos Ypsilantis.

---

[157] Gregory Ars: "How the Greek Revolution began in Iasi", E-Historically, p. 11 (in Greek).
[158] Wladymir Brunet de Presle et Alexandre Blanchet : La Grèce depuis la conquête romaine jusqu'à nos jours, Firmin Didot, 1860 (in French).

Following these events, the Ottoman army invaded the Principalities in Moldovlachia, in violation of the treaties enacted under the guarantee of Russia, and militarily suppressed the movement. The military of Ypsilantis was finally destroyed in the battle of Dragatsani on June 7, 1821, and retreated to the Austrian border. The reasons for its failure should be attributed mainly to the superior power of the opponent, along with the absence of adequate military might of the rebel forces. The leader of the Romanian Vlachs Tudor Vladimirescu, who, as a pro-Russian, was expected to support Ypsilantis, ultimately refused to assist him financially or militarily. He allied with the local boyars to banish the Phanariotes and take their place as hospodars - rulers.

The campaign in Moldovlachia that ended with disaster in June 1821 could strategically be regarded as belonging to the ecumenical rather than national perception of the liberation of the Greeks. Ypsilantis probably considered that his plausible victory would have most likely aided Russia's plans against the Ottoman Empire and could have therefore brought the desired assistance from the Czar. His military engagement was more an act of war rather than a revolution - rebellion of the inhabitants of a region.

Considering the eventual failure of the operation, the great historical significance of this movement lies in the fact that it was undertaken in the context of the Friendly Society's plan by its head, Alexander Ypsilantis. The legacy of the movement of heroic Ypsilantis is immense for the joint affair of the Greeks, as it signaled the launch of the Revolution, which was diligently prepared by the Friendly Society.

The eruption of the Revolution in Moldovlachia became known to the Sublime Porte on March 1, 1821, when the revolutionary proclamation

154

of Ypsilantis was delivered to it. Sultan Mahmud II and the Ottoman government were outraged by "the betrayal and the audacity of the infidels". The Ambassadors of the Great Powers were summoned to the Porte, to hear the intense protests of the Turks. Russia's Ambassador Stroganovdeclared that his government was not involved and that Russia deplored Ypsilantis' revolt before even receiving specific instructions. Austria and Britain, for their part, sought to avoid a new Russian - Ottoman war and advised the Sultan's government to respect the treaties and restore the status quo. They also proposed, as per the national aspirations of the region, the appointment of rulers from local boyars, since the Sultan had lost his confidence in Phanariotes.

When the news of the Revolution arrived, the rulers of the European Powers were discussing in Laubach (Ljubljana) ways to suppress the various subversive movements that had erupted on the Iberian and Italian peninsulas. Under these circumstances, the Greek Revolution could not but receive the general disapproval of the rulers that had gathered there, without a shred of sympathy.

The only one that the Greeks thought might provide some form of support for their cause was the Czar of the coreligionist Russia, with the added element that Ioannis Kapodistrias was his advisor, and Alexander Ypsilantis was the Czar's trusty aide before becoming the leader of the Revolution. After all, since 1774 with the Treaty of Kaynarca, and especially with the interpretation given to this treaty by Russia which the Porte had accepted, it was understood that the Czar had been granted the right to protect the Orthodox Church with the power of intervention at the internal matters of the Ottoman Empire, in the event of a breach of the privileges granted by the sultans.

But Czar Alexander I had a mercurial temperament, and Chancellor Metternich had no difficulty convincing him that the Greek Revolution was germane to the subversive movements in Spain and Italy. The Czar could not openly show support for Greeks since this could be interpreted as Russia's complicity with radical movements, the very act that the European Powers were trying to suppress. With this in mind, the Czar publicly denounced Ypsilantis and banished him from the ranks of the Russian army. He also signed, on May 30, 1821, with the Emperor of Austria and the King of Prussia a joint declaration, where although there was no direct reference to the Greeks, it contained a clear allusion to the denunciation of the events in Balkans.[159]

The situation in Constantinople

The Sultan had difficulty believing that Russia was absolved of involvement in the events in the Balkans. He wanted assurances regarding the Czar's intentions before proceeding on acts against the Greeks. In responding, Ambassador Stroganov reiterated his statement on Russia's disapproval of the revolutionary movements, as per instructions he had received. This assurance calmed the Sultan briefly. He decided to grant amnesty to the rebels of Moldovlachia, on the condition they declared submission, excluding only Ypsilantis and ruler M. Soutsos. On March 3, he sent a "ferman" (decree) to Patriarchate, where he stated that " After finding out about the rebellion of some reckless individuals in Moldova, the Sublime Porte, deplores them, and urges the Great Church to advise the faithful citizens of the mighty Empire under its pastoral, not to get enticed and befall in its righteous and relentless indignation, as well as that of the faithful Ottomans".

[159]Anastasis Vistonitis: "To Vima" 19.3.2017 (in Greek)

At the same time, the wish of the Porte that the Patriarchate issues resolutions to strengthen the Sultan's ferman was relayed orally.

Meanwhile, Turks became aware of the strength of the Friendly Society as a secret organization whose objective was the division of their Empire. When, along with news of massacres of Turks in Moldovlachia, it came to light that some members of the Friendly Society, having been warned, had fled Constantinople, it was resolved to proceed on harsh measures, with the Rums of the city finding themselves under a state of siege. All the stately Phanariot families inhabiting the European coast of Bosphorus were ordered to move immediately to Phanari to prevent their escape. Turks began massacring Greeks who had relatives in Moldovlachia and arrested the Metropolitan of Ephesus Dionysios Kalliarchis, who was the brother of a former fugitive ruler of Moldovlachia and happened to be at that time in Constantinople. All Greeks who were not residents of Constantinople were ordered to depart.

On Sunday, March 6, 1821, Gregory V was summoned to the Sublime Porte by the Minister for Foreign Affairs, Reis Efendi. He was accepted by the Minister along with the Great Interpreter of Greek origin Mourouzis. The Minister announced to the Patriarch the Sultan's mandate for the supervision of the Serbs who lived in Galata neighborhood, confirming the trust of the Porte to the Patriarch and underlining the duty of the latter to ensure the allegiance of his flock to the Sultan.

On the other hand, the resentment of the Turkish mob in Constantinople was escalating with each passing day. Rampage against the Greek element that had begun with the first news of the Revolution in Moldovlachia had reached the point of mobs murdering in cold blood Greeks on the streets. Attacks on homes and shops, insults, beating,

157

stabbing, and raping were on the daily agenda. The relocation of the Phanariotes had started at once, but the Patriarch considered that this measure intended to amass victims destined for slaughter. An assembly of dignitaries and the Holy Synod was convened at the Patriarchate to confer on the quandary.

In this assembly, it was decided to submit a petition to the Porte stating that all the dignitaries of the genus vouch for each other's stay in Constantinople, as loyal subjects of the Sultan. It was also agreed to articulate in the report that the genus had no knowledge of the existence of a revolutionary society and that they had denounced Ypsilantis' movement. They stated that they were "ready to assist the mighty Empire to suppress such pernicious movements". The petition was drafted in the Turkish language by the former ruler of Vlachia Skarlatos Kallimachis and co-signed by the 49 clergy and laymen who took part in the meeting. The report was presented by the Patriarch accompanied by three senior priests to the Sadrazam on Sunday, March 13, 1821.

But the realization of the activities of the Friendly Society and the revelation of the plans for action in Constantinople had created among the Turks and the Sultan Mahmud II feelings of rage on the one hand - but of horror as well. Considering that he was surrounded by secret and overt enemies, the Sultan saw no other solution but the general massacre of the raya, "culprits" or not, even though he had announced shortly before the beginning of the events, that as long as the Rums respected his authority, their life and fortune would be secured to the same extent as those of Muslims.

For the carrying out of his decision on the all-around slaughter of Greeks, Sultan Mahmud II asked for the approval of the supreme religious leader, Seyhulislam Haji Halil, with the issuance of a pertinent fetva. At the same time, he declared a state of emergency and called the mob and Janissaries from Anatolia to come to Constantinople to implement his decision. But while the violence, looting, and sporadic slaughtering of Rums in the streets continued, the Sultan faced the dissidence of the supreme religious leadership to his decision of the concerted slaughter. Seyhulislam refused to issue the fetva, on the grounds that the massacre in the absence of differentiation between guilty and innocent did not conform to the religious order. Sadrazam Said also voiced his objections to the idea of a total slaughter along with the same rationale.[160]

Patriarch Gregory V had not stayed idle. As soon as news of the impending massacre became known, he visited Seyhulislam at his residence together with the Patriarch of Jerusalem, who at the time was visiting Constantinople, as well as with three dignitaries. He gave assurances about the non-involvement of his flock in the Revolution and appealed for the life of the Greeks in Constantinople. Seyhulislam Haji Halil, although resorted to delaying tactics for a while, eventually decided against issuing the fetva. For his courageous and honorable stance, he lost his life. He was dismissed from his position and was exiled to Limnos. On his journey there, he was killed by his escorting guards on the behest of the Sultan. Sadrazam Said was deemed ineffective and unworthy of the circumstances and was also dismissed of his duties and replaced by Ali Benderli Pasha, who, after eight days, lost not only his position but also his head because of the blind wrath of the Sultan. Salih Pasha, who was appointed Sadrazam next, adopted a merciless policy and let the mobs carry on the atrocities.

---

[160] The Turkish Government acted in like manner, in the preparation of the pogroms against the Greeks of Istanbul in 1955.

Eventually, the general slaughter of the Greeks of Constantinople was not carried out, most likely not only because of internal reactions but also for fear of provoking Russia's intervention. The new Seyhulislam Feiz Imam was forced to issue a fetva on a more tenable judgment that allowed the punishment (slaughter) of transgressors, and surely accomplices and "outright suspects". Based on this fetva, a ferman was issued providing amnesty (sic), on the premise that the Greeks will reject any idea of revolution and remain under the reign as raya. On March 20, 1821, the Porte handed over to the interpreter Mourouzis the amnesty decree to translate it. At the same time, Sultan issued a mandate to the genus and Patriarch, packed with reprimands, demands, and threats.

Sadrazam Salih, while handing the decree to Patriarch, relayed an order of the high command to unequivocally issue an ex-communication against A. Ypsilantis, M. Soutsos, and the rebels across the Danube. As the Sadrazam inferred, only this aphorism could shed some hope of postponing "the sword of the Sultan that was hanging over the heads of Greeks". Under this plight of extortion, the Ecumenical Patriarch convened an extraordinary, comprehensive clergy-laity meeting with the participation of the Patriarch of Jerusalem, twenty-one senior priests, and many dignitaries. Among those who took part, was Skarlatos Kallimachis, the Great Interpreter of the Sublime Porte K. Mourouzis, and the Interpreter of the Fleet N. Mourouzis. The delegates faced the dilemma of succumbing to the blackmail or rejecting the will of the Sultan and thus endangering Hellenism to imminent comprehensive slaughter, a threat that seemed feasible and very likely, considering what was happening on the streets.

After a lengthy debate, it was decided that the laity would submit a petition to denounce the Revolution and declare allegiance of all provinces to the Sultan. At the same time, the clergy would compose the act of ex-communication. On Wednesday, March 23, 1821, the two Patriarchs and twenty-one senior priests signed a text of ex-communication, which was addressed to all the senior priests and clerics of the Empire. In this text, an effort was made to include as few of the common aphoristic expressions as possible. On Sunday, apparently, after the demand of the Sublime Porte, a new document was signed using stronger censuring language, which was however addressed only to the Metropolitan of Moldovlachia. With this, the all-around slaughter of the Greeks of the Empire and especially of those in Constantinople, was temporarily averted.[161]

Gregory V was harshly criticized by many Greek historians, mainly of the left-leaning, for the ex-communication act and the consequences it could have had -although it did not- in the outcome of the Revolution. If the facts are looked upon not with the cold-hearted hindsight, but bearing in mind that the protagonists were enduring a climate of terror that Turks know how to create in perfection, it becomes crystal clear that the Patriarch and the entire leadership of Hellenism in Constantinople were facing dreadful extortion. The lives of hundreds of thousands of civilian Greeks were in imminent danger. The act of ex-communication should be judged in this context.

The various allegations that the Patriarch did not long for the Revolution, and therefore reacted in a conceding way, remain unproven, even though it is

---

[161]Petros A. Georgantzis: the "Aphorism" of Alexander Ypsilantis, Kavala, 1988

very likely that Gregory was advocating a different approach to it. Notably, several indicators point out to the assessment that the Patriarch, as well as Kapodistrias, believed that the timing for the attempted movement was not conducive and that he explored for an evolutionary and not revolutionary approach towards the desired goal. That notion would be akin to the Ecumenical (global) national idea laid out by the Phanariotes. The Patriarch feared that a rushed revolution could have harmed the Greek National Idea.

THE REVOLUTION IN GREEK TERRITORIES

The Outbreak of the Revolution in Mani

On the order of Ypsilantis, Perraivos, a member of the Friendly Society, went to Mani and informed the Greeks there, the approaching of the start of the Revolution, and asked them to make the necessary preparations. Ypsilantis relayed that he would not be able to satisfy the financial demands of Mani because of the large expenses he faced in organizing an army in the Danube principalities.

Meanwhile, the ruler of Mani, Petrobey Mavromichalis, had long been a suspect in the eyes of the Ottomans on account of his reluctance to obey the order of handing over Kolokotronis and Papaflessas. He was forced to send his two sons as hostages, one to Constantinople, the other to Tripolitza. The Ottomans, although they did not react drastically, they had been aware of the Friendly Society and tracked the movements of the Greeks. In the meantime, the Friendly Society of Constantinople had helped Petrobey's son George, who was held by the Turks hostage in Constantinople as a guarantor of paternal faith to the Sultan, to flee and come to Mani. This act did not sit well with the Turks, who already seemed to have been planning to depose Petrobey as Bey of Mani.

Petrobey had succeeded in concealing the presence and actions of the chieftains in Mani. The chieftains, for their part, believed that Mani should have the primary role as it was the most suitable place to start the Revolution. However, money and ammunition were missing and were solicited from the Friendly Society. The Society, however, did not prioritize the events in Mani and instead insisted on

163

payment of its contribution (February 1820), as Moldovlachia had the precedence. The final decision of commencing the Revolution in Peloponnese had not been reached yet.

On the other hand, any assurances of involvement and assistance from Russia did not materialize for Mani – or for that matter, for anywhere else. Information could have been requested outside the channel of the Friendly Society, but of course, it would not have been prudent to attempt any communication through an external channel or hold discussions in this sensitive time, right before the outbreak of the movement in Moldovlachia. Any undertaking in this direction was inevitable to fail, as was the case with the mission of Petrobey's advisor, but not a member of the Friendly Society, K. Kamarinos to A. Ypsilantis.

Despite the prevailing adverse conditions, it became apparent in Mani that inaction would lead to disaster. The Ottomans had been aware of the "conspiracy" and would not stand still facing a new movement like Moldovlachia. The danger was imminent, and the chieftains pushed for a rapid call to arms. At any rate, the secret of the Society was revealed, and "all sorts of people", including the Ottomans, were aware. Petrobey hesitated, not for the Revolution itself, but rather for the timing regarding preparations, and while his son was in Tripolitza hostage to the Ottomans. At any rate, his prestige and influence on the population of the province made it imperative for Petrobey to participate in the uprise. The time for the Greeks to charge ahead had come, and if they failed to do so, the Ottomans would move and slaughter them.

Kolokotronis, a member of the Friendly Society since 1818, had meetings with other associates in Zakynthos, and as he alleged, received letters from A. Ypsilantis asking him to get ready for

March 25, 1821, though it cannot be corroborated. The British in the Ionian islands were also informed about the preparations. Kolokotronis stated that in 1820 he went to Corfu and met with Kapodistrias, but did not elaborate on what was discussed in the meeting.[162] If there was any exchange between the two on the planned movement, it was most likely that Kapodistrias would have tried to be discreet. In January 1821, after a three-day trip, Kolokotronis arrived in Mani (southern Peloponnese) and disembarked in Kardamili. Apparently, he went there after an invitation from either the head of Mani Petrobey or chieftain Mourtzinos, most likely from the latter. Kolokotronis was not too keen on Petrobey, although he acknowledged that Petrobey did not hand him over to the Ottomans, who were aware of his journey to Mani and had requested related information. However, Kolokotronis believed that at any rate, Petrobey could not have betrayed him "since betrayal was not a trait ascribed to Mani".[163]

The pivotal moment had arrived. It was not the right time, but the timing would never be entirely proper. Greeks were not ready, but no one could ever be entirely ready. At the invitation of Petrobey, all Maniates chieftains assembled on March 17, 1821, in Tsimova (Areopoli), the capital of Mavromichalis, where they "agreed to take up arms against the Turks". So, in Mani, they were compelled to move "sooner rather than later".[164]

There was no central plan, no structured army, no commander in chief. "On the day of the Annunciation, everybody should be ready. Each province will move against the local Turks and besiege

---

[162] Theodoros Kolokotronis by hand of G. Tertsetis: Narration of events of the Greek race from 1770 to 1836, p. 57 (in Greek).
[163] Th. Kolokotroni Ibid., p. 59.
[164]Theod. Kolokotroni: Ibid., p. 59

the local fortresses, the Arcadians Neokastro, the Methonians Methoni, and so on", noted Kolokotronis. In the first revolutionary military action, the Greeks entered Kalamata on March 23, 1821, and liberated the city without a fight. It was a first bloodless victory, significant both from a military standpoint and in terms of impressions.

Until the entry of the army to Kalamata, the Revolution was led by the Bey of Mani, Petros Mavromichalis. Immediately afterward, Theodoros Kolokotronis took up command and implemented his plan for the uprising of each province independently. Already, from Patra to Monemvasia, everyone was alerted through the Friendly Society. A small number of armed rebels set forth from Kalamata to Methoni and Koroni to the west, while others to Karytaina and the northernmost cities of Peloponnese, to facilitate the Revolution that proved to be successful militarily, at least until the eternal feuds of Greeks were resurrected. On April 1, 1821, Kanellos Deligiannis, in charge of several fighters, declared the Revolution in Langadia. The meeting of Kolokotronis in Gortynia with the heads of the region sealed the partnership of dignitaries and chieftains. On April 28, 1821, the dignitaries in Karytaina named Kolokotronis commander-in-chief.[165]

The Greeks, with Kolokotronis, Nikitaras, Anagnostaras, Papaflessas, and other chieftains, proceeded to the liberation of various areas of Peloponnese. The Turks retreated to fortresses and towns, mainly in Tripolitza. The nine fortresses, Athens, Patras, Mystra, Acrocorinth, Methoni, Koroni, Navarino, Nafplio, and Tripoli, were besieged.

---

[165] Ioannis Philemon: Ibid., V.3 p. 437

The local polities

The need for political representation in legitimizing the revolutionary acts was promptly raised with the founding of the Messinian Senate on March 23, 1821. The President of the senate was Petrobey Mavromichalis, the ruler of the region of Mani, while its composition consisted of locals. Its first action was to issue a Notice to the Europeans (April 9, 1821), declaring their fight for freedom and asking for their aid. The islands had set up a special senate, while in central Greece, there was no political organization at the outset.

Between May 20 and 26, 1821, a new, more representative assembly, the Peloponnesian Senate, was convened in Kaltetzes with the participation of 29 dignitaries from Peloponnese under Bishop Anthimos. Among the chieftains and dignitaries who participated, Petrobey Mavromichalis (a dignitary) was elected President and Theodoros Kolokotronis (a chieftain) Vice President. The Assembly concluded by adopting a codified text "The general organization of Peloponnese" that was accepted later at the session of Zarachova in Verveni in August 1821. The Peloponnesian Senate was transformed into a central authority with a five-member council based in Stemnitsa to be the first revolutionary government. The places of origin of the members of the council were various cities of Peloponnese that, in a way, they represented. Its authority lasted until the liberation of Tripolitza on September 9, 1821.

The advent of Dimitrios Ypsilantis to Astros on June 8, 1821, as a proxy of his brother Alexander and his assumption of power on June 21, 1821, as well as the arrival of Constantinopolitan Alexandros Mavrokordatos in Messolonghi on July 24, 1821, created a specific political climate and new adversaries. The Peloponnesian Senate remained intact with the addition of only a few new members,

167

Archbishop Germanos and politician Asimakis Zaimis, at the request of D. Ypsilantis. Mavrokordatos, after consultation with D. Ypsilantis, undertook the organization of the western mainland Greece and the Constantinopolitan Theodoros Negris of the eastern.

A meeting was convened in Messolonghi on November 4, 1821, with the participation of 32 dignitaries and chieftains that established the Senate of west mainland Greece under the chairmanship of Mavrokordatos, which took over the governance of the region, while in the same period an assembly in Amfissa under Negris drew up a text referred to as Legal Order. On account of this document, a local government called Areios Pagos (the name of the supreme court in ancient Greece) was formed by 14 members and two divisions: the political under Negris and the judiciary under Talantius Neophyte. All these local polities contained, albeit imperfectly, principles of political self-determination and individual freedoms that Greeks were striving to attain. At the same time, they exposed the appeal for legal administration and state laws by elected rulers while adopting some of the ingredients of the traditional Greek society.

The capturing of Tripolitza

With the beginning of the Revolution in Peloponnese, Dimitrios Ypsilantis, who was assigned to represent his brother, Alexander Ypsilantis, the General Commissioner of Authority (of the Friendly Society) in Peloponnese, took over on June 20, 1821, the command of the rebels and attempted to organize

168

a tactical army. Victories in the Battles of Valtetsi,[166] of Doliana, and Grana, followed.

The necessity of capturing the capital of Peloponnese Tripolitza was strongly advocated by Kolokotronis, who managed to persuade chieftains and dignitaries on this move. During the siege of Tripolitza, Khurshid was busy in Ioannina. Although he sent some additional reinforcements to Tripolitza under Kioshe Mehmet Pasha, the Greeks prevailed, and after sieging it, they eventually seized the city on September 23, 1821. For Greeks, the liberation of Tripolitza was a milestone in their struggle for their prevalence in Peloponnese. The massacre of the Ottomans of the city that followed, although deplorable, should be judged in its historical context. It was the result of accumulated rage and seemed to have been carried out as retaliation to atrocities the Turks had committed. Among them, the destruction of Aigio and the massacres in Galaxidi that occurred a bit earlier, in Constantinople, Anatolia, and other regions, as well as the massacre of three thousand Christians in Tripolitza that took place on holy Monday, March 29, 1770, together with the assassination of the Metropolitan Anthimos and five other clerics, was cited. Nevertheless, Kolokotronis' promises to those he had come to an understanding, had been respected and were spared.

The five-month siege of Tripolitza had the peculiarity of transactions between besiegers and besieged, within the moral code of a primordial society. The two sides had dialogues between them regarding the getaway of some of the besieged, through financial incentives - bribing. Strangely, the harem of Khurshid in the occupied Tripolitza escaped

---

[166] Iakovos Michaelides: Theodoros behind Kolokotronis, 2014, p. 46 (in Greek)

unharmed along with many of the proceeds from collected taxes.

Later, Khurshid was accused by the Sultan that he had embezzled a large amount of the treasury of Ali Pasha of Ioannina, as what he claimed he had found was much less than what Ali's officials confirmed were there. Khurshid pleaded that it was slander and did not respond to the request of the Sublime Porte to give a detailed account. This fact convinced the Porte for the righteousness of the accusations, and the Sultan deposed him from his post as Prefect of Peloponnese, replacing him with Dramali. Khurshid, fearing the worst, committed suicide later in Constantinople.

The liberation of Tripolitza was until then the most remarkable military success of Greeks. However, the massacre of the Turks marred the glory of victory and provoked the aversion of the philhellenes abroad. It was another episode between D. Ypsilantis, who had instructed to abstain from aggressions, and warlords who had committed them. To avoid events akin to Tripolitza, D. Ypsilantis personally oversaw the surrender of Corinth, although his supervision was not entirely adequate. However, the siege of other fortresses, such as Nafplio and Patras, failed mainly because of the purveyance of supplies to Turks brought in by sea, at times by European ships.[167]

Dramali Mahmud Pasha from the city of Drama and cousin of Ibrahim, the son of Mehmed Ali of Egypt, with the eruption of the Revolution, was appointed by the Sultan commander of an army of about 42,000 men. After suppressing the movement in Thessaly, Dramali reached Thebes on July 1, 1822, and torched the city. Following that, he occupied Attica, Corinth, and on July 12, arrived in Argos.

---

[167] Iakovos Michaelides: Ibid., p 54

There, he met the strong resistance of a small infantry of Greeks under the command of D. Ypsilantis, who had barricaded themselves inside the acropolis of Argos. While the Turks were blockading the acropolis, Kolokotronis ordered the contamination of water sources and the burning of crops of the plains of Argos to starve the Turkish army. When the siege failed, Dramali decided to return to Corinth, passing by the valley of Dervenakia. On July 26, when the Turks attempted to go through the passes of Dervenakia, they were crushed by Greeks who had entrenched in the surrounding hills. After this victory against Dramali, Kolokotronis returned to Tripolitza. Dramali eventually managed to reach[168] Corinth, but the campaign in Peloponnese was disastrous for his army. Turkish historians attribute this failure to both burnt crops and poisoned waters, and the reluctance of other Ottoman Pashas to assist Dramali in order not to inflate his sway over the Sultan. Of the approximately 30,000 men who eventually participated in this expedition, only 6,000 returned to Corinth. In October of the same year, Dramali died in Corinth from typhus at 42 years.

The Revolution had now prevailed in Peloponnese, and the message of the forthcoming freedom resonated throughout Greece, arousing the hopes of enslaved Greeks.

Patras

Patras, at the time of the Revolution, was the largest and most prosperous city in Peloponnese, a commercial gateway to Western Europe. The Revolution erupted there almost simultaneously with Mani, with an uprise of the inhabitants. The news of the revolt angered the Turks, who countered with

---

[168] Iakovos Michaelides: Ibid., p. 65

arsons and murders, that ignited the conflict. The inhabitants, primarily from the island of Kefalonia and Zakynthos (Zante) took up arms while the Turks took refuge in the fortress of the city, bombing the Christian neighborhoods. In the meantime, several chieftains arrived with a few hundred armed irregulars.[169] The fort was besieged, but Greeks were unable to seize it.

A revolutionary authority, the Directorate of Achaia that would cover the area of northwest Peloponnese, was quickly established. A proclamation was delivered to the European Consuls in Patras, communicating the decision of Greeks to fight for freedom or death and appealed to Europeans for assistance in the Greek conflict. The declaration was signed by Archbishop of Patras Germanos, the Bishop of Kalavryta Prokopios, chieftains, and dignitaries. A few days later, however, a powerful Ottoman army arrived, ending the siege of the fortress. It destroyed and plundered Patras and then headed towards the interior of Peloponnese.

After the liberation of Tripolitza, Kolokotronis wanted to confront the Turks in Patras. Still, as per his written narration, he was prevented by the local people for fear of looting the spoils of the city! After the battle of the monastery of Nursing Home, the Turks once again barricaded inside the fortress, but setbacks of Greeks on various other fronts eventually forced them to dissolve the siege. Patras remained in the hands of Turks until their final departure from Greece.

Central Greece and Epirus

In Eastern Mainland Greece, despite the prevailing state of submissiveness, the presence of

---

[169] D. Tzaki: Achaia, Ibid., p. 39.

172

Kleftes, Armatoloi, and local chieftains, inspired and encouraged the people to fight for freedom.

Once news of the revolutions in Mani and Patra spread, Greeks of the Sterea (mainland) region went to the monastery of Prophet Elias and declared the Revolution there. Levadia, under Ottoman rule, had become an administrative center decades ago, with heads of community there, securing privileges and freedoms. The central role of the city in the region of Rumeli had drawn the interest of the Friendly Society that attracted several dignitaries in its ranks.

The Revolution was declared on March 27, at the Monastery of Osios Loukas near Levadia, with the presence of chieftain Athanasios Diakos and dignitaries of the area. Levadia was liberated after the namesake battle. The liberation of Amfissa and Thebes followed.

In Attica, the revolutionary Athenians blockaded the Acropolis, and on May 7, 1821, liberated their city. In Western Central Greece, the local rebels freed Messolonghi and besieged Vonitsa. Revolutionary movements were taken place in Parnassos under chieftain Androutsos and Archimandrite Anthimos Gazis, a member of the Friendly Society. Gazis, in May 1821, declared the Revolution in Thessaly and Magnesia from Milies, Pelion, where he taught at the school he had founded. The Revolution was aided with ships that came from Hydra and Spetses and the support of Armatoloi. While the castle of Volos was besieged without success, Velestino was liberated by the revolutionaries. Powerful Ottoman forces, however, succeeded eventually in expelling the rebels.[170]

---

[170] Thanasis Christou: E-Historically, "The declaration in Salona and Levadia" p.p.73-78 (in Greek)

Victories and defeats took turns but overall, the balance tilted in favor of the Greeks. The undisciplined irregular chieftains, despite their bravery on the field, resorted at times to massacres and looting. There were also instances of transactions with the enemy. The ordinary Greek fighters fought "for God and Country", and for everything they believed and considered important. Though perceived the supremacy in weaponry of the Turks, they always hoped that at some point, Russia would show up and assist them in their struggle.

Omer Vryoni was a Turkish-Albanian officer from the city of Vryoni near Verratti in Albania. From Ioannina, he went to Egypt and helped Mehmed Ali at war against Mamelukes. Upon his return, he took over as treasurer of Ali Pasha in Ioannina but defected when the Sultan disowned Ali. The Sublime Porte rewarded him with his appointment as Pasha of Verratti. With the outbreak of the Greek Revolution, Omer Vryoni was appointed commander of the Turkish forces and was mandated by Khurshid to move against the Greeks. Vrioni departed from Ioannina on April 9, 1821, and tried to bribe Greek chieftains to renegade, without much success.

In April 1821, Athanasios Diakos, in collaboration with other chieftains, had occupied the fortress of Levadia and, using it as his base, fought many victorious battles. He took over the Bridge of Alamana, and on April 22, 1821, he fought with the troops of Omer Vryoni. In this battle, he was arrested and transferred to Lamia, where he was murdered.

Before Omer Vryoni commenced his campaign against Peloponnese, he ordered corrupted chieftains of Western Greece faithful to him to gather in Gravia Fokis, to join him in his campaign to Peloponnese later on. He sent a special messenger to chieftain Odysseus Androutsos, whom he knew from Ali's court, to announce the death of Athanasios Diakos.

He conveyed that if he came to Gravia with the other chieftains, not only would forgive him for the murder of Hasan Bey Geka, a Turkish-Albanian bey but that he would give him the command of Liakoura. Androutsos refused.

In the battle of the Inn of Gravia, which took place on May 8, 1821, Odysseus Androutsos, heroically fighting with only 118 men, defeated the army of Omer Vryoni, inducing significant losses with hundreds of dead Turkish soldiers, and succeeded in escaping with his team almost unscathed. This tactical defeat and the many casualties of Omer Vryoni in the battle resulted in a strategic success for Greeks. It prevented the descent of the Ottoman army into Peloponnese and facilitated the victory in Valtetsi that further inspired the Revolution.

Before the outbreak of the Turkish offensive against Souli, the Greeks of Peloponnese received calls from the mainland to send reinforcements. The campaign's head was the Constantinopolitan member of the Friendly Society Alexandros Mavrokordatos, who gathered a regular army of 3,000 and a squad of philhellenes, whose leadership was assigned the German officer Karol Norman. The first victorious battle was fought at Koboti Arta on June 10, 1822. "Neither Greeks nor Turks could be blamed for lack of courage. Both sides fought like lions. But injustice... is defeated... ".[171]

Three weeks later, at the heights of Peta, the two armies faced each other in a decisive battle, where Greeks and philhellenes suffered a debacle. All Western Central Greece was left in the hands of the Turks. The defeat in Peta led to the dissolution of the organized Greek forces of the region. Turks, despite their partial failures, advanced to Messolonghi. Vrioni and Mehmed Reshid Pasha joined forces in besieging

---

[171] General Makrigiannis: Memoirs, p 32 (in Greek)

Messolonghi in October 1822. Vrioni, apparently with the motive of looting the city "with order", sought to take over the city intact and, instead of attacking immediately, started negotiating despite the objections of the commanders of his troops. The town of Messolonghi had a weak fortification and few defenders. Mavrokordatos, who had fled there, organized the defense using all methods of the art of fortification as well as the subterfuges he was able to devise and commissioned Marko Botsaris to start discussions with the besiegers to save time. Botsaris, during the negotiations, succeeded in instigating the rivalry among the Pashas. Greeks continued discussions until early November. When reinforcements arrived from Peloponnese by sea, Greeks broke off the negotiations. The Turks decided to attack the night of Christmas Eve of 1822 to take Greeks by surprise. But the secret leaked out. The Turks were repelled, suffering heavy losses at this first siege of Messolonghi. The success in Messolonghi offset in some way the defeat of Peta. Vrioni, as a result of the Ottoman failure and his contention with Mehmed Reshid, was recalled from the Sublime Porte in 1824.

In the summer of 1823, Markos Botsaris attempted to halt the advancement of the Ottoman armies toward West Rumeli. On August 8, leading 450 rebels from Souli charged the 5000 Ottoman and Albanian mercenaries of Pasha Mustafa of Skodra that had camped in Kefalovriso of Karpenisi. Botsaris died in the battle of Kefalovriso and despite the partial victory in the battle, the progression of Pasha went on.

Macedonia: Halkidiki and Naoussa

Halkidiki was involved from the outset in the struggle for the liberation of the Greek nation on

176

account of the patriotism of Macedonians, its relatively favorable geographical position, and its proximity to Thessaloniki. At the time of the Ottoman domination, the peninsula of Halkidiki was a refuge and sanctuary for persecuted populations. The relatively good living conditions in Halkidiki not only deterred the migration of Greek inhabitants out of the area but also appealed to refugees from elsewhere, resulting in the increase of its Greek population and the unscathed preservation of Hellenism, its privileges, and churches. The monastery city of Mount Athos, the community of ore-producing villages, and the federation of towns of Kassandra contributed to this success. The participation of the inhabitants of the region in the uprising in Halkidiki was prompt and comprehensive.

The revolutionary campaign in Halkidiki began near the end of March 1821, with the arrival in Mount Athos of Emmanuel Papas, a wealthy merchant and member of the Friendly Society from Serres. Papas, on orders of Alexander Ypsilantis, procured weapons and ammunition in Constantinople and sent them by the boat of Antonis Hadzi Visvizis to Macedonia. He later also departed for Mount Athos, which considered most suitable as a base for the operation, because many monks had already been initiated into the Friendly Society. Also, its access by Turks from the sea was difficult, along with the fact that it was guarded only by a small Turkish garrison.[172]

The initial clashes began in Polygyros on May 17, while the fierce retaliation of Turks in Thessaloniki that followed elicited an opposite effect, evoking the spreading of the Revolution in Halkidiki. The Revolution in Halkidiki was declared at the end

---

[172] Aikaterini Flassianou: E-Historically, "Eruption of the revolution in Halkidiki" p. 43

of May 1821, and Emmanuel Pappas was declared the "leader and defender of Macedonia". Cassandra also rebelled under the leadership of the dignitary Hatzihristodoulou. The rebellious troops of the irregulars were separated into two major squadrons: one led by Emmanuel Papas led the first and Stamatis Hapsas the second. After early Greek victories, fierce battles broke out, with Turks counterattacking while possessing the superiority in arms. Bayram Pasha, heading to Peloponnese, was instructed to move against the Halkidiki rebels, who were in a dire position due to lack of supplies and money.

In October, a powerful Ottoman expeditionary force was sent to Cassandra, Halkidiki, under the new Pasha of Thessaloniki Mehmet Emin, who attacked in November 1821. The women and children took refuge in Mount Athos. In the deadly battle at the Isthmus of Cassandra, the Greeks, considerably outnumbered, were forced to retreat, leaving the Ottomans to plunder the land, slaughter residents, and enslave others. Cassandra was deserted while the monks of Mount Athos surrendered. Emmanuel Papas escaped by boat to Hydra, but along the way, he died of a heart attack.[173]

The failure of the Revolution in Halkidiki is attributed to the lack of money and military experience of the rebels, the proximity to the military centers of the Ottomans, and the absence of any coordination with the uprisings in other regions. Nevertheless, both revolutions in Moldovlachia and Halkidiki impaired the efforts of the Ottomans in coping with the rebellion in Peloponnese.[174]

---

[173] Konstantinos Papoulidis: E-Historically: "Mount Athos, when the "untrodden" of the Holy Mountain was violated", p. 50 (in Greek)
[174] Aik. Flerianou Ibid., p. 48.

Even though Macedonians were devastated by the defeat in Halkidiki, they started recovering their hopes as a result of the overall successes of the Greeks and the encouragement they got from Dimitrios Ypsilantis and Alexandros Mavrokordatos. As the preparations of the Greeks became known to the Turks, the revolution date in Pieria was moved up to March 8, 1822, when it started with the attack against the Turks in Kolindros, though without attaining a decisive victory. In Naoussa, the Revolution was declared on February 19, 1822. The first attack of the rebels in the region of Veria failed. Greek insurgents fled to the monastery of Dovra, where a victorious battle was fought against the Turks who had besieged them. Following that, by order of the Sultan, the Turks resorted to looting and slaughtering civilians. The rebels barricaded themselves in Naoussa, while the Turks began its siege on March 27. On April 13, the Turks entered the city and crushed the Revolution, drowning it in blood. The primary reason for the failure of the Greeks in Macedonia can be attributed to the fact that the Revolution had not started in a coordinated way, with simultaneous outbreaks, as it had happened in Peloponnese, and thus allowed Turks to repress the movements one by one. Moreover, Macedonia was near the military centers of the Ottoman administration.[175]

The Greek islands and the war at sea

Hydra, along with Spetses and Psara as well as Kasos, played a decisive role in the Revolution of 1821, aiding the cause by dispensing their merchant and war fleets and providing fighters and money. The contribution of these islands was significant. When

---

[175] Annita N. Prassas: E-Historically, "Naoussa: The Revolution and the destruction of the city" p. 53-60 (in Greek).

the Revolution erupted, they were economically prosperous, mainly due to their successful involvement in the grain trade during the Napoleonic Wars. The first Greek fleet under I. Tombazis from Hydra consisted of 21 ships, with the numbers increasing with time. Every island had its Admiral and Vice Admiral.

Moreover, the crews had amassed a great deal of know-how in naval warfare from their clashes with pirates from Algeria. In the decade 1810 - 1820, especially in Hydra, the downturn of the Greek merchant marine had created some social unrest. However, the islands' dignitaries were let in on the secret of the Revolution by the Friendly Society since 1820. Following the declaration of the Revolution in Peloponnese, on March 24, 1821, the dignitaries of Peloponnese, by way of a letter, sought the assistance of the islanders of Hydra and Spetses for the naval blockade of the enemy.[176]

The flag of the Revolution was raised in Spetses by members of the Friendly Society who were initiated in Constantinople. The female member of the Friendly Society Laskarina Pinotsi "Bouboulina" offered significant services to the common cause with the expeditionary force she created, the "Spetsiotes", and her fleet. However, the anguish the island suffered from its participation in both the Orloffics and the movement of Lambros Katsonis was not yet forgotten and a certain hesitation lingered. There was even a thought-out strategy with Hydra for a concurrent revolutionary commencement, as per the "General Plan" countersigned by A. Ypsilantis, the implementation of which would take effect after the destruction of the Ottoman fleet in the Navy Yard of Constantinople (that, however, did not prove

---

[176] Konstantina Adamopoulou – Pavlou: E-Historically, "Economou delivers Hydra to the struggle" p. 61 (in Greek).

possible). The participation of Spetses in the Revolution started with the blockade of the fortresses of Nafplio and Monemvasia.

The daughter of the member of Friendly Society Nikolaos Mavroghenis, Mando Mavroghenous, went to Mykonos and took part in the campaign. With ships equipped at her own expense, she pursued the Algerians who flocked to the Cyclades and later fought in Karystos and other places.

Hydra, however, appeared more reluctant to rise immediately, remembering, on the one hand, the disasters that had suffered in the previously failed uprising of 1770, and on the other, fearing the military superiority of the enemy and the subsequent risk of losing what they had come to have. The initiative was undertaken by a captain from the middle-class A. Economou, a member of the Friendly Society. Confronted with the procrastination shown by the dignitaries, Economou took it upon himself to proclaim the Revolution in Hydra on March 27, 1821. The arrival of Gika Tsoupa from Spetses dispersed any lasting reservations, and Hydra, on April 14, 1821, joined the ranks of the Revolution.

Psarians who had participated in the Russo-Turkish war and were involved in the destruction of the Turkish fleet at Chesme in 1770, as well as in the effort of Lambros Katsonis, responded positively to the calling of the Friendly Society as early as 1818. On April 10, 1821, the call for the Revolution was enthusiastically accepted. Psara declared the Revolution eight days later. After creating a fleet of 16 ships, Psarians were the first who dared to attack the enemy on the coast of Smyrna, defying any consequent danger emanating from the proximity of their island to the bases of the Ottoman fleet.

Samos, although near to the coast of Anatolia, had few Turkish inhabitants. By the time of the Revolution, many Samians had already been initiated into the Friendly Society. Samos declared the revolution on May 8, 1821, led by Lykourgos Nomothetis (Georgios Paplomatas), leader of Carmagnoles, who arrived from Smyrna, together with chieftains of the island. Samos functioned as a stronghold, advanced outpost – embankment and base for the Revolution. It was organized politically with the adoption of the "Report of the Local System of Samos" in May 1821, while during the Revolution, Samos maintained a local administration that was named "Military – political System of Samos ". The Samians carried out raids on the Turkish coast and repelled the Ottoman's landing force. Although Samos was not included within the borders of Greece after its independence, they continued their struggle until 1834 when Samos was recognized as autonomous hegemony, a tax vassal statelet to the Sultan.[177]

The Greeks of Samothrace had connections with their compatriots in Constantinople, and through the sermons of Metropolitan Constantine, they were already prepared for the Revolution, and they took up arms in August 1821. The Ottomans reacted and, in September 1821, dispatched a strong naval force to Samothrace. The destruction was devastating. The island was looted, the Turks slaughtered thousands of men while the women and children were sold as slaves.

On March 11, 1822, with the landing of an expeditionary corps from Samos, Chios also joined in the revolution. The rebellious Greeks besieged the castle where the Ottomans had barricaded themselves in. On March 30, however, the Ottoman

---

[177] Konstantina Adamopoulou – Pavlou: E-Historically, Ibid., p.p. 69-72

fleet arrived. After breaking the siege in April with the participation of irregular Muslims who had come from the opposite coast of Anatolia, they massacred the Greeks.

The sea battles generally favored the Greeks. The ships of Spetses, after the naval blockade of Nafplio and Monemvasia, destroyed three Turkish ships near Milos. The boats of Psara, after excursions to the coast of Anatolia, captured several Turkish ships near Chios. Greek ships bombarded fortresses and set on fire the Turkish vessels, a form of naval combat that proved highly effective. Even though September 1821 turned out to be a month of successes for the Ottoman fleet, after its departure, Greek victories were restored.

In June 1822, after the Greek fleet failed to save Chios from the massacre, it was decided to set on fire the Turkish fleet. Konstantinos Kanaris from Psara and Giorgos Pitinos from Hydra managed to enter the port of Chios with their boats on the night of June 6, 1822, and set on fire the flagship of Kara Ali, the head of the army who had slaughtered the inhabitants and burnt the island. This scorching of the flagship became one of the most singular events of the naval battles and made a great impression in Europe. Many philhellene writers and authors, including Victor Hugo, Lord Byron, and the historian Thomas Gordon, who also volunteered for the ultimate endeavor of Greeks, extolled the heroic stance of Kanaris. This success propelled the Revolution by elevating the spirit and morale of Greeks in their struggle for freedom. Kanaris, the "Pyrpolitis" (torcher), became a hero.

The Greek Navy succeeded in the coming years to continually inflict damages to the Ottoman fleet, hindering the navigation of Turkish ships in the Aegean. But the lack of resources created problems. It led to some sailors taking ships, raising a flag of their choice, and engaging in piracy. Kanaris, on the other hand, was successful in maintaining discipline among his crew and continued his attacks.

The Ottoman commercial and warfare navigation was heavily impeded in the Aegean by the Greek fleet. Psara was a strong base for Greeks because of its geographical location and the bravery of its inhabitants. In June 1824, the Ottoman government decided to send a strong force not only to subdue the revolutionary island but to avenge the disasters suffered by Ottoman ships. The Ottomans landed a large military regiment, against which the Psarians fought heroically. After the battles ended, the Ottomans proceeded to the sweeping massacre of the heroic inhabitants, with only a few fleeing with remaining ships. The Turks pillaged and burned the island; "on Psara's blackened hill... glory walking alone... ".[178]

The circumstances in Cyprus

The hierarchy of the clergy and the dignitaries of Cyprus were informed by the Friendly Society about the impending Revolution through its envoys. However, because of the island being far away from the rest of the centers of Hellenism and its vicinity to the Anatolian coast, Cyprus was not considered at the outset as qualifying for an uprising. It was therefore decided that the island's contribution would be limited to material aid that would be provided to the rebels. According to another opinion, however, Cyprus fulfilled the conditions to support an armed partnership with other Greeks since the ruling class was financially robust, and the population density of Greeks on the island was large. At the same time, the Greek navy dominated the marine region of Cyprus.

---

[178] Poem of D. Solomos (in Greek)

Subsequent events showed that this view was somewhat flawed.

Archbishop Kyprianos was considered a member of the Friendly Society, but there is no evidence of this since he had apparently destroyed any relevant correspondence following the Society's tactics. However, it is known that in 1820 he hosted D. Ipatros, a member of the Friendly Society, and at his request, the Archbishop had promised him financial aid supporting the Revolution. It is also known that in October 1820, the member of the Friendly Society A. Pelopidas was in Cyprus as an envoy of Alexander Ypsilantis to receive the contribution of the Archdiocese. However, Kyprianos himself had to consider the safety of his flock from the enemies and avert a massacre.

When the Revolution began, Sultan Mahmud ordered the disarmament of the Cypriots that was carried out without resistance. Archbishop Kyprianos tried to persuade the Cypriots to obey and reassured the Ottoman commander, Kuchuk Mehmed, of the obedience of the Greeks. At the same time, Kyprianos tried to keep up appearances for the Turks about the Friendly Society and the impending eruption of the Revolution on the island. Despite these efforts, Archimandrite Theophylactos Theseus distributed notices in Larnaka for rallying the Greeks of Cyprus. It was also widely known that Konstantinos Kanaris' ships had docked for a few days in June 1821 in ports of the island and had received support for the Revolution.[179]

Following that, Sultan Mahmud authorized Kuchuk to arrest, confiscate the estate, and execute those involved in the planned Revolution. Church leaders and dignitaries of Cyprus were summoned on

---

[179] Dionysios Dionysiou: E-Historically "Kanaris in Cyprus", p. 115 (in Greek).

July 9, 1821, in Nicosia by the Ottoman commander, while the Sultan had already given his approval for the executions. Archbishop Kyprianou was executed by hanging, followed by the decapitation of three Metropolitans, Chryssanthos of Pafos, Meletios of Kition, and Lavrentios of Kyrene on the same day.[180] Many of the clergy and laymen were also executed, including Kapukehaya (Portal representative) George Masouros and other Greek officials of the Ottoman administration. Churches and monasteries were looted and the fortunes of the executed confiscated. After the massacres of Kuchuk Mehmet in Nicosia, all revolutionary activities on the island were suspended, while many local fighters and members of the Friendly Society fled to safe havens in Greece and foreign countries. The island's dignitaries took refuge in consulates of the European forces and later fled abroad.

Executions, persecutions, destructions, and looting constituted the prologue of a series of terrorist acts and repressive measures against the Cypriot population. The Ottoman commander in order to usurp the properties of the most prominent men on the island, accused many Cypriots as conspirators and sent a list with their names to the Sublime Porte. Of these, 74 were executed while others managed to flee the island.

In the autumn of 1822, there were new massacres, arsons, and destructions. This time, many Cypriots were rescued by the arrival of the fleet of Psara that evacuated them. After the Revolution started, mass involuntary Islamizations had intensified. In 1827, persecutions were unleashed anew against the Christians of the island regardless of their nationality. The Ionians were considered

---

[180] Petros Papapolyviou: E-Historically "The Revolution of 1821 and Cyprus" p. 113 (in Greek)

Ottoman nationals despite the reactions from the British Consul, while foreign Consuls were forbidden to hire raya as interpreters. Finally, marriages of European states nationals with women of Ottoman nationality were banned. The Ottoman garrison of Cyprus was later reinforced with military force from Egypt that terrorized the population of Cyprus and discouraged any thoughts of participation in the armed struggle.

Cypriots who fled to Greece joined as fighters in the Revolution and excelled for their bravery and self-sacrifice. Among the Cypriot-born activists of the Friendly Society was the teacher Charalambos Malis from Nicosia, who had accompanied Papaflessas in Peloponnese and emerged as a significant and active personality among the Cypriots in Greece.

The Revolution in Crete

The Revolution in Crete was declared as early as April 1821. The big island was quite remote from the remainder of Greece, and therefore dispatch of military aid was difficult. Moreover, a substantial Muslim minority of almost one-third of the population resided in Crete. Despite these adverse conditions, joining the Revolution was raised in meetings with chieftains and dignitaries in Sfakia, and a decision to revolt was taken there. The Turks reacted by hanging the bishop of Kissamos, imprisoning others, and by proceeding in the persecution of clergy and laity of the region.

The first major victory of the rebels occurred on June 14, 1821, in Chania, where a unit of Janissaries was defeated, and their leader was killed. The Turks responded with looting and slaughtering of civilians. However, battles with victories of Greeks continued in July 1821, but in August, a powerful Ottoman force arrived in Sfakia, defeating Sfakians

187

and proceeded to commit brutalities and carry-out murders. But the uprising did not stop. Dimitrios Ypsilantis, at the request of Cretans, appointed Michael Komninos Afentoulief as general commander of the Revolution in Crete. Despite the failure of an attempt to capture Rethymno, the Greeks achieved victories in the region of Mylopotamos, as well as outside the Fortress of Chania.

Petros Skylitsis Omiridis arrived later in Crete as the representative of the central administration of Greece. A local assembly was held, the result of which was the institutionalization of the "Transitional Polity of the Island of Crete" (May 21, 1822). Afentoulief, with his title of "General prefect of the island", took over as general leader of the Greek Revolution in Crete.

In May 1822, an Egyptian fleet sailed to Souda with many ships. Several thousand infantrymen (mainly Albanian mercenaries) and several hundred horsemen, led by Hassan Pasha, landed on the island. In its first clash with the Greeks, the Turkish-Egyptian army was defeated in Malaxa, but right after, the Greeks succumbed to the counterattack of the Ottomans, who had the upper hand in weaponry.

Akin to the internal quibbles of the Peloponnese, there were clashes between the chieftains and Afentoulief, resulting in his ousting and waste of stamina in trivial internal conflicts. Hydraean Emmanuel Tombazis replaced Afentoulief. Tombazis' presence reinvigorated the Revolution, especially in western Crete. The fortress of Kastelli (Kissamos) was captured. This was followed by the siege of the fort of Kandanos in Chania; however, this victory was overshadowed by the breach of the agreement drawn up with Turks, when Cretans attacked and killed many of the departing Muslims. This unfortunate action led the Turks to no longer accept assurances by Cretans and thus not to surrender voluntarily. In June 1823, another Egyptian fleet arrived, and a massive tactical Egyptian army with French officers under Hussein Bey landed in Crete. The result was the stifling of the Revolution in Crete.

Tombazis failed to unite the chieftains in a joint action against the enemy while it was not feasible to secure reinforcements from Greece. The Egyptians, with great strength, continued to suppress the Revolution. Hussein Bey marched against Messara and invaded Rethymno.

In March 1824, Hussein moved to Sfakia, which constituted the headquarters of the Revolution. The fall of Sfakia squelched the morale of the inhabitants of many regions who finally capitulated. On April 12, 1824, the governor of Crete Emmanuel Tombazis left the island. The Revolution in Crete had ended. The clashes against the Egyptian-Turks, however, continued in the mountains with sporadic guerrilla acts.

The provisional prevalence of the Revolution

The revolutionary army was characterized by the fact that it was voluntary. This inherently possessed positive attributes – the fighters were fighting with heroism and self-sacrifice for the success of the cause they believed wholeheartedly. But at the same time, the organization was plagued with some ills. Besides, most warriors did not have military training. Apart from specific tactical units, sometimes under the command of the European military, the Greek army consisted of corps under various chieftains. The relations most of the time were competitive instead of cooperative. Some defeats were caused by miscommunications among the warring Greeks.

On the other hand, the Turks fought with spite. Competitions among pashas also existed on the Ottoman side. The decisive factor, though, was that the battles took place on Greece's territories, in the court of Greeks, and on a terrain that was conducive to guerrilla tactics.

Despite the interspersed victories and defeats and in contrast to the revolutionary movement in Moldovlachia, which was relatively quickly suppressed, the Revolution of March 23, 1821, that started in Peloponnese was unyielding. The Ottoman side could not muster sufficient resistance as its troops were occupied concurrently with Ali of Ioannina. At the same time, Greeks fought with bravery and stamina inculcated by the Friendly Society. The rebels blockaded the Ottoman ships in the Mediterranean; the Sublime Porte, being unable to send ammunition to its armies in Peloponnese, suffered shortages even in Constantinople because of the impediments in shipping.

The Greeks attempted to secure international alliances, mainly through the vision of Alexandros Mavrokordatos, in three directions; with Mehmet Ali of Egypt and Beshir of Lebanon with the purpose of striking agreements against the Sultan, as well as with Milos Obrenovic of Serbia, who sought independence from the Ottoman Empire. Ambassadors were dispatched to facilitate this - Bishop Gregory Dendrinos and Haji Stasi Rezi to Syria and Lebanon, Papoutzalov and Anastasiou to Serbia and Montenegro. The assistance of the French Jourdan and Favier was requested by approaching Mehmet Ali. All efforts failed, as both the Serb leader and Mehmet Ali weighed in their interests and decided against any involvement. An earnest alliance with Beshir was impossible, as Greeks could not offer and notably could not expect any assistance from Lebanon.[181]

Initially, the news from Europe for the Greeks was not encouraging. However, the great victories of the Greeks at land and sea, as well as the resonance in Europe of the atrocities committed by the Ottomans, led to the public opinion to turn in favor of Greeks. The Western European states recognized the dynamics of the Revolution and the weaknesses of the Ottoman Empire, along with the fact that the Ottoman Empire was going through a period of decline. Britain, France, and Russia began to assess their profits from the new political environment that had risen and figure out ways to preserve them. Austria surmised from the beginning that the developments in Greece were not favorable for its interests.

---

[181]Spyros Dim. Loukatos: E-historically "The attempts for alliances and their fate" p. 101-104 (in Greek).

THE REPERCUSSIONS OF THE REVOLUTION

Europe's posture on the Greek Revolution

The Greek Revolution marked the first instance of the prevalence of the national doctrine; however, this revolutionary movement was not exclusively the result of progressive ideas that were prominent at that time in Europe. The Greek Revolution began under the adverse conditions of the principle of legality, having to confront it both militarily and diplomatically.

Regarding the positions of European Powers, France initially remained indifferent to the Greek Revolution –with French officers taking part in Mehmed Ali's army– while Britain and Austria attempted to stem Russia's sympathetic stance towards the Greeks, although Alexander I was entirely in accord with the spirit that prevailed in the European Directorate. Alexander I, grandson of Catherine the Great, was crowned Czar following the assassination of his father Paul I in 1801 and remained on the throne until 1825. He was characterized as lacking the virtue of possessing a resolute mindset. At first, he promoted a series of liberal administrative and social reforms, only to revert later to conservatism and retract them.

The "Greek scheme" of Empress Catherine had been abandoned by her successors. At the same time, Chancellor Metternich, in his contacts with Alexander I, had also vilified the Greek Revolution for being part of a more general subversive movement in Italy. Austria held a hostile posture against the

193

revolutionary Greeks from the outset, sided diplomatically with the Ottoman Empire, and appeared to be the one that had advised Mehmet Ali's involvement in the operation. At the same time, Austrian ships helped Ottomans with supplies to Turkish guards and fortresses.

The unfavorable, even hostile stands of European Powers towards the Greek Revolution, are of no surprise to modern well-versed observers. Byrons may fight for the rights of the Greeks, Delacroixs depict their torments, Hugos praise their exploits, and the auspicious public opinion of France may strengthen the morale of the struggling Greeks, yet European states' foreign policy decisions are driven by self-serving criteria.[182]

At the time, Austria and Britain were focusing on safeguarding the Vienna regime in Europe, even though the Vienna Congress had not dealt with the issue of the Ottoman Empire. France and Britain, in the context of the doctrine of the balance of power in Europe, sought not only to prevent Russia's descent into the "warm" seas but also to curb Russian influence in the Balkans. The Czar foresaw, of course, the opportunity presented for the pursuit of Russia's standing policy on extending southwards, as well as, felt compelled to respond to prevalent "public opinion" that existed in Russia. However, eventually, he was obliged to concur with the rest of the Powers in order not to appear as challenging the status quo.

Metternich had several political reasons to oppose the Greek Revolution. The eight ethnicities that comprised Austro-Hungary could create problems for the Government in Vienna if they started harboring national ideals. Also, Russia would have gained a foothold in the Eastern Mediterranean. An

---

[182] Vasilis Moutsoglou: The criteria in international politics, Edit. Papazisi, 2015(in Greek).

independent Greek state could compete against Austria's national interests through the creation of commercial centers and the development of a strong merchant fleet. Greece was a poor district of the Ottoman Empire. Still, from the outset, it had the prerequisites for growth since Greeks had excelled in commerce and shipping, and the geographic locale of the new state would be particularly conducive in this aspect.[183]

Britain, France, and Russia wanted to ensure that the outcome of the war in Greece would not undermine their interests. The Great Powers, in general, were facing the Eastern Question, i.e., if they should sustain a faltering Ottoman Empire or face an uncertain future by allowing it to collapse. The British, primarily the civilians, were sympathetic to the Greek cause in part because of the classical studies. Still, politically, the state was reluctant to render the Ottoman Empire so weak as to allow Russia to regain control of the Straits and threaten the trade in the Mediterranean. On the other hand, the Russians viewed with sympathy their Greek coreligionists, although feared both the notion of Revolution and the possibility that an independent Greek state could turn out to be an ally to Britain. France's interests were partly economic partly strategical. Its trade with the Ottomans was important and French investors kept in their portfolio large numbers of Ottoman bonds, worthless in the event of the Empire's dissolution. At the same time, France was seeking its re-entry into international politics after its defeat in 1815. Thus, all Great Powers involved tried to safeguard their interests based on transnational relations and away from sentimentality that entered the debate only as a matter of public opinion influence on Government. However, even the authoritarian governments, which were the norm at

---

[183] A.G. Protopsaltis: Ibid., p. 22.

the time, were compelled ever so often to respect the general sentiment, to a certain degree.[184]

A significant factor was the widespread philhellenism that manifested itself both in France and Britain. The element of Christian Orthodoxy played a critical role in shaping Russia's positions, always to the degree that the official policies were influenced by the then-current public opinion.

However, in contrast to the philhellenism of the public opinion of the 19th century, there might have also existed a "governmental pro-Turkism" notion. The reference pertains to the development within the Ministries of Foreign Affairs and governments of policies that transcend the interests and other contractual decision-making criteria in international relations and are traced back to the realm of emotion. This phenomenon had been observed in Austria and Britain at the time.

The atrocities in Constantinople

Following the events in Moldovlachia, the aphorisms and the manifestation of full subjugation of the Constantinopolitans had temporarily saved them from the danger of general slaughter, but when the news of the uprising in Peloponnese arrived, the Sultan proceeded to additional horrid measures. The first led to the gallows was the Ecumenical Patriarch Gregory V. The execution was committed on April 10, 1821, on Easter Sunday, in front of the main gate of Patriarchate by irregular Janissaries, but the text posted as justification proved that he was executed on Sultan's order. The execution of senior priests who had been arrested as hostages followed. Metropolitan Dionysios of Efessos was hanged in the central market of the Greek-populated Pera, Baloukpazar;

---

[184] S.W. Sowards: The Balkans, 1996.

Eugenios of Aghialos in Galata, while Athanasios of Nicomedia died from hardships of his imprisonment and torture. Retribution against the Greek populace of Constantinople was widespread and brutal. Mass hangings of laity took place on April 19, 1821. Nicholas Mourouzis, the Interpreter of the fleet, was murdered on May 6. On the west coast of Bosphorus, Metropolitans Ioannikios of Tyrnovos, Dorotheos of Adrianoupolis in Megalo Revma, Ioseph of Thessaloniki in Nihori, and Gregory of Derkon in Therapia were hanged on June 3. On the same day, Alexandros and Skarlatos Kalatsoudis, who had been appointed ruler of Wallachia after the eruption of the Revolution, were exiled to east Anatolia.

According to news arriving from Greek territories, real or fabricated, a state of terror reigned in Constantinople over the Greeks. The reckoning of casualties, Greeks, and Armenians or Christians from European countries, was in the thousands. It was a sign that the general massacre in the City had commenced. Among the Greek victims were also those to whom the state owed money, with the expedient practice of Turks to evade, at times, repaying government debts by declaring their creditors as traitors whose property was to be confiscated.[185]

European countries remained indifferent[186] , but the Czar evoked the right to be involved in the fate of the Sultan's Orthodox Rum subjects, based on the Treaty of Kaynarca of 1774 and the Treaties of Iasi of

---

[185] Petros A. Georgantzis: Ibid. E. G. Protopsaltis: Political History of the Hellenic Republic v. B′, Athens 1973, p.p. 7-10. Re. E. Vakalopoulos: Ibid., Volume V, p. 499.
  Also D. Fotiadis: The revolution of ' 21, D. Kokkinos: The Greek Revolution, as well texts of T. Kandilora and Sp. Trikoupi. (all in Greek)
[186] As they did during the pogrom against the Greeks of Constantinople in 1955

1792 and Bucharest of 1812, and requested the fulfillment of four conditions: The Ottoman Empire would undertake the obligation to rebuild or repair churches destroyed by the mob; The Sultan would ensure the genuine protection of the Orthodox Christian Church; The Ottoman government would differentiate between "culprits" and "innocent" Christians, and not harm those who would declare allegiance within a certain period. And above all, Principalities of Moldovlachia would revert to the previous regime, and the Ottoman army that had invaded the principalities would retreat under the prerogatives established in favor of Russia according to the treaties. It added that in case the Sublime Porte did not abide by these demands, it would constitute a justification for Russia to intervene to uphold the treaties' accords.

The Czar set forth the content of the ultimatum to the attention of the rest of the European Powers. He underlined that his stance towards the revolutionary movements had not changed and that it was presumed for Russia, as a neighboring country, to consider itself responsible for restoring order in the Balkans.

Ambassador Stroganov did not get an answer from the Sublime Porte within the deadline he had set and left the Ottoman capital in early August 1821. For their part, Austria did not want Russian influence to extend to the Balkans and was also afraid of the outbreak of similar movements in its territory. Britain believed that the Sultan provided the best guarantee for the safety of the road to India. They both requested from their Ambassadors in Constantinople to try to extract some concessions in favor of Greeks, even in appearance only, just to offer some gratification to the Czar in order to not proceed with his war plans.

Shortly before the Revolution erupted, Kapodistrias systematically discouraged the Greeks

198

from resorting to this resolution as he considered it untimely and reckless, given the prevailing conditions. But after the eruption of the revolutionary movement, he used his persuasion towards the Czar to provide armed assistance to the Greeks. At this point, the concerted action of Austria and Britain prevented the Czar from declaring war at that time.[187]

Meanwhile, Patriarch Gregory V had not remained inactive throughout the tragic days of March and April 1821. He had repeatedly visited the Ottoman authorities, presided over meetings, and seemed to have tried, as much as possible, to reduce the impact of the ex-communication. By his martyrdom, he became a symbol for the revolt of the nation, offering his ultimate sacrifice on the altar of the Revolution. Thus, history's glorious consecration of the Martyr was well merited.

Throughout the period, from the eruption of the Revolution to the official acceptance by the Sublime Porte on April 12, 1830, of the three Protocols of London February 3, 1830, the Greeks of the Empire and especially of Rumeli and Constantinople had been exposed to the atrocities of the mob and the vengeful fury of the Sultan. Although the situation had not culminated with implementing the threatened comprehensive massacres at the start of the Revolution, it had continued to be extremely brutal for the Rums. Despite all this, the Greeks of the Ottoman Empire were enheartened by 1827, when after the naval Battle of Navarino, they had discerned that the course of events toward freedom of the genus was irreversible.[188]

---

[187] S. Th. Laskaris: Diplomatic History of Greece 1821-1914, Athens 1947 p. 1-24. (in Greek).
[188] Manuel Gedeon: 1800-1913 Notes of Chronograph, Athens 1932.

THE REVOLUTION AND THE OTTOMANS

Ottoman administration's initial assessment about the insurrection in Peloponnese considered it as an ordinary uprising similar to those that periodically erupted in Rumeli and elsewhere, that were successfully quelled. As soon as the uprising began, the Ottoman state followed a policy of repression, taking countermeasures in the revolutionary regions. However, contrary to what the Sublime Porte predicted, the Revolution in Peloponnese spread rapidly to a large geographical area because large segments of the Rum population supported it. To counter that, the Ottomans took extensive security measures in vital regions of Anatolia and Rumeli to prevent any further escalation of the Revolution.[189]

In the Balkan region, just before the Greek Revolution, the Ottoman state had successfully suppressed insurgencies by Serbs and Tepedelenli Ali Pasha of Ioannina. It presumed that in the same manner, it could quell the Greek revolt and tried to take measures in that direction. Moreover, it had misinterpreted the Greek movement initially as an "upheaval" rather than what it was in substance, a separatist campaign directed against the state. As neither historical knowledge nor tools to distinguish between social or class movements and national ones existed at the time, everything was dealt with in the

---

[189] Filiz Yashar: Journal of Faculty of Literature, 2015, https://scholar.google.com/citations?user=g4IPzAsAAAAJ&hl=en #d=gs_md_cita-d&u=%2Fcitations %3Fview_op%3Dview_citation%26hl%3Den%26user%3Dg4IPz AsAAAAJ%26citation_for_view%3Dg4IPzAsAAAAJ%3AzYLM7Y 9cAGgC%26tzom%3D-120 (last access 03/09/2020) (in Turkish).

light of the legitimacy of the power that entailed economic benefits. It soon became apparent that the rebellious spirit of Peloponnese had expanded rapidly to the Balkans, the Aegean, and western Anatolia, and from the point of view of the Ottomans, it had evolved to a real "Revolution".

The "Greek Revolution" or the "Hellenic War of Independence" was the first political movement among a sequence of many other insurgencies that aimed at independence and resulted in a loss of the Empire's territory. In this sense, the Ottoman state, seeing the effect of the Revolution on many regions of the Empire, felt the urgency to take strict security measures in specific areas. The measures had been particularly austere and contributed to the crippling of the potential for Rums of these regions to rebel.

From Ottoman's viewpoint, the uprising included Peloponnese and the areas around it, where the Rum population outnumbered other ethnicities. The movements initially spread to the Aegean, Egriboz (Ottoman name of Evia), Camlıca (Spetses), Suluca (Hydra), and Psara. The large ships of these islands were utilized for revolutionary purposes, and according to Turkish accounts, they took on piracy that subverted the security of the Mediterranean. They would raise various flags and cause damage to Muslim ships they encountered in the Aegean.

In Ayvalık (Kydonies), in Cunda (Moschonisi), in Sisam (Samos), the populace joined in with rebels attacking Ottoman ships and coastal villages where they found support from local Rums.

The Supreme Council convened in the Porte described these attacks as "predatory" and announced that the aggressors intended to gather and entrench in a large area like Peloponnese or Crete. Although the Ottoman state initially characterized the move as sedition, as time passed, it

202

realized that the revolutionary spirit among "the race" of Rums was getting stronger. Ottoman documents indicate, though, that the administration had not realized, at the time, that the uprising was a fight for independence. The concern was confined to the unrest that had risen in the area. The wretched and scornful characterizations used by the Ottoman state for the rebels seemed to have been an attempt to confront them through contempt.[190]

Contrary to the Ottomans' expectations, as time passed, the movement of Rums intensified, and attacks against unarmed Muslims began. The Sultan himself wrote that Rums, who rebelled all-around, had revealed their intentions through their conduct, and thus none could be trusted and that it made no sense to attempt to make them compliant. It was a subtle message insinuating the slaughtering of Rums. The direct message would follow later.

The Sultan kept the same stance in the coming months. The conflicts were no longer between revolutionary forces and the state but had transformed into a regular war between nations. The Turkish historiography cites, for example, the Rums of Chios, who rose twice between 1821 and 1828. The ruthless clashes between Rums and Ottoman soldiers, the blockade imposed by revolutionary ships on the island and the siege of the Turkish fortress, the conduct of the Ottoman soldiers who broke the blockade and arrested the local population as captives taking their fortunes as spoils (Turk historiographers do not speak of massacres), brought to mind war between states.

According to Professor Ali Fuat Orenc, the Greek Revolution soon evolved into a ruthless religious and ethnic war. He wrote that "the Greeks, with the support of Europe, set as a goal to fight until

---

[190] They were called Izbandit from the Italian word Sbandato.

there was not a single Turk left in Peloponnese. He added that by the time the Revolution was over, the Muslims of Peloponnese had vanished from the historical scene".[191]

As the Revolution expanded, the Ottoman agitation in Constantinople grew. In addition to war operations, other ways were sought to suppress the Revolution. Among them were the arrests of Metropolitans and other dignitaries of rebellious islands and their transfer to Constantinople, as well as the cessation of appointments of Rums to public posts and confiscation of the property of Rums that were involved in the Revolution. Because of the continuation of the "mutiny" (the exact terminology of the mandate), it was also decided to stop the handling of bureaucratic matters relating to Rums.[192]

Apart from Rums, measures were also taken against Ottoman administrators, with the punishment of local bureaucrats and military officials who did not display the zeal required to suppress the Revolution. Following this, Salim Kaptan, who had not rushed to help the Ottoman fleet during the naval battle that took place between Chios and Karaburun, was executed.

The Ottoman administration, in light of the increasing daily insurgencies, issued mandates for the preparation of a mission of assistance from Anatolia in the form of food and human resources to

---

[191] Ali Fuat Orenc: Mora Turkleri, 2009, (in Turkish). The same writer, who spoke about the support of Europeans to Greeks, writes in the same paragraph that from accounts of European eyewitnesses, the events in the insurgent areas were such, that sometimes death was a salvation for the Turks. Conflicting claims both being incorrect. Five hundred thousand of Muslims left in 1923 with the exchange of populations (except for the Muslims in Thrace). Greece has accepted hundreds of thousands of Muslim refugees fleeing Turkey, from 2015 onward.
[192] Filiz Yashar: Ibid.

fight the rebels. The fastest route to dispatch the help was via the Aegean, where Greek "pirates" dominated. Consequently, it was decided that the Ottoman fleet should get involved. Indeed, the fleet, a few months after the start of the Revolution, overpowered the revolutionary "pirates", ousting them from the coasts of Rumeli and Anatolia. But once the fleet departed, the rebels in Peloponnese and the islands resumed their operations.

The central government believed that "erasing" the element that revolted would end the Revolution. It took a while to realize that these local uprisings were aspects of a more general movement of independence.

The countermeasures of the Ottomans

The Revolution initially broke out in Peloponnese and its periphery, islands, and coasts, but a little later, the Ottoman state realized that a similar threat existed both in Rumeli (Europe) and in Anatolia. A document sent to the Ottoman administration of Vlore stated that "Rums have committed all forms of treachery, ravaging and burning everything at sea and land", with the complaint that despite all efforts, it was impossible to appease them.

The Ottoman authorities of Eastern Thrace wrote in April 1821 that they were under the threat of Rum inhabitants of the region, while the Revolution appeared to engulf coastal cities in Anatolia such as Ayvalık (Kydonies) and Halicarnassus. They wrote that "Despite the measures implemented to suppress the Revolution, Rums persisted on, and in areas where it had been suppressed new uprisings had resurfaced."

While initially the repressive measures of the Ottoman State were limited to Rumeli (in Peloponnese, a full-scale war was in effect), a couple of years later, it became clear that Anatolia was also under threat, and orders were given for measures to be taken there. With time, the Revolution spread to all regions inhabited by Rums. Despite the characterization of the events initially as a mutiny by the Ottoman state, it was understood that all Rums in some way were implicated in the Revolution.

The confrontation with rebels was difficult as Rums resorted to guerilla warfare. Their attacks were precipitous in retaking an area, and the regular Ottoman army could not hold out against them. The unconventional war of Greeks did not permit strategic warfare schemes, and the Ottomans were unaccustomed to such a wide-ranging guerrilla war. The roadways were in bad condition, and the Rum "pirate" fleet obstructed the navy. As a result, the mission of providing military aid and supplies was severely hindered.

The documents arriving in Constantinople from Varna, Chios, and the opposite mainland coast, Tekirdag (Raidestos) and Malgara in Thrace, reported that Rums there had been mobilized and had begun attacking Muslims, particularly, in the region of Raidestos where the Muslim population numbered 200 while Rum inhabitants were of the order of ten thousand. Further, as Rums frequently traveled to the western Balkans for trade-related businesses, the Ottomans suspected that all of them had fully embraced the principles of the Revolution.

The Revolution had evolved beyond being an internal dissent and threatened the political, administrative, and social structure of the Empire. Rums constituted a significant portion of the population, both in Rumeli and in Anatolia. The areas where they lived formed strongholds of the Empire against external dangers, whereas the revolutionary mobilizations in Eastern Thrace brought the center of the Empire directly into contact with the Revolution. Although the Revolution had not spread substantially to the regions in question, the Ottoman State saw fit to take rigorous measures there as well. The areas were separated into sections according to the Ottoman system of roads, as Right (east), Middle (Constantinople area), and Left (west).

In this context, the Ottoman State took a series of measures (Tedabir-i Osmaniyye) in what considered "dangerous" areas of the Empire, particularly in parts of Rumeli and Anatolia that were near the Aegean Sea. A Turkish study highlights three categories of measures:

1. The definition of a border containing the Eastern, Western and Middle regions of Rumeli and Anatolia and the protection of areas within them.

2. The confiscation of the weaponry held by Rums there.

3. The control and requirement to obtain authorization to enter and exit these areas.[193]

Although there is no mention of it in the Turkish study, an additional implicit measure had been the intimidation of the populace. The rampant slaughter and destruction of entire Greek villages in Aegean islands, especially in Chios and Psara, in order not only to crush in blood any revolutionary movement but also relay an underlying message. On the other hand, the selective executions in Constantinople that were not part of the Sultan's blind fury and vengeance were carried out as punishment and aimed at wiping out the nation's leadership and squelch the Revolution. They were

---

[193] Filiz Yashar: Ibid.

intended to serve both as a warning and threat to those involved.

The shores and periphery of the area from Strantza in northern Rumeli to Hendek, Girit (Heraklion, Crete), including the capital city of Constantinople, were considered as top-level areas of defense. Any transgressions in these regions would be punished forthwith. The measures taken were similar to contemporary wartime emergency conditions. The measures were also extended to ships, mostly Russian, crossing the Straits. With the mandates sent to local authorities, a new, peculiar legal situation emerged, whereby the Ottoman state was at war with a part of its population. Armed conflicts with Rums, confiscation of their property, and their captivity were considered legitimate.[194]

The measure of collecting weaponry held by Rums in areas outside Peloponnese yielded a vast array of pistols, swords, and sabers. The action was extended to the Muslim population from which weapons were also taken from. These were dispatched to places where the Ottoman state faced uprisings that were flourishing in Rumeli, Aegean, as well as in Anatolia to the extent of unnerving the administration, as It can be attested from Ottoman documents.

From 1822, the Ottoman administration had perceived that Greeks traveling from Rumeli to Anatolia and back, particularly when passing from Constantinople, not only conveyed information and orders, but they were also spying. To curb this, they imposed the measure of travel constraints. The

---

[194] Therefore, no cowardice, as D. Ypsilantis claimed, was shown by Xanthos during his passage from Constantinople, hidden in a Russian ship's hull in September 1827, as he knew about the searches and his fate if he was discovered. See. Xanthos: Memoirs, Letter of D. Ypsilantis. October 6, Nafplio

measure covered both land and sea transport. To restore order as it was alleged, the action was also extended to the travels of Muslims since it seemed that Rums occasionally would dress up as Muslims and, with their flawless Turkish accent, could not be detected. For the authorization of permits, information regarding departure and destination of travelers and reasons for the journey was mandatory.

Whether, of course, all these detailed orders of the Ottoman State were implemented effectively and justly by an intolerant administration would never be known for sure. However, they succeeded in imposing the Ottoman order and confront the revolutionary movements in large areas of Rumeli and Anatolia.

The Ottoman measures did not differ from the usual steps taken by the Ottoman State in wars, and in that sense, they are indicative of the extent of the Revolution. The designation of Rums as enemies and the call to Muslims for a "holy war for Islam (Gaza)" reinforces the view that the Ottoman State ultimately had realized that it was not facing a revolt but an all-out war.

THE FORMATION OF THE GREEK POLITY

The victories in the military field led to the need for establishing some sort of institutions that would take over the political leadership of the campaign. However, it is evident that there were difficulties in establishing an organized state under the prevailing conditions. Among the many military and political leaders, social and historical reasons did not allow the emergence of a single leader that could be recognized by all. Prominent figures like Ioannis Kapodistrias or Alexander Ypsilantis -at the beginning of the revolution- who both possessed the leadership qualifications needed, were not available at the time. Any political figures that arose in succession were the result of compromises and conflicting ambitions, and whenever governments tried to exert proper power, it resulted in a civil war.

The roots of the misfortune of the Greek State extend to the beginnings of its founding, for lack of a democratically established central authority that would be able to exert its sovereignty indisputably. On the contrary, there existed a multitude of small power clusters who were trying to become part of the emerging governing entity. The chieftains considered that sway stemmed from the might of their weapons. The politicians, on the other hand, claimed that their mastery in state affairs was not only indispensable but also constituted the source of the power of the new State, in the creation of which themselves had played the central role setting up the link between the foreign Powers and the Greek State. The fact that most chieftains hailed from Peloponnese, whereas many politicians were from Constantinople and other cities of the Greek diaspora as well as from towns of

211

wider Greece, created additional grounds for resentment.

After the failure of the movement in Moldovlachia, ecumenism, the plan of the Friendly Society for the liberation of a wider part of Hellenism was abandoned. The members of the Society were sidelined. They did not excel in arms, while their middle-class origins, as well as the lack of academic accomplishments and titles, did not allow them to assume an essential political role in state affairs.

Despite the operation of local administrations, all Greeks realized the need to establish a strong central government. This unanimity led to the convening by D. Ypsilantis on December 20, 1821, of the first National Assembly for the formation of a general government. The convention, which was held near Epidaurus, declared the independence of Greece and proceeded to the sanctioning of the " provisional regime" on January 1, 1822. It was designated as temporary in order not to alienate European monarchies with the adoption of a republican regime at such an early stage. This action had been extremely significant as it was no longer a revolutionary group of rebels who had risen against a ruler but a state fighting on equal footing with another. Nevertheless, the voting for a republican constitution in Epidaurus had provoked distrust for the Greek cause at the Courts of European monarchies even of Czar Alexander I.

The Constitution of Epidaurus defined in its preamble the purposes of the revolution: "The Greek nation, under the intolerable Ottoman oppression, could not bear any longer the heavy yoke of tyranny, and having broken free from its chains with great sacrifices, declares today...its political existence and independence". The first Constitution of Greece, drafted with the legal aid of Italian lawyer Vincent Galina, provided protection of individual freedoms, the principle of representativeness, and the separation of powers. The political power, i.e., the Administration, according to the Constitution of Epidaurus, was divided into two supreme authorities, the executive and the parliamentarian, both with specific tasks, two collective bodies with a one-year term, "equal" in the legislative process. The "Judicial" branch, on the other hand, consisted of eleven members, and it was a unit independent from the other two powers.[195] The rendering of justice was assigned to the "Criteria" (courts).

The military branch was also organized. The revolutionary army consisted mainly of irregular bodies together with a small tactical force. The Naval division was headed by a three-member committee composed of representatives of Hydra, Spetses, and Psara. The Community system remained intact. In the Constitution, there was no reference to the Friendly Society, something that would make sense since Greeks had to keep their distance from Carbonari type movements in order not to alienate the conservative European Courts.[196]

Thus, the foundations for a modern democratic state were set. All Greeks were equal before the law. Every indigenous Christian was declared Greek. Those who came from abroad and resided in the Greek territory were equal before the law with the natives. The possibility of naturalization would be available to them. The estate, honor, and safety of Greeks were protected by law. All proceeds would be rightfully distributed, and no taxation would be assessed without a law.

A state seal was adopted, and the colors of the flag were chosen as blue and white while the executive was assigned to determining its form. At the

---

[195] Greek Parliament: Constitutional history
[196] Vasilis Kremmydas: Ibid., p.110.

outset of the revolution, as there was no single administration, each military unit borne its own flag. The revolutionary flags were tricolor (white-black-red) with the symbols of the Friendly Society (such as the reborn Phoenix or anchor) that the flags of the islands mainly adorned. Alternatively, they followed the banners and pennons of chieftains graced by a cross with saints or an eagle. Meanwhile, many villages rebelled under the banner of the Church of their parish. Many of the flags of the revolution brought one of the phrases "Freedom or death", "I tan I epi tas" of the ancient Spartans (with the same meaning), or specifically in Mani, "Victory or death".

Meanwhile, political formations had started to emerge. The first political strife appeared among those who sought to introduce European morals as they had developed in western settings and those who followed a line that reflected local upbringing. The first group, the "Foreign Party" including mainly those who had come from abroad, were led by Mavrokordatos and echoed rational views, while the second, the "Domestic Party" represented the dignitaries, the chieftains, the clergy, all those who had some authority during the Turkish occupation. The power of the latter came from tested positions and leadership skills along with the power of the weapons of the chieftains of Peloponnese. The "Domestic Party" was not aligned with doctrines prevailing in Europe; its leaders despised the press; its followers did not desire compliance with the law and did not respect hierarchy. The local populace, in general, felt more at ease with them, and therefore the "Domestic Party" initially had the upper hand. However, the party had shortcomings in its organization, lacked inner unity, and had suffered from mutual rivalry and distrust, personal interests, and family passions.[197]

Eventually, though, displaying the firm resolve of Greeks for progress and organization of a modern state, a component of the character of the Greek people, the "Foreign Party" that also included the progressive islanders prevailed. The political program of the party, inspired by the principles of enlightenment, made provisions for the sovereignty of people, equality of rights, and freedom of the press. At any rate, the morals of Europe could not easily be impressed upon peoples who had lived for centuries in slavery, more so when the regimes there were autocratic.

At first, the awareness of necessity kept everyone together and cooperating. Later, military victories and rationing of spoils began to create suspicion and dissensions. After the defeat of Dramali, Kolokotronis was asserted on the consciences of many as the undisputed military leader. The authority that came with it led him to make unilateral decisions without any consultations with the Government. There was thus discord among the adversaries to the degree of threatening a civil war at a time when the danger from the Ottomans seemed to have been thwarted. But, this was not the case as it turned out to be, not long after. Already after the ravaging by Dramali in August 1822, the Government's credibility had diminished significantly from the chieftains' perspective. The failed Greek mission at the Conference of the European Concert meeting in Verona, where even the reception of the Greek Delegation had been denied, further denigrated the perception of the Government as an effective entity.[198]

---

[197] A.G. Protopsaltis: Ibid., p.p. 31-32.
[198] A.G. Protopsaltis: Ibid., p. 29.

There were no substantive cases to be made against the Government, however. The role of the State in coordinating its efforts to provide for the dire necessities of its populace on the one hand, while simultaneously trying to protect it from the multitude of dangers it was facing was not well understood. Resentment against the Government stemmed from the nature of peoples who would expect the Government more than it could offer. The lure of power has always remained the perpetual bedrock of political evolution, having as a set point of reference the human nature as well as the social and partisan distortions that prevented and nullified the already reduced possibilities for resolving a multitude of problems. The fierce rivalries, with tendencies - legitimate or not- of incrimination of the opponents, rendered the national affair prey to political passions.

Thus, the Government convened the second National Assembly in Astros to revise the Constitution of Epidaurus. The convention, in which the former dignitaries had the majority, carried out its work between March 29 and April 13, 1823, and was deemed a success. The new Constitution, which was a simple revision of its antecedent, was called the "Law of Epidaurus". It was technically more sophisticated, establishing a slight primacy of the legislative body over the executive. It reformed the rights of the executive regarding the drafting of laws, prohibited any legislation against the system of Government, improved the provisions on individual rights, and altered the electoral law rendering it more democratic. All the local governing systems that had been operating since the beginning of the revolution had been abolished.[199]

The Assembly appointed a new executive under the chairmanship of Petrobey Mavromichalis,

---

[199] V. Kremmydas, Ibid., p. 126.

while Mavrokordatos was elected President of the Parliament. The executive included Kolokotronis, Andreas Zaimis, A. Metaxas, and S. Charalambakis. The martial issues were assigned to a three-member committee with representatives from mainland Greece, Mani, and the rest of Peloponnese. Efforts were made to complete the State's organization and to centralize the powers. The drafting of criminal law was sought, and the need to secure an external loan was acknowledged. The three islands' pecuniary requirements were examined, although some of them were deemed excessive.[200]

In the meeting at Astros, a dispute broke for the first time between Greeks born outside Greece and the indigenous people with protagonists, the group of reformers for the former, to which Mavrokordatos belonged, and the dignitaries and chieftains for the latter.

The political evolutions

At the second National Assembly, the rivalry between civilian and military factions became pronounced.[201] Mavrokordatos, being in charge of the "political" bloc that included the brothers Koundouriotis, Ioannis Kolettis, along with chieftains from Rumeli, managed to prevail overall. His election to the position of president of the parliament, while he was the first secretary of the executive, stirred up a political storm and the intense protests of the "military", especially Theodoros Kolokotronis and K. Deligiannis with whom Petrobey Mavromichalis also collaborated.[202]

---

[200] E. G Protopsaltis: Ibid., vol. B, p. 30.
[201] V. Kremmydas, Ibid., p. 127.
[202] V. Kremmydas, Ibid., p. 129.

Kolokotronis, having been the target of many attacks, left dissatisfied mainly with Mavrokordatos. In this context, the antagonisms that had taken root in a divisive background with the potential for civil war were further intensified. There was an opposition of the executive to the parliamentary; Greek forces split up and began to turn against one another in an internal conflict. The parliamentary had no means of prevailing over the executive. Since its existence was itself in danger, it was forced to relocate its post often until eventually was split, with one base remaining in Argos under Bishop of Vresthenis and the other in Nafplio under Gregory of Methonis.

The party of Mavrokordatos, by way of the majority of the parliament in Argos, sought the fall of the executive branch whose power was consolidated under Kolokotronis. To this end, the House of Argos requested the executive branch to render an account of its financial management. This claim angered its president, Petrobey Mavromichalis, who sent a team of gunmen to Argos, expelling the members of the parliament to Kranidi. On the other side, Kolokotronis formed a military government and captured the fortresses of Palamidi (Nafplio) and Acrocorinth.

However, the parliament in Kranidi, who had the support of Kolettis and was influenced by Mavrokordatos, terminated the mandate of the executive accusing it of the incidents in Argos and appointed a new executive branch. Ioannis Kolettis participated in the new executive under G. Koundouriotis, while Mavrokordatos was appointed Secretary. The new Government secured some internal supremacy thanks to the weaponry of Kolettis, and a reputation abroad, thanks to Mavrokordatos. The other faction, however, controlled individual provinces and confronted the Government of Koundouriotis.

218

The new executive authorized a three-member committee to go to London and attempt to get a loan. The Commission succeeded in February 1824, with the help of the philhellenes there, to secure a loan, but upon their return, they were blamed for the high interest-rate of the loan and waste of large sums of money during their stay there. A year later, a second loan twice the amount of the first was attained but on burdensome terms, resulting in large part of the loans never reaching Greece.[203] The procurement of these loans through which the Greek state established international economic relations was regarded as important as the recognition of the state.

The civil war between the two factions erupted when the first loan's money arrived. The Government of Koundouriotis, despite its large debts to the chieftains and the dignitaries, decided to allocate the funds to the preparation of the fleet to avoid a new disaster in Samos after that of Psara. Besides, this was the main reason the money was rendered in the first place. Hydra and Spetses received most of the money, and this was attributed to the support of the islanders to the Government but also to Koundouriotis' origin from Hydra. The chieftains, who did not receive the money owed to them, protested strongly and, in September 1824, rebelled against the Government under the leadership of Kolokotronis. Yet several Peloponnesian chieftains aligned with the Government.

After the expulsion from Nafplio of the "politicians" by Petrobey Mavromichalis and Theodoros Kolokotronis, the executive branch was reorganized in Kranidi under George Koundouriotis. The executive of Kranidi, the "legal" Government, declared the rebellious "executive of Tripolitza" as the «enemy of the nation». The Government, strengthened

---

[203] S. Th Laskaris: Ibid., p. 17.

with the money of the British loans, decided to suppress the rebellion by force. Kolettis took over the staffing of the troops that would be used in the conflict with the "military". The government forces of the administration of Kranidi, under Papaflessas, took Tripolitza in early October, while warriors from Rumeli, who had fled, crushed the rebellion within two weeks. The homes of the leaders of the mutiny were looted, chieftains were captured, and Kolokotronis, who surrendered, was imprisoned in Hydra.[204]

After these events, the Government commanded the respect of all. However, a new cause of discord started to emerge between the followers of Kolettis, who with the increasing power gained with the victory in the civil war had founded the "French party", and the supporters of Mavrokordatos (subsequent English party) who considered Kolettis a more dangerous adversary even than Kolokotronis.

The diplomatic developments

The service to the Sublime Porte of the Russian telegraph of June 16, 1821, by Ambassador Stroganoff took Europe by surprise. The potential mobilization of the Russian army in the event of a victory could have instigated a border change in favor of Russia. The Powers reacted to preserve peace and the status quo. France rejected Czar's request to send a squadron of the fleet to the eastern Mediterranean, as the government of the Second Restoration considered that France would gain nothing from a possible prevalence of the Greek revolution. An independent Greek state would be under the influence of Russia, while a French intervention with Russia would jeopardize the long-lasting Franco-

---

[204] V. Kremmydas: Ibid., p. 130 – 136.

220

Turkish friendship and could even result in a confrontation with Britain and Austria, countries friendly to Ottoman Empire with interest in preserving its territorial integrity.

Austria feared that a successful national revolution could have inspired the ethnicities in the Habsburg Empire to revolt, while Britain considered that a stable Ottoman Empire would better ensure the route to India. Thus, the orders given to the Ambassadors of Britain and Austria in Constantinople were to try to wheedle out some small concessions from the Sultan in favor of Greeks with the hope of calming Russia.[205]

Czar Alexander I was worried lest a common front would be created against him by Britain and Austria. He remained indecisive, sometimes influenced by Metternich, sometimes swayed by the arguments of Kapodistrias. Austrian Chancellor Metternich, in his correspondence with Czar, recognized Russia's rights on the Danube principalities but argued that the Greek issue being of general interest should be examined separately at a conference in Vienna among the representatives of the Sultan and the Powers. Metternich intended to stall the discussions to give time to the Sublime Porte to confront the revolution of Ali Pasha and suppress the movement of Greeks with more ease.

When in May 1822, the Sultan withdrew his army from the Danube principalities, the Czar, despite Kapodistrias' suggestion, accepted the proposal of Chancellor Metternich, and Russia participated at the conference in Vienna at the end of June 1822. The meeting was held under the "guardianship" of the Chancellor to the extent that Metternich himself drafted the reports that Czar's

---

[205] S. Th. Laskaris: Ibid., p. 13 (in Greek).

representative Tatistcheff sent from Vienna.[206] The views of the Chancellor finally prevailed. Metternich's victory at this stage was thorough as Kapodistrias had not succeeded in convincing the Czar of the deceitfulness of Metternich. Kapodistrias was removed from his duties in June 1822 in the Russian government by the Czar and retired to Geneva. [207] There, he became the soul of the entire philhellenic movement in Europe. Once again, the Czar had placed the interests of his dynasty above any other issue.[208]

The Sultan, for his part, rejected any interference of Europe in the interior affairs of the Empire, arguing that the issue of its Orthodox nationals could not constitute a subject of international debate.

Russia, through a circular letter to the Powers, announced on September 14, 1822, the conditions under which it would resume diplomatic relations with the Ottoman Empire. In this letter, all that was included in favor of Greeks were some measures for restoration of order by peaceful means. It also mentionned a joint effort for granting amnesty to Greeks by the Ambassadors in Constantinople. The restoration of the status quo antebellum at the Danube principalities was Russia's primary interest. It was evident that Alexander I had similar positions with the Austrian Chancellor as it was confirmed at the Congress of Verona of October 1822, which had

---

[206] Guillaume de Bertier de Sauvigny : *Metternich*, Paris, Fayard, 1998.
[207] Kapodistrias at the Congress of Vienna in 1815, as Russian minister, had counteracted the overwhelming influence of the Austrian minister Prince Metternich and had obtained international guarantees for the constitution and neutrality of Switzerland through an agreement among the Powers.
[208] S. Th. Laskaris: Ibid., p..14.

been convened particularly regarding the situation in Spain.

Meanwhile, on August 12, 1822, the Turcophile Lord Castlereagh committed suicide, and the Foreign Office was undertaken by George Canning, who believed that Britain should take steps in such a way that if Greeks were to prevail, they should be under the impression that they owe their success to Britain. The first display of the reversal of British politics was the recognition at the beginning of 1823 of the Greek blockade of Turkish coasts declared on March 25, 1822.[209] Following this, in 1824, Greeks succeeded in securing a loan from Britain.[210] The loan was approved by the British government mainly in support of the British interests in the Eastern Mediterranean regarding navigation in the region.

This politicking of Britain was a cause for concern to Czar Alexander, who feared that Russia might lose the upper hand in the Greek affair. Besides, the Russian Council in Petersburg was never friendly to the Ottomans. In this context, Russia complained that the conditions set out in its circular letter had not been fulfilled, particularly regarding the issues pertaining mainly to its relations with the Ottoman Empire. Thus, after discussions with the Powers, it drew up a new memorandum made public in early 1824, where it included references to the Greeks' liberation from the Turkish yoke.[211]

In its memorandum of January 9, 1824, Russia called for establishing three autonomous sovereign principalities in Greece, tax vassal to the Sultan, like those in Moldovlachia. The first would include the eastern mainland (Sterea), Thessaly, and

---

[209] G. B. Zotiadis: Political and diplomatic History, 1973 (in Greek).
[210] S. Th Laskaris: Ibid., p. 18.
[211] S. Th Laskaris: Ibid., p. 19.

Macedonia along with Thessaloniki; the second, the old Venetian (west) coast, Epirus, and Akarnania; the third, Peloponnese and Crete. The islands would retain their privileged status. Russia had alleged that otherwise, the establishment of an independent Greek state might end up becoming a refuge for rebels from all over Europe. The memorandum was rejected by the European Powers, who considered that the plan intended to increase Russia's influence and power at the expense of the Sultan.

When the Russian proposals leaked through a British indiscretion and were published in a French newspaper, both Ottomans and Greeks protested strongly. The Greeks, who at that time thought they were outmatching the Ottomans, did not want under any circumstances the continuation of the dominance of the Sultan. At the same time, they saw their longing for a single independent State to be fading as rumors spread by Britain suggested that the purpose of Russia's proposal was the partition of Greece. The Greeks understood that they should not be alienated from Britain and, in a memorandum sent to London, expressed their opposition to the Russian project. Later, however, the rejection of this proposal was criticized, especially by the Russophile Greeks, since the acceptance of the plan would have avoided, as they argued, the prolongation of the war along with its consequences for the next six years, let alone its highly dubious outcome and the very narrow borders that independent Greece eventually ended up with. It is impossible to second-guess what would have happened if the Russian plan were to be accepted.[212]

After the British opposition, the two conferences of St. Petersburg on the Russian proposals failed with the only conclusion of authorizing the Ambassadors in Constantinople to

---

[212] A study by Periklis Argyropoulos (in Greek).

persuade the Ottomans to seek the mediation of the Powers voluntarily - something, of course, that was never going to happen.

Philhellenism

Governments arrive at decisions on the foreign policy according to specific criteria; however, the public opinion in countries is set by different standards. Regarding the Greek Revolution, the criteria initially considered by the European States led them to a friendlier stance towards the Ottoman Empire and the safeguarding of its territorial integrity rather than the quest for independence of Greeks.[213]

Yet the public opinion in Western European countries was shaped under different criteria. Westerners had a profound admiration for ancient Greece and associated that fondness to modern Greeks not only because of the same locale but also of the spoken modern variation of the same language, given that the historical continuity of Hellenism through the Byzantines had not yet been evinced, while there were disputes, which were later expressed by Fallmerayer in his essay "On the origin of the contemporary Greeks".[214] Jakob Philipp Fallmerayer, already in the preface to the "History of Morea during the Middle Ages", published in 1830, argued that "the genus of Greeks has vanished from Europe and not even a drop of genuine Greek blood flows in the veins of the Christian population of Greece".[215] He openly

---

[213] Vasilis Moutsoglou: The criteria in international politics, Athens 2015 (in Greek).
[214] Nefeli Editions 1984
[215] However, the theoretical allegations of Fallmerayer about Slavic origin etc. of the modern Greeks, were shot down by modern research through DNA, without of course this being of fundamental importance since a nation is not based on racial affinity.

stated in his works that his political goal was to prevent Slavic expansionism. However, the ideas of the German historiographer did not find any resonance with the rest of Europe, mainly because of his ulterior political motives.

The Enlightenment had led to the strengthening of the liberal current, which from the start was sympathetic to the Greek cause. The liberals through the Greek Revolution found a way to express their opposition to the backward-thinking Sacred Alliance, under the guise of Christian solidarity and charity, since they could not freely express their opposition to their own autocratic governments for fear of persecution.

At the time, the romanticism dominating in letters and arts, along with the always present classicism, made philhellenism a general tendency in European societies. The pious sought the prevalence of Christianity; the intellectuals expected the reemergence of classical Greece, while others considered it their obligation to assist contemporary Greeks as a gratitude to the endowments of ancient Greeks. Poets and painters discovered new themes for their works in the dreamy Elysian Fields or Ancient Athens. Even in the woeful Anatolia, archaeologists believed that they could proceed to excavations that would punctuate ancient Greece (and their work). The military saw new fields of glory. The traders expected new markets and trade routes in the eastern Mediterranean with their prevalence. The idealistic philhellenes, on the other hand, without expecting any benefit, came and fought sometimes to the bitter end, inspired by the ideal of freedom for which the Greeks fought and died for. They were mainly British, Italians, Germans, French, Swiss, Belgians, Dutch,

Danes, Americans, Swedes, and Poles, creating battalions of philhellenes who fought heroically.[216]

Poets of the romanticism movement glorified Greece: "To Greece! To Greece! Come on now, it's time..." urges Victor Marie Vicomte Hugo, "Greece, taken to be dead, here she is standing up, here she is marching on..." called Percy Bysshe Shelley. "Forwards, stand up, Greece, you rebel, hold on to your arms in your hand! Olympus, Pindos, Thermopylae did not rise in vain for your glory", cries out Aleksandr Sergejevic Pushkin, "Without freedom, what would you be, Hellas? Without thee, Hellas, what would the world be?" wonders Johann Ludwig Wilhelm Müller, the Greek Miller. François-Auguste-René, Vicomte de Chateaubriand, and Johann Wolfgang Goethe both write in favor of Greece, adding their prestige to the cause, while British poet Lord Byron, George Gordon Byron, "dreams that Greece might still be free" and dies from illness in Messolonghi, alongside the fighting Greeks.

Ludovico Lipparini, Ary Scheffer, Eugene Delacroix, Ambrose Louis Garneray, Karl Krazeisen, Peter von Hess, Auguste Vinchon, Adam Friedel, François-Émile de Lansac, Louis Dupré, philhellene painters and not only -famous or less famous- take their themes from the revolution, the heroic fighters and Greece.

Even from the beginning of the revolution, philhellenic societies were established in Switzerland, Britain, and Germany. With the money they collected from donations and events, they recruited volunteers and bought weapons and ammunition that they sent to Greece through the ports of Marseille and Livorno. In November 1823, the philhellenic committee of London was founded and dispatched its representatives to Greece to encourage the rebels.

---

[216] S. Th. Laskaris: Ibid., p. 18.

Later, the movement extended to France, where philhellenic associations run by known personalities were also established. Especially in France, artists and intellectuals expressed vigorously in their creations their philhellenic tendencies.[217]

The news of the Greek Revolution was positively received by the public opinion in the United States, where philhellenic committees were also founded. Among those who advocated US assistance to Greeks were Edward Everett and Daniel Webster. Despite initial enthusiastic sentiments, however, the response of the US administration and Congress was limited only to expressions of support for the Greeks' conflict and a message of encouragement, with a resolution in favor of Greece signed by President James Monroe in 1822, with no dynamic intervention in either military or diplomatic field. According to the neutrality or isolationist doctrine[218], US Secretary of State John Quincy Adams was more skeptical on the issue of Greeks at the diplomatic level than President Monroe. The State Department also argued that the US was not strong enough to assist the Greeks.

Ordinary citizens manifested philhellenism in the United States in many ways. Americans such as Samuel Howe, George Jarvis, and Jonathan Miller came and fought for Greece. Kolokotronis also acknowledged the American contribution to the struggle.[219] The American humanitarian mission (1827 -1828), which saved the lives of thousands of Greeks, came exclusively from the private charity, and Ioannis Kapodistrias publicly thanked the

---

[217] E. G Protopsaltis: Ibid., p. 38.

[218] Monroe doctrine was a principle of US policy, originated by President James Monroe, stating that any intervention by external powers in the politics of the Americas is a potentially hostile act against the US. In return US would not intervene in European affairs.

[219] Research of the Dept. of historical archives, MFA, Greece.

American Government. For several Greeks but mainly for two influential liberals, Adamantios Korais and jurist Anastasios Polyzoides, United States constituted a political and institutional model. Polyzoides translated all the founding texts of the United States (Declaration of Independence, Constitution & Amendments) and circulated them in Messolonghi in 1824.[220]

Among the protagonists of the American Revolution that were still alive, the father of the then Secretary of State, the second president of the US John Adams, was an enthusiastic philhellene. Meanwhile, Thomas Jefferson (who corresponded with Korais) was more cautious, and although he had prepared a detailed outline for the constitution of the new Greek state, he avoided criticizing the official neutrality of the US administration. The most important success of philhellenism was the clear pro-Greek stance of President Monroe in his State of the Union addresses from 1822 to 1824. The American recognition of the strive of the Greeks was considered as direct and unambiguous, and although it may not have been documented formally, it carried great diplomatic weight as the US was the first significant country to do so.

---

[220] Aristeidis Hatzis, 2019 (in Greek).

THE GREEKS IN DIRE SITUATION

The initial Greek successes were bound to cause great discomfort to the Ottoman authorities in Constantinople. In the face of the weakness of the Ottoman army and the problem with the Janissaries, the Sultan called as early as January 1823 the Pasha of Egypt Kavalalı Mehmed Ali to help with his tactical army the Ottomans that were being defeated in Peloponnese.

The military and naval forces of Egypt had a European organization with strategic make-up and many weapons. The organization of the army had been undertaken by officers of Napoleon that had fled to Egypt after the restoration of the dynasty in France, while France of Bourbon after 1824 had set up there a military mission. Therefore, the assignment of the case to Mehmed Ali had a significant guarantee of success for the Ottomans.[221]

Ibrahim Pasha, son of Mehmed Ali of Egypt, was appointed leader of the campaign in Peloponnese, in order to have a unified administration took charge of the entire Ottoman army there. Ottoman auxiliary ships sailed from Constantinople and gathered in Alexandria. After the embarkation of soldiers, the navy departed for the campaign in Greece. Mehmet Ali had acknowledged the difficulty of the operation in advance, and the army was properly readied.

Ibrahim's fleet, after Crete and Rhodes, arrived in Marmaris, Anatolia, where it picked up several thousand soldiers. It sailed in January 1825 for Crete to recruit Turkish mercenaries and from there sailed for Peloponnese. The Egyptian-Ottoman army landed in Methoni in February, defeating the

---

[221]A.G. Protopsaltis: Ibid., p. 40.

weak Greek vanguard. The Greek government, engulfed in internal discords coupled with a lack of organizational structure, was neither committed nor strong enough to mount an adequate stand. Thus, it failed to foresee the danger and demonstrated catastrophic indolence.

Ibrahim's army was by far more powerful than the Greek military, as French and Italian officers commanded many of its units. Austrian merchant ships provided supplies to the Turkish guards in Methoni and other forts and ports. It was clear that the support of foreigners was not confined to the philhellenes who fought alongside the rebels but extended to the Egyptian invaders with whom they were fighting along. Greeks underestimating the power of the Turkish-Egyptians failed to take necessary measures in time.

While the Egyptian bridgehead was expanding, the Greek government had just come out of the civil war and was forced to take action that proved to be somewhat feeble finally. The first real battles took place in Neokastro. Greeks were defeated in Kremmydi in April 1825 and again in May in the area of Pylos, losing among others the islet of Sfaktiria at the entrance of the Gulf of Navarino.

The situation in Greece

The period after the invasion of the Ottoman-Egyptian army in Peloponnese (Morea) in February 1825 marked the end of the first period of military victories and brought the Greeks in an extremely difficult position due to the military superiority of their adversaries. The weaknesses of the military organization brought about by political extremes, arrogance and thoughtlessness of chieftains, and the lack of discipline of the irregular army, led the devastated by the civil war Greeks close to

232

devastation. All hopes were entrusted to Kolokotronis, who was released from imprisonment in Hydra and undertook the general command of the army in May of the same year. However, the state of the military and Government was described as woeful.[222]

The Greek fleet struck back with some successes in Methoni and Kafirea, but they were followed by the defeat in Maniaki on May 20 and the death of the heroic Papaflessas. The Egyptians sallied out to the interior of Peloponnese while Kolokotronis attempted to confront them at the borders of Messenia – Arcadia without any success. Ibrahim invaded Argolis and, having taken Tripolitza, advanced towards Nafplio. Meanwhile, many refugees had amassed in Nafplio, causing life in the city to become intolerable, while many more refugees were scattered outside the walls attempting to enter the city. Nafplio was not seized eventually, likely due to the lack of cooperation of the local Ottoman army with the Egyptians. Dimitrios Ypsilantis, with Makrigiannis, faced the army of Ibrahim at Myloi (June 13, 1825), and with their victory, the Greeks were able to briefly feel at ease. However, this victory was followed by the defeat of Kolokotronis in Trikorfo on June 23-24, 1825. The Greeks were also defeated at sea by the superior enemy fleet.

In the summer of 1825, in response to information received by Lazaros Koundouriotis, a squadron of the Greek Navy was sent to Alexandria with E. Tombazis and A. Kriezis at the helm along with a few other ships. Among those was that of K. Kanaris, who attempted to torch the Turkish-Egyptian fleet docked at the port.[223] Despite the

---

[222] Apostolos E. Vakalopoulos: Ibid., Volume VII, p. 118.
[223] John C. Loukas: E-Historically "the Greek Fireboats in Alexandria" p.p. 83-86 (in Greek).

bravery shown by Kanaris who approached his ship - on which he had hoisted a Russian flag- to the enemy fleet to set it afire, he was eventually prevented by a sudden dead calm and the French ship "L 'Abeille" being nearby. The Greek fleet was forced to withdraw from Alexandria without any success.[224]

If the situation in Peloponnese was dire, in the Mainland (Sterea), it was much worse with Greeks confronting the Sultan's army without any substantial assistance from the troops in Peloponnese. Androutsos, disappointed by the Government, took a suspicious stance and consequently was arrested by the Greeks and put to death in June 1825. The Turks seized Salona (Amfissa) in May, plundering and enslaving the inhabitants. They were confronted sporadically by Greeks with G. Karaiskakis at the helm, but the situation remained stagnant for about five months, after which the Turks departed voluntarily. After the withdrawal of the Turks from Lamia, the residents felt somewhat relieved.

The Ottomans had begun the siege of Messolonghi in April 1825, with continuous attacks successfully repelled by far fewer Greek defenders of the city. In October, the blockade continued, but the Sultan with his ferman of October 28, 1825, indicated that he was pleased with the prefect of Rumeli and his army "who purged the mainland so as not even an inch of land was left in the hands of giaours (infidels)". He also expressed his certainty for the takeover of Messolonghi "that was somewhat delayed".[225]

In Peloponnese, Ibrahim carried out "purging operations" against the Greeks. He continued advancing by taking villages and arresting and

---

[224] A. Vakalopoulos: Ibid., p. 173.
[225] A. Vakalopoulos: Ibid., p. 205 refers to Vasdravelli, Archive of Thessaloniki.

imprisoning inhabitants. The Greek front had almost collapsed. In September 1825, there was an attempt to recapture Tripolitza by the Greeks without any success.

In the meantime, the despondent Greeks sought the aid of the Great Powers. Political factions based on hopes entrusted to one of the three Powers for national rehabilitation started to emerge in the Greek political scene. These trends later coalesced in forging the three parties, the English, the Russian, and the French. The three Powers were trying to expand their influence through various means, including rather unfounded promises by their representatives. At the same time, the leaders of the three parties ironically went claiming that they disdained the involvement of any foreigners in the country's internal affairs.[226]

Nevertheless, the situation on the battlefield seemed hardly correctable, and the Sublime Porte felt quite confident for its victory. Facing this dire situation and after their defeat in Trikorfo, the Greeks realized that the conflict among the three Powers was weighing against them and decided to seek the guardianship of a single country. Leaving aside their intense disagreements, and with the urging mainly of Alexandros Mavrokordatos and Spyridon Trikoupis sought the protection of Britain requesting from the latter to undertake the mediation with the Ottoman Empire.

The Anglophile committee of Zakynthos also promoted this idea. Alexandros Mavrokordatos, while in the service by his uncle Karatzas, ruler of Wallachia, was frustrated with the persistent Russian interventions; consequently, he was not fond of Russia. Even though the Greeks did not believe that they would receive any favorable response from

---

[226] A.G. Protopsaltis: Ibid., Issue B, p. 33.

Britain, with this action, they tried to encourage their striving soldiers. Greek envoy Dimitris Miaoulis, son of the glorious admiral who was dispatched to London to inquire for a loan, received the order to raise the issue with the British Government and, at the same time to investigate the possible assignment of Prince Leopold as head of independent Greece. The reason probably was to attract the interest of Europe's royal Courts, as the monarchy was the norm at the time.[227]

The Porte and Austria were concerned about this development, and Austria contacted London seeking to learn about the objectives of the British Government regarding the Greek request. Secretary of State for Foreign Affairs Canning assured Austria that he did not intend to do anything, while Miaoulis was not even officially accepted to present the Greek petition. Britain also published a decree prohibiting the conscription of British nationals by the Greek Government and the equipping of warships intended for Greeks in ports of the country. Simultaneously, however, two Greek frigates were built in the Thames, and the contracted loan money was sent to Greece. No definitive answer was given to Miaoulis at the time. Still, in the European courts, the idea of rendering some form of independence to the struggling Greeks had begun to ripen. The solicitation of British protection was rejected by French philhellenes, while the pro-France circles in Greece started discussing the candidacy of Duke of Nemours for the throne of Greece.[228]

In the military sector, Kolokotronis once again resorted to guerilla war, as he did not see any other way to combat the regular army of Ibrahim lacking adequacy in arms and the sheer number of fighters. The Greeks scored victories in Piana and Davia on

---

[227] S. I. Laskaris: Ibid., p. 23.
[228] Apostolos E. Vakalopoulos, Ibid., vol. C, p.p. 255-256.

August 12-14, 1825, but the Egyptian army invaded Laconia and clashed with the Greeks in Trinisa.[229]

In the camp of the Greeks, debates and consultations were held, and actions were initiated for amending the army organization. The need for the realignment of the fighters was acknowledged, and it was decided to reinforce the regular army (which was downgraded after the defeat in Peta in 1822) with the assignment of the French Colonel Favier to his leadership. But the defeats persisted. In February 1826, a campaign of the regular army in Evvoia was launched with no success. The headquarters of the regular army was transferred to Athens. At the same time, efforts were undertaken to modernize the navy by securing a loan and placing an order for steam-powered warships. Nonetheless, the situation in the sea remained ambiguous with combats and victories for both sides.

After 1824, incidents of piracy intensified in the Aegean by the islanders who had suffered devastations from the Ottoman raids and were obliged to seek supplies. Although acts against enemy vessels would be justified in a general war, the piratic acts of the islanders spread out even to neutral ships. Piracy resulted in the weakening of the diplomatic clout of Greece. In any case, the proliferation of piracy in 1826 and especially in 1827 created severe problems in the relations of Greece with various European countries, forcing the Greek Government to invoke some strict yet difficult to enforce measures against these acts.[230]

---

[229] A. Vakalopoulos: Ibid., p. 263.
[230] A. Vakalopoulos: Ibid., p.376.

Crete

Cretan patriots who had fled to Peloponnese asked the government for assistance in seizing the fortress of Imeri Gramvousa, a small rocky island at the western end of Crete, which was protected only by a few guards. In August 1825, three ships were dispatched, and a few hundred men disembarked in Castelli (Kissamos), capturing the area. The few Turkish guards of Gramvousa handed over the fortress without a fight via a deceptive ploy. The absence of Egyptian troops and this success encouraged the Cretans to rise again. However, the lack of organization and concord among the rebels prevented them from achieving real progress. The government could only provide limited reinforcements while the governor of Crete Mustafa was a persistent adversary. Defeats and disappointment followed after the fall of Messolonghi. Despite the efforts of both Cretans themselves and the Greek government, it was not possible to secure a decisive victory in Crete.[231]

The campaign to Lebanon

The matter of mounting a campaign to Lebanon had been on the table from October 1824, when a proposal by the Emir of Lebanon Bashir was conveyed to the Greek Parliament for establishing an alliance with the Greeks against the Turks. Bashir, offering fighters and horses, requested, in return, naval help to succeed in his cause to acquire autonomy from the Sultan. For their part, Cypriot refugees in Greece were pushing for a campaign to liberate their island. With that in mind, they were in secret contacts with chieftains and captains to divert

---

[231] A. Vakalopoulos: Ibid., p. 169.

238

the campaign to Lebanon to a commando operation in Cyprus.

The Parliament accepted the Emir's proposal to create a distraction to the forces of the Sultan and Mehmet Ali. A three-member group of appointees was dispatched to Lebanon in 1825 and held lengthy negotiations with the Emir. Nevertheless, the liberation of Cyprus had always been part of the discussions for the campaign to Lebanon. Eventually, however, the whole project was considered too risky and was abandoned by the Greek government. The thinking was that it would have extended the battlefront too far along with the prospect of having to face great difficulties and possible defeats. Once again, another attempt to help the liberation of Cyprus fell by the wayside.

Nevertheless, few chieftains who became aware of the plan for Lebanon and Cyprus took it upon themselves to organize and carry out the campaign. Their initiative, however, came to the attention of Cypriot Charalambos Malis, who had in mind only the strive of Cyprus. Malis disagreed with the unilateral initiative by a few chieftains and denounced the planned operation to the Parliament on January 29, 1826, insisting that the Greek government should formally take over any campaign in Lebanon and Cyprus.[232]

Despite Malis' notification and without the approval of the executive, the three chieftains who had the initiative, bolstered by the support of others, gathered in Kea and sailed in late February 1826 with several men and ships. A few days later, in early March, the fleet arrived in Lebanon, where it landed near Beirut, seized a coastal stronghold, and right away indulged in looting. The Emir of Lebanon Bashir

---

[232] George H. Orfanos: Article in Rethymno News, 2016 (in Greek).

soon found out that the leaders of the rebel force lacked any official letters of credence and ordered them to immediately depart with the threat of attacking them if they disobeyed. They left Lebanon on March 25, 1826, and set sail to Cyprus, where once again, they engaged in rapacious acts. Eventually, they were ousted, and that is how this scheming operation ended.[233]

Messolonghi and the provisional defeat

In October 1825, the second phase of the siege of Messolonghi commenced. The city's heroic resistance spanning several months had become a symbol of the campaign for freedom. The Greek government, for its part, could not be of any adequate help. In Messolonghi, pages of glory and heroism were written. Small forces arrived from other places[234] - "...but Turkish force and Latin fraud/would break your shield/however broad..."[235]. Ibrahim carried out a fierce bombardment of the city while hand-to-hand combat in the bastions abounded. But "...the rifle is heavy, and Agarinos knows it".[236] Solomos, while in Zakynthos, heard the sounds of the bombings and felt that "my eyes have not seen a more glorious place than this patch of land". Eventually, hunger and exhaustion led the "Free Besieged" to a dramatic exit. Only a few survived. Ibrahim seized the perished Messolonghi on April 10, 1826 - "...deafening silence of tombs, in the plains reigns". Greeks had been

---

[233] A. Vakalopoulos: History of the New Hellenism, 1980, p. 537-540, D. Dionysios E-Historically "Kanaris in Cyprus", p. 110 (in Greek).

[234] The fighters that came from Samarina became a legend echoed in the popular folklore song with the title "Children of Samarina".

[235] Lord Byron: The isles of Greece.

[236] From the poem of Solomos "Free Besieged". Agarinos means Arab.

240

forsaken; it seemed that they had been defeated, with everything and all had conspired against them- "Arabian horse, French mind, Turkish bullet, English gun". Despair.[237]

But the tragic exodus of Messolonghi stirred emotions of valor in the circles of Philhellenes in Europe and sent the message that indeed this heroic people deserved freedom.[238] Kapodistrias, who had not yet assumed the leadership of the government, tried to encourage and inspire the nation. He wrote that he was "far from being scared"; "Initially rumors were spread that the entire garrison of Messolonghi had succumbed. Today, recent news gave us the certainty that the most formidable group of these heroes have survived. Whereas all European governments, with no exceptions, seem to have abandoned Greece to its demise, the humanity and piety of the people of all nations are giving us a helping hand." The Greeks were determined to fight to the death.[239]

The third National Assembly met in Piada (new Epidavros) on April 6, 1826. The situation in Nafplio was chaotic due to the conflicts of the Mainland chieftains. The administration suffered from the strife of the prevalence of the three Powers via the Greek politicians who were partial to them. The main issues of the National Assembly under the chairmanship of P. Notaras were the revision of the Constitution of Epidaurus and the ways to stop the offensive of the joint Ottoman-Egyptian force. The news of the fall of Messolonghi arrived during this first period of the Assembly. The Assembly, in a declaration sent to the European Powers, declared the nation's united resolve to fight to the bitter end and

---

[237] A. Vakalopoulos: Ibid., p. 419.
[238] A. Vakalopoulos: Ibid., p. 481.
[239] I Kapodistrias Ibid., p. 32, Letter to his brother Viaro.

241

rejected any idea of subjugation to Turks. It elected a three-member Administrative Committee chaired by Andreas Zaimis and the committee of the National Assembly constituted by 13 members under Archbishop Germanos. Kolokotronis was appointed General of the Army for Peloponnese, whereas the western Mainland was entrusted to Gouras and the eastern to Karaiskakis. The committee of the National Assembly would undertake the negotiations pursuing an immediate armistice under the guarantee of Britain and acceding to a solution that would secure for a state, tax- vassal to the Sultan.[240]

After the fall of Messolonghi, the garrison of the city withdrew to Nafplio, and the western Mainland surrendered. The prefect of Rumeli, Kutachi, marched to Attica and captured Athens (August 3, 1826) apart for the fortress of Acropolis that resisted.

In the meantime, Sultan ordered Kutachi to co-ordinate the Turkish forces with Ibrahim, but he procrastinated. Eventually, the Turks attacked Ilia and Achaia (western Peloponnese) and headed towards the Messinian castles in the south. Greeks confronted the advance of Ibrahim towards Mani in the battle of Vergas. Ibrahim retaliated by marching to the center of Peloponnese and engaging in the battle of the Caves, while in July 1826, he raided Corinth. The Greeks resisted with guerilla warfare, but the sole beneficial effect was the moderate depletion of the Egyptian invaders.[241]

Greeks were able to hold on to only Nafplio, Mani, part of Achaia and Corinth, and the islands of Spetses and Hydra, as well as the Acropolis of Athens that was besieged by the Turkish troops. The Greeks were able to create a small bridgehead in Eleusis,

---

[240] Apostolos E. Vakalopoulos, Ibid., p. 613.
[241] Ali Fuat Orenc History Magazine Number 46, 2007 (in Turkish).

242

Attica. The administrative committee, under the leadership of Karaiskakis organized the army of Attica to confront the Turks.

The first battles of the Greeks in Attica took place in Haidari while fighting continued outside the Acropolis of Athens. Battles raged throughout Boeotia as well as in Attica until February 1827. While the position of the besieged in the Acropolis worsened, Karaiskakis arrived in Keratsini in March 1827. In the ensuing decisive battle of Analatos, however, Greeks were defeated on April 24, 1827, a day after the hero George Karaiskakis was killed. Following that, Acropolis was handed over to the Turks on May 24.[242]

Ibrahim continued his operations in Ilia and Achaia, but the Greeks did not put their weapons down and continued the fighting wherever and in any way they could.

The European Repositioning

With terms adverse to Russia, Britain offered to mediate between the Sublime Porte and the rebels. Metternich, to give time to the Porte to suppress the Revolution, pushed for the assemblage of a conference in St. Petersburg in early 1824. There, once more, Russia found the opportunity to raise the issue of the liberation of Greece. Austria, on this occasion, failed to achieve its objective.

The unfavorable developments at the battlefronts had led the Greeks to request in the mid-1825 the complete protection of Britain. The Greek demarche, in which Greeks themselves had laid little hope, did not yield any direct results, but in September 1825, the British government issued a declaration of neutrality signaling the recognition of

---

[242] A. Vakalopoulos: Ibid., p. 640-663.

Greeks as an embattled party. After all, neither Britain nor Russia were pleased with the French influence on Mehmed Ali of Egypt and sought ways to respond.

On December 1, 1825, during a journey to southern Russia, Czar Alexander I died unexpectedly of natural causes. He was succeeded by Czar Nicholas I, who was more proactive and advocated more fervently in favor of the Greeks' strive for freedom. Nicholas initially held out accepting the throne and only agreed to it after his elder brother Constantine had removed himself from the line of succession definitively. The day after his inauguration, he faced the Decembrist domestic uprising that, with the pretext of protesting his enthronement, sought socioeconomic reforms.

The rise of Nicholas I to the throne led to the hardening of the Russian position regarding the unresolved business with the Ottoman Empire in the context of the Eastern Issue. With a new ultimatum, Russia requested the reinstatement of the previous regime in the Danube principalities and the full implementation of the measures agreed in 1812 in favor of Serbs. At the same time, it called for the delegates from the two parties to meet at a border town for the discussion and resolution of its concerns without making any reference to the Greek issue. The other European Powers recognizing the renewed danger of a Russian-Turkish clash rushed to advise the Sultan to consent, with which he complied.[243]

The meeting of the two parties, Russians and Ottomans, was held in Ackerman, where the Russian side found an opportunity to raise the Greek issue once more. However, the Ottoman government remained intransigent on the Greek matter and, with the confidence of the military victories achieved by

---

[243] S. Th Laskari: Ibid., p.25

244

Mehmed Ali, sought a diplomatic resolution on the Russian concerns to relieve the pressures of the Great Powers. To this end, it concluded an agreement with Russia (October 7, 1826) that was devoid of any reference to the Greek matter. With the agreement of Ackerman, the hospodars of Moldova and Wallachia would be elected by their respective Divans (Boards) for seven-year terms with the approval of both Russia and the Ottoman state. The Ottoman forces that had entered the Danube principalities in 1821 to confront Ypsilantis would retreat. The Ottomans agreed to grant Wallachia several ports on the Danube. The Serbian issue was also somewhat regulated by granting Serbia autonomy and ceding back certain territories, while the Serbs would have the right to move freely in the Ottoman Empire.

The British, however, felt that they were left out of the developments, and noting that an association of Russia with the Ottomans was not in their interest, they sent the Duke of Wellington to Russia supposedly to congratulate the new Czar. There, the Duke secured the accord of the "Saint Petersburg Protocol" on April 4, 1826. Based on this agreement, Russia and Britain would act in the name of religion, justice, and humanism to halt the conflict in Peloponnese by creating a tax-vassal Greek principality. If the Sublime Porte did not accept the mediation of Britain and Russia, the two parties would consider the terms of the Protocol as the only basis according to which the pacification of the near east could be achieved with the intervention of both Powers or one of them.[244]

With this, Britain theorized that it had undermined the further rapprochement of the Ottomans with the Russians since, for Britain, the foremost purpose of the Ottoman Empire was to

---

[244] S. Th Laskaris: Ibid., p. 26.

prevent Russia's descent to the warm seas. There, "Britain should dominate". Britain had no aspirations for peace between the two neighboring states, which it considered foes. Further, such a peace would pose risks to Britain. It is noted that no official action by the Great Powers, including Navarino, was inspired by sheer "philhellenism". The Great Powers are obliged to act for their interests, but sometimes they did "succumb" to public sentiment, always in the framework of the interests of their rulers.

The Saint Petersburg Protocol was communicated confidentially to Austria, Prussia, and France. Austria and Prussia did not take in favorably the content of this Protocol, as they did not wish in any way for the territorial integrity of the Ottoman Empire to be affected. On the contrary, France, both, because it did not desire to be left outside of European developments as a somewhat sidelined Great Power and due to the widespread philhellenism that prevailed there, expressed its willingness (but rather half-heartedly) to cooperate with the other two Powers.[245] At the time, France was in the Second Restoration period with Prime Minister Villèle and Foreign Minister Ange Hyacinthe Maxence de Damas under the Reign of Charles X, Comte d'Artois.

The two warring parties were initially not notified of this Protocol. For the Greeks, 1826 was a tragic year on battlegrounds, and they could no longer object to the servitude term. The Ottomans, on the other hand, should have certainly been informed by the Austrians. The Protocol was communicated officially to the Sublime Porte only in January 1827. The embassies of Russia and Britain in Constantinople issued harsh notifications where it could be inferred that they viewed the conflict as a controversy of Christianity versus Islam. Britain's

---

[245] S. Th Laskaris: Ibid., p. 28.

Ambassador Stratford Canning (Stratford de Redcliff) probably overstated the mandate he had, while the Russian envoy even more bluntly threatened that if the Protocol were not accepted, his country would regard Greece as an independent state. Russia, after receiving what it bargained for with the Ackerman agreement, had reverted to its old self: The rival of the Ottoman Empire, which stood as an obstacle to its descent to the south. Although the Porte said it considered the Protocol to be a "blank paper" without any authority, it did not terminate the debates and pointed out to the Powers that their moral support to the rebels impeded the resolution of the issue.[246]

France, for its part, demonstrated a lukewarm attitude since it had economic benefits from its cooperation with the Ottoman Empire and because of its association with Egypt and Mehmet Ali. Its Ambassador to Constantinople, Earl Guilleminot (Armand Charles), however, tried to persuade the Sublime Porte to accept the Protocol. The Ottoman Foreign Minister replied that what had already been agreed on in Ackerman constituted "a sword on the neck of the Ottomans", and that they would settle "easily" the issue with the Rums when (and not if) the Europeans departed.

Political Developments in Greece

Both the defeats and the historical necessity of the time led the Greeks to political deliberations on establishing some form of monarchy. Kolokotronis seemed to embrace the idea. But the choice of the proper person for the position did not turn out to be an easy task. The meaningless and without real purpose political contentions that resulted mainly from personal rivalries, along with the involvement of

---

[246] Ali Fuat Örenç: History Magazine No. 46, 2007 (in Turkish).

European Powers seeking to enforce their influence, prolonged the debates, and relayed adverse signals to all directions. French propaganda for the nomination of the Duke of Nemours as ruler of Greece intensified. At the same time, it appeared that the arrival in Greece of Bavarian Colonel Karl Heideck with a group of officers, an expression of the true philhellenism of Louis I, Otto's father, may not have been without political motives judging by the eventual outcome. Other philhellenes in Greece focused their attention on either Britain or Russian courts.[247]

The internal political disputes in January 1827 focused on the venue of holding the continuation of the 3rd National Assembly of Epidaurus, which was interrupted after the Fall of Messolonghi. Two "opposing camps" were formed; those who opted for Aegina and others who chose Hermione. The involvement of foreigners and the continuing realignment of members of the Friendly Society and other influential politicians with each of the three Powers provoked additional disagreements among the Greeks. In addition to the multitude of externally derived problems, there emerged endogenous political afflictions and blatant distortions with socio-economic underpinnings. New elections held to complement the vacancies of each side worsened the situation, with the risk of formation once again, two governments. There was no time to promote the necessary resolutions that could have reversed the existing divisive mentality. Arguments brought up by conflicts of personal interest, selfishness or rivalry, led to miscommunication and inability to elect a unified government and any consequences that it entailed. Any potential and prospect for a strong defense against the common enemy eroded. However, in Hermione, it was decided on March 2, 1827, that the polity will be

---

[247] Apostolos E. Vakalopoulos: Ibid., 7th vol., p. 691.

parliamentary with separation of the three governing branches, legislative, executive, and judiciary, which constitute the foundation of a democratic regime in the modern sense. In the meantime, the situation on the battleground was dreadful because of the continuing defeats and ammunition shortages.

With the help of British military personalities and given the grave situation, it was decided to compromise and transfer the venue of the Assembly in Troezen, half away from the Aegina-Hermione route. The proceedings commenced on March 19, 1827. The 3rd Assembly of Troezen recognized the decisions of Hermione and, among recriminations, appointed as commanders in chief the British general Church for the army and the French admiral Cochrane for the navy. As for the governance, with the military defeats ascribed to the multiheaded executive branch, it was agreed that the consolidation of power on one individual for an extended period was the best alternative in tackling the dire circumstances.

Of course, no governor could be found from a European sovereign parliament for a collapsed country that was not yet recognized by any Great Power. At the time, among the Greeks, there was no personality revered more than Kapodistrias commanding global prestige and moral glamour. The initiative in the election of Kapodistrias was taken by the heroes and marshals of mainland Greece and Peloponnese, G. Karaiskakis, and Th. Kolokotronis, respectively.[248] In this context, Ioannis Kapodistrias was elected governor of Greece for seven years, not without discontent since he was considered a friend of Russia. Until his advent, a three-member provisional commission took over the governance.

---

[248] E.G. Protopsaltis Ibid., p. 63.

249

The Constitution of Troezen was drafted, having as a model that of Epidaurus, the third during the Revolution, and although criticized as haphazard by politician M. Dragoumis, it was the most democratic. The "Political Constitution of Greece" passed in Troezen in May 1827 remained in history as one of the most liberal and democratic constitutions of its time. The Assembly wanted to give the country an absolute democracy inspired by democratic and liberal ideas and the "Polity of the Hellenic Republic" of Riga. Thus it proclaimed in the new Constitution for the first time the principle of popular sovereignty: "Sovereignty exists in the nation, all governance derives from it, and endures to protect it". Moreover, it explicitly established the separation of powers; it assigned the executive power to the governor and the legislative power to the House of the representatives of the people, the Parliament.[249]

It recognized the Greek territory as single and indivisible, including all the areas of Greece that had risen. The governor was inviolable, while accountable were his ministers.[250] The Constitution stipulated the equality of all citizens and the protection of their life, honor, and property. In particular, in accordance with the provisions of the Constitution of Troezen, detention without an arrest warrant was prohibited, no one could remain in prison beyond 24 hours without a charge or three days without commencing of an interrogation, congress members could not be imprisoned during parliamentary sessions, accused ministers would be referred to a special court, no one would be considered guilty before conviction, no one could be tried twice for the same offense, torture and confiscations were prohibited, and the law did not apply retroactively.

---

[249] Greek Parliament: Constitutional history (in Greek).
[250] E.G. Protopsaltis Ibid., p. 56.

A Supreme Court was appointed at the headquarters of the Government, and no extraordinary courts were allowed. Expropriation of estates with compensation for public use was allowed. Slavery was forbidden, and any slave upon entering Greek territory would be regarded free from that moment. Titles as his Brilliancy, his Excellency, etc. were banned.[251] The clergy were excluded from political positions, and the legislature was renamed Vouli, the name of Parliament in ancient Greece.[252] With a special decree, a naval court was also formed to combat piracy. Even though the polity of Troezen was liberal, it was received rather with indifference by the people who at the time were facing major challenges. After all, the implementation of most of the provisions was unattainable, and there existed no strong state force to enforce them.

After the dramatic fall of Messolonghi and the defeat of the battle of Analatos in Attica with the death of Karaiskakis and the loss of Acropolis in Athens one month later, the military position of the Greeks had deteriorated considerably, having lost their two bastions in the mainland. Ibrahim's troops continued to devastate Peloponnese. But Greeks did not give up; they persisted and continued to fight since they were convinced that the conditions before the Revolution, the status quo ante, was no longer tolerable, and to die while fighting for freedom, was preferable.

---

[251] Makrigiannis, in his memoirs, uses the title "Brilliant" for Kolettis.
[252] Apostolos Vakalopoulos: Ibid., 7th vol., p. 710.

THE NAVAL BATTLE OF NAVARINO

Mehmed Ali of Egypt accepted the invitation of the Sultan to assist the Ottoman army with his forces against the Greek rebellion not only for the promised incentives but also to reinforce his prestige. What he did not consider was that the Great Powers, mainly Great Britain, would not tolerate Egyptian domination under the sole influence of France in the eastern Mediterranean that would subvert the balance of power. Later on, this concern was destined to be decisive for the shaping of the stances of Britain and Russia in favor of the Greek cause, positions which would gradually coerce reluctant France under the pressures of its public opinion and its Parliament to change its views. At first, however, the European states' responses remained at a rhetorical level.

After the victories of Mehmed Ali's army in Peloponnese, Sultan Mahmud of the Ottoman Empire broke the silence he had kept until then. In a statement issued, he declared that he was an independent sovereign, that the Greeks had rebelled against the legal authority, and that an emperor Sultan could not negotiate an agreement with "a bunch of bandits". He challenged the principles of neutrality and freedom set forth by the European states and rejected any external interference on the issue of the Greeks.

After the categorical rejection of the protocol of St. Petersburg (April 4, 1826) by the Ottomans, new discussions among the Powers regarding the freedom of Greeks began in London in March 1827, for preparing a new protocol that would validate the content of the prior one. Prussia and Austria once

253

again did not consent. The new protocol, recorded as the Treaty of London, was signed by Britain, France, and Russia on July 6, 1827, and foresaw establishing an independent Greek Principality. The Greeks would recognize the Sultan's superiority and pay an annual tax. They would elect their authorities. The Greeks would also become masters of Turkish estates in the areas of the Principality, paying compensation to the legal owners.

In secret articles of the Treaty, it was stated that in the event the Ottomans did not accept the terms of the Treaty, the fleets of the three Powers would cut off the naval transport between Egypt and Peloponnese. Moreover, the Powers would prevent any hostilities of the Ottomans against the Greeks and would even recognize their independence. The Treaty of London appeared to be indicative of the intentions of the European Powers to resort even to violence to achieve their objectives. However, it could be argued that it was characterized by ambivalence, "a creative ambiguity", regarding the means to attain that. Britain, in addition to international policy issues, had already been exposed, having recognized Greece as an embattled party through the 1825 neutrality declaration. Britain was also aware that for Greece to repay its loan, it needed to attain some form of a legal entity.

With the London Treaty, the three Powers transformed the case of Greek independence into a European "internal" matter within the framework of the continent's order. Without waiting for the Ottoman government's response, on July 12, 1827, a joint order was sent to the Admirals of the fleets in the Mediterranean regarding the content of the Treaty. The three fleets would be considered equal from an administrative point of view (although the British Admiral Codrington believed that he had the primacy), they would be in contact with the

254

transitional Greek government, and if the latter agreed to negotiations, they would seek a way to cease hostilities as soon as possible.

For its part, the Ottoman state, as per Turkish historians, despite the strategic errors it had committed from the start of the conflict, made every effort to suppress the Greek movement. The first objective considered was the destruction of the Greek naval "pirate" forces in order to facilitate the dispatch of munitions. The maritime administration was entrusted to the son of Mehmed Ali, Ibrahim so that the entire Ottoman forces would be managed under a unified command. A small Ottoman fleet of 24 ships passed from the Straits on May 6, 1827, and sailed to Navarino at the end of the month. Later, it became known that the Egyptian fleet had also arrived in the bay of Navarino on September 9. An indication of the way that the Ottoman Empire handled its relations with Europeans and especially France was its attempt through Mehmed Ali, who maintained ties with France, to establish a loan from Europe, its adversary, given its increased needs due to war. Its effort was not successful.

In August 1827, the fleets of Britain under Admiral Sir Edward Codrington and France under Admiral de Rigny (Marie Henri Daniel Gauthier) were anchored in the Gulf of Smyrna (Izmir) when they became aware of the movements of the Turkish-Egyptian fleet. Even if the intention were there, they would not have had the time to halt the course of the Ottoman fleet to Pylos. Instead, they headed towards Zakynthos, where they waited for the arrival of the Russian squadron under Admiral Hayden,[253] which navigating through the English Channel, arrived at Navarino on September 13, 1827.

---

[253] S.Th. Laskaris: Ibid., p. 31.

Meanwhile, the Austrian Embassy in Constantinople had leaked the contents of the Treaty of London to the Ottomans, although it is not known whether the Embassy informed them also of its secret articles. Subsequently, the Powers, after informing the Ottoman authorities of the Treaty on August 4, 1827, reduced the Ottoman authorities' response time to their declaration from one month to fifteen days, as a result of the Austrians' breach. The allies made it clear that in the event of a negative response, they would take every necessary action to force an agreement. The Ottoman administration held Russia responsible for the Treaty of London, especially since it considered that Russia, with the Treaty of Ackerman, had committed to remaining neutral on the Greek issue. The Ottoman Government, therefore, attempted to relay the message to Russia that with this new Treaty, Ackerman's undertakings would cease to exist.

At the same time, according to the Turkish sources, during the internal conferences at the Sublime Porte, the view to reject all demands of the European Powers prevailed, despite the voicing of moderate opinions suggesting partial acceptance of the terms of the Treaty. The moderates acknowledged that although accepting the terms of the Treaty would result in an odd situation of a government within the government, they projected that by relinquishing some limited form of independence to the Greeks, the Empire would rid itself from this carcinoma and annoyances the revolted Greeks were inflicting. In opposition to this, it was argued that Christian Russia would continue to incite the Greeks against them, and therefore the situation would not get any more tranquil.[254] The Ottoman side, unable to predict Russia's foreign strategic posture towards a quasi-independent Greece, found itself facing a form of the

---

[254] Lutfi: History (in Turkish), Istanbul, 1999.

256

"prisoner's dilemma".[255] In the end, the view of non-cooperation prevailed, and the proposal of the Allied Powers was rejected. The Ottoman government, according to Turkish sources, replied to the Embassies of France and Britain that the terms of the Treaty of London on the issue of Morea (Peloponnese) caused grief to the Ottomans, adding that the state would resolve the matter within the framework of its laws. However, no official response was dispatched promptly.

The Allies came back with a new Joint Communique on August 27, 1827, insisting on the acceptance of their proposals of August 4, in order to retain their friendly relations with the Sublime Porte. Sultan Mahmud, however, remained adamant. On August 31, Reis Efendi formally responded to the Embassies that the Sublime Porte "cannot and would never listen to anything sanctioning support to the Greeks and that this declaration is definitive, unequivocal, and irrefutable".[256] At the same time, Sultan Mahmud sent orders to Ibrahim to destroy Hydra and then Spetses that were still in the hands of the Greeks, to restrict the action of Greek ships in the Aegean that hindered the supply of Turkish military guards in various remote areas.

Meanwhile, the Ambassadors notified the Admirals of the expiration of the deadline and asked them not to allow neutral ships to carry supplies to the Turks on the battlefronts. They also asked them to restrict the Greek naval activities only in the area

---

[255] The prisoner's dilemma is a paradox in decision analysis that examines the strategic choices of reasonably thoughtful players involved in competitive situations in which both players could benefit from collaboration or suffer failure by acting, but find it impossible to coordinate their activities for the success of the problem they face.
[256] A. Vakalopoulos Ibid., p.830 cites Driault, Histoire, 1   p.375-377.

the Admirals had blocked, from the Gulf of Volos to Aspropotamos along with the Saronic Islands and the Cyclades. [257]

In the meantime, on September 2, 1827, the Admirals of the Allied fleet informed the Greek government of the terms of the Treaty, as per the instructions given. The terms were accepted by the Greek government on the next day, as at the time it was clear that there was no margin for negotiation. At the same time, the Admirals sent a delegation to Alexandria to inform Mehmed Ali of London's decisions and to persuade him to halt the hostilities but to no avail. By then, the British and French fleets had set Peloponnese under naval blockade, but without the Russian fleet, they refrained from taking any further action.

With the Allies failing to persuade Mehmed Ali, the Admirals visited Ibrahim in Navarino on September 25, 1927. They warned him that they had orders to block the operation he was preparing against Hydra and that they would destroy the Ottoman fleet if it did take place. Ibrahim replied that he had specific orders to continue the war in Morea and attack Hydra, but that he would inform Constantinople and Egypt of the developments. It also appears that he promised that he would not leave Navarino until he received a response from the Sublime Porte. Ibrahim then convened a council of all the commanders of warships, who concurred with Ibrahim's reply to the Admirals. In a joint report sent to the Sublime Porte, they noted that their fleet could not successfully confront the joint fleets of the three Powers along with the "pirate" Greek ships. They prophetically added that an untimely action could destroy the Turkish-Egyptian fleet.

---

[257] A. Vakalopoulos: Ibid., p. 830.

On September 29, Greek ships with the help of their allies engaged a section of the Turkish fleet in the Bay of Itea and sank it, enraging Ibrahim. In early October, Ibrahim attempted to send food supplies with 20 ships to Turks besieged in Patras while ordering 18 warships to leave Navarino to accompany them. It took only a few hours after their departure that British ships sailed to confront them, assuming a battle position.[258] The Turkish ships were forced to return to their base. In a new document sent by Ibrahim to Constantinople on October 7, 1827, he noted that under the existing conditions, the Ottoman fleet was unable to partake in any action against the Greeks.[259] Ibrahim, therefore, considered it appropriate to revert to land operations. After reinforcing the fortifications in Sfaktiria and other surrounding areas of Navarino Bay, he divided his army of 30 to 35 thousand into three branches and proceeded inland, causing significant casualties to Greeks. The Turk-Egyptians, enraged primarily by the debacle of their fleet in the Gulf of Itea, attacked whatever they encountered, uprooted trees, demolished houses, and slaughtered the weary and starving inhabitants.

These developments mobilized the three Powers that believed that Ibrahim had promised he would not take any military action on his own. By a common demarche, the interpreters of their Embassies in Constantinople asked about the orders that had been given to Ibrahim. The Sublime Porte's response was, in essence, "How dare you to ask such a question?". The Allies responded that they were just trying to confirm if Ibrahim, contrary to what he had promised, had left Navarino without a mandate from Constantinople. They inquired whether the Sublime

---

[258] S.T. Laskaris: Ibid., p. 31.
[259] Ali Fuat Orenc: History Magazine Issue No. 46, 2007 (in Turkish).

Porte would view an armed conflict that might result from this dispute with Ibrahim as a cause for war. The Porte answered that the order given to the Prefect of Morea was the suppression of the revolution of the Greeks. Further, that Ibrahim had no jurisdiction to negotiate and draw an agreement on anything with the Admirals of the fleet, and that even if such an agreement existed, it would be null and void for the Ottoman administration, and therefore there was no obligation for its implementation. Finally, in an unequivocal tone, the Porte concluded that the Ottomans would not entertain in perpetuity any offers or deals from the Allies with regards to the Greeks. With contemporary technical analysis, one could infer that the situation at hand had evolved into a predicament that in the theory of games could be characterized as the "Nash equilibrium".[260] The negotiations had hit a wall with no apparent steps for a resolution. Since there was no change on the part of the Ottomans, the Allies had to change their - passive up to then- stance.

In the aftermath of this unfriendly and uncompromising attitude of Ottomans, the Allies decided to get engaged in a chicken game.[261] They decided to enter the Bay of Navarino with the intent of pushing the Turkish – Egyptian fleet towards Constantinople and Egypt. Even though the Ottoman fleet outnumbered the allied fleets, it lagged in expertise and firepower. The Ottoman commanders of the fleet had already informed Constantinople that

---

[260] The Nash Equilibrium is a decision-making theorem within game theory that states a player can achieve the desired outcome by not deviating from their initial strategy.
[261] A chicken game is a game theory set up, that typically describes two players heading toward each other. If the players continue on the same path, they bump into each other; if one swerves out of the way and the other doesn't, the former "loses" and is labeled the chicken, while the second, implicitly braver player, wins.

they could not defeat the Allied fleet. The Allies' hopes that the Ottoman fleet would eventually retreat and not engage with a superior power were well-founded. The warfare, at least for the British and French, was undesirable. On the other hand, mainly Britain would not consent to a strong hostile fleet controlling the East Mediterranean Sea.

After all, the entry of the allied fleets to Navarino was necessary.[262] The British, French and Russian ships had anchored a few miles north, and because of the approaching winter, they could not remain there. On October 19, a French ship entered the Gulf of Pylos and delivered a letter addressed to the French Officers stationed in the Egyptian fleet, indicating the possibility of a conflict. It accentuated that they should not be fighting against the ships of their homeland and that they should abandon the Muslim ships. After delivering the letter, the French vessel withdrew undisturbed. Ten Frenchmen serving in the Egyptian fleet, who expressed the desire to leave, boarded an Austrian ship that was with the Ottoman fleet and departed, with only their captain remaining with the Ottoman fleet. It was a clear, explicit threat of the allies against the Ottomans, which the latter either did not comprehend or carelessly ignored it. This constituted the first move in the chicken game.

The Allied ships had devised a naval warfare plan before entering the Navarino Bay. On the morning of October 20, ships of the Allied fleet began to enter the Bay of Navarino with war readiness. The Ottoman fleet also assumed a battle position by aligning its vessels in a semicircle.[263] Nothing happened right away, but the chicken game had started.

---

[262] S.T. Laskaris: Ibid., p. 32.
[263] A. Vakalopoulos: Ibid., p. 841.

According to Turkish sources, on the afternoon of the same day, two boats of 40 men each descended from the frigate Dartmouth and headed towards the Ottoman ships. Their purpose was not evident. It could have been an act of provocation, or most likely, according to the same sources, the delivery of an ultimatum. However, the ambiance was tense. The ships were wooden, and the Turkish-Egyptians knew that Kanaris and Pipinos had set fire to the Turkish flagship in Chios in this way. The enemy boat approaching posed a mortal danger to their ship.

As the boats approached, the Ottomans, after giving them a warning, started shooting, wounding several British sailors.[264] Following that, Dartmouth fired its cannons. The Ottomans did not respond at once, but when a French ship (the Sirène) also opened fire, they answered back with their artillery. The naval battle of Navarino had commenced.

The British side claimed that it had sent a single boat with Lieutenant Fitzroy to request the repositioning of a Turkish fireship that was too close to the frigate and that the naval battle started when the lieutenant fell dead from gunshots. Allied ships fired back to protect the retreat of the boat, and the Turkish-Egyptian ships responded with their cannons.[265] The British demand, as articulated, constituted a provocation. There is a difference of opinion regarding Navarino between the Turkish and European historians, which draws from the different narratives of the two sides, each attempting to justify its own actions.

The battle lasted three and a half hours in the afternoon of October 20, 1827, and ended in the

---

[264] Ali Fuat Orenc: History Magazine Issue No. 46, 2007 (in Turkish).
[265] A. Vakalopoulos: Ibid., p. 842.

destruction of the Ottoman fleet that lost more than two-thirds of its ships. The naval Battle of Navarino shifted the balance in favor of the Greeks in their struggle for freedom. In addition to the loss of naval support for the Ottoman campaign, another significant consequence was the loss of supplies to feed the 40 thousand Muslims of Peloponnese, residents and soldiers alike, that had sunk along with the ships. Ibrahim, who was involved in military ground operations in Peloponnese, returned to Navarino at once. The commanders of the Ottoman ships alleged that the claims of the Allies that the Ottomans were the ones to fire first were false. They did admit that they initiated the shooting but considered the gunshots to be a military incident, whereas the cannonade launched would have constituted the start of a naval battle.

On the other hand, the Admirals of the allied fleet warned that the likelihood of an Ottoman retaliation would be considered casus belli (cause for war). In a conference on an allied ship with the Ottoman head of the remaining fleet Tahir Bey, allied commanders, blamed the Ottomans. Tahir Bey fearing that contradicting them might lead to the sinking of the remaining ships remained silent. Following this conference, British and Russian ships left for Malta while the French headed for Toulon. The Ottomans were informed of the destruction of their fleet by the Austrian Ambassador in Constantinople, who expressed his regrets.

If the intent of the Powers were the resolution of the Greek issue, the fleets would not have left. They would have consolidated their victory by remaining in the area and demanding the withdrawal of Ibrahim's troops from Peloponnese. Rather than expressing regrets, they would have demanded immediate concessions from the Ottoman Sultan in favor of the Greeks. It seems that this was not their objective.

263

The Admirals of the Allied fleet, in their dispatches sent to Constantinople, reported the destruction of the Turkish-Egyptian fleet triumphantly. In Britain, however, the result was not viewed favorably. Wellington, who had just taken over the government in London, claimed that the rendering of the Ottoman force inactive, a party that functioned as a counterbalance and an obstacle to the Russian expansion in the eastern Mediterranean, was contrary to Britain's interests. He criticized Admiral Codrington for having exceeded his jurisdictions and shortly thereafter deposed him of his duties. In his inaugural address to the House of Commons, the King of Britain characterized Navarino as an "unfortunate event" and the Ottoman Empire as an allied country. In France, the reception of Navarino was more favorable, and Admiral de Rigny attained popularity, although concerns were raised regarding the expansion of Russia in the eastern Mediterranean. Russia was the most content with the outcome and tried to persuade the other two Powers to exploit the weakness of the Ottoman Empire and declare war against it.

Metternich's Austria portrayed Navarino as some sort of tragedy, as it probably put an end to the European Concert that had been formed. It was mainly concerned with the strengthening of Russia. Nevertheless, he replied only orally through the Austrian Embassy in Constantinople to a letter from the Ottoman Sadrazam about Navarino, where he alluded to the need to come up with some form of a compromise. To a question from his Ottoman interlocutor regarding Austria's positions, the country's Ambassador replied that circumstances had changed and that everyone should adapt to them.

Navarino for the Ottoman administration was a «Black Swan event",[266] given its incompetence in carrying out technical assessments that could allow it to appraise the developments and adequately maneuver accordingly by offering some timely concessions to the Greeks. Sultan Mahmud expressed his regrets (and perhaps his wrath) for Navarino, portraying this synergy of the three Powers as a new crusade. The Allies' Ambassadors in Constantinople were called to the Porte for explanations.

Russia's Ambassador de Ribeaupiere brought forth that they had informed Ibrahim beforehand of the need of the Allied fleet to enter the Gulf of Navarino as winter was approaching. This request, he explained, had sparked tensions, and the conflict started when the Ottoman fleet opened fire. He added that the Allies' losses were also significant, failing to convince the Ottomans. Moreover, the Ottomans considered that the Russians were the main culprit for the Navarino debacle. At a subsequent meeting of allied Ambassadors with the Ottoman Foreign Minister Pertev Bey, they declared that their countries wished for peace. Still, Pertev Bey replied that with regards to the Greeks, the politics of the Empire would remain unchanged.

After that, the Sublime Porte, with a Note to the embassies, called for moral gratification and compensation for the destruction suffered by the Ottoman fleet, and once more emphasized that the Ottomans would never accept allied demands in favor of the Greeks. In response, the Ambassadors reiterated that their countries stood for peace and

---

[266] The black swan theory is an unpredictable event that is beyond what is normally expected of a situation and has potentially severe consequences. It is often inappropriately rationalized after the fact with the benefit of hindsight.

security in Greece and that the Ottoman fleet was the one to open fire first, and therefore there was no question on the matter of compensation. Concerning the issue of fulfilling moral gratification, they pointed out that they had already expressed their regret. Thus, they considered that much respect for the Ottoman State had already been demonstrated on many levels. They added that if their offer for mediation on the Greek issue had been accepted, the conflict could have been resolved peacefully. After all, they observed that if the intentions of their fleets were hostile, they would not have fled but would have continued the fighting.

From the Ottoman side, Mehmed Ali, in a letter to the Sultan, wrote that war should be avoided, as Austria having the same religion might join the three Powers against the Empire. Consequently, he thought it would be helpful to make some small concessions to the Greeks.

The diplomatic tug of war in Constantinople continued with the Ottomans remaining intransigent on their position to restore the pre-revolution administrative system. The Ambassadors threatened to leave Constantinople, something that they finally did on November 29, 1827, breaking up the diplomatic relations of Britain, France, and Russia with the Ottoman Empire. Despite the debacle in Navarino, the Ottomans insisted stubbornly on the non-acceptance of the Powers' brokerage and continued hostilities in mainland Greece.[267] At the same time, the Ottomans began preparing for a new war. Although they were considered a naval force to be reckoned with, the Ottomans no longer had a fleet. First, they tried to render operational the new military corps they had established and sought to construct a

---

[267] Ali Fuat Orenc: History Magazine Issue No. 46, 2007 (in Turkish).

new fleet to deal with the Russians in the Black Sea and the Mediterranean.

THE DENOUEMENT

The Era of Kapodistrias

Ioannis Kapodistrias was residing in Paris at the time of his election. Before returning to Greece, he visited several European power nations to establish contacts and promote the Greek positions. He first stopped by St. Petersburg to visit Czar Nicholas I and submitted his resignation from the Russian service. Whereas his visit was very well received in Russia, at his subsequent stops in both Berlin and London, his discussions were not constructive. This was to a certain degree expected, as Kapodistrias had served under the Czar, and both nations regarded his views as pro-Russian. After Paris, where his reception was more accommodating, he boarded a British ship at Ancona. First, he stopped in Malta, where he met with Codrington, who had arrived there after the naval battle of Navarino. Kapodistrias finally arrived in Nafplio on January 18, 1828, ten months after his designation by the third National Assembly of Troezen as Governor of Greece. In Nafplio, he was received enthusiastically and four days later went to Aegina, the then capital of the state. Shortly after that, it was decided that Nafplio would become the capital of the Greek state.[268]

The state that I. Kapodistrias came to govern was virtually non-existent and unmanageable, and the Governor refused to accept the decisions of the National Assembly that elected him.[269] Despite the existence of the Constitution of Troezen under which it was presumed that he would exercise power, Kapodistrias, citing the disarray and difficulties that made his governance difficult, recommended to

---

[268] A. Vakalopoulos, Ibid., p.p. 867-879.
[269] Vasilis Kremmydas: Ibid., p. 197.

Parliament to resolve itself by early January 1828. The Parliament accepted to suspend its operations as well as the implementation of the Constitution. Instead of the Parliament, a new advisory body, the Panhellenic, was established. The Panhellenic worked together with the Governor in administrative matters. In essence, of course, the power was exercised by Kapodistrias himself, who had gathered all political powers in his own hands, formally by a popular mandate that it would be renewed via elections in a representative system.[270] The system of Kapodistrias, as it was manifested with his actions in the internal affairs during the brief period of his administration, was the expression of an "enlightened despotism".[271]

Petrobey Mavromichalis accepted the election of Kapodistrias as Governor of Greece, and after Kapodistrias' arrival, he was appointed member of the presidency of the Panhellenic and later of the Senate (1828). Kapodistrias sought to set up a state from a nation riddled with anarchy. As he wrote to Andreas Moustoxydis, "Everything here is in desolation, ruins, and disarray".[272] As Governor of Greece, Kapodistrias introduced important reforms for the restoration of the state machinery and the establishment of the legal framework of the state necessary to institute order. He founded primary schools and courts, tried to curb Greek piracy, and sold national land to farmers to facilitate the development of agriculture.[273]

He also reorganized the armed forces under a single command. However, the mindset that would recognize the importance of the central authority within a democratic framework had not yet evolved among Greeks. At the same time, Kapodistrias

---

[270] Greek Parliament: Constitutional history.
[271] V. Kremmydas: Ibid., p. 198.
[272] I. Kapodistrias: Texts, Athens 1976 p. 50 (in Greek).
[273] V.Kremmydas: Ibid., p. 199.

ignoring the general tendencies of the Greek Society for a progressive trend, failed to take any initiatives for ensuring the smooth transition to this democratic framework.[274] The armed forces often revolted. Kapodistrias, with a stern letter, asked the chief of the Army Dimitrios Ypsilantis to ensure that the troops abstain from such acts. He also relayed a message to Petrobey Mavromichalis, indicating how much easier and more fruitful his endeavors for fatherland would come to be if only those who held high positions in the political system of the country put aside their personal interests and helped him in good faith.[275]

Kapodistrias, right from the outset, also faced reactions in the political arena, as he did not recognize the need to form political alliances. Consequently, he tried to rule out all those who could share power with him and especially Phanariotes,[276] as well as the members of the Friendly Society who had not forgotten his refusal to assist the Society when he was asked. The first reactions appeared in Hydra as a result of Kapodistrias' strict stance on continuing piracy. More serious, however, was the reaction of the Francophile and Anglophile politicians who considered him an instrument of Russia. The formations of the three major parties, the English under A. Mavrokordatos, the French under I. Kolettis, and the Russian under A. Metaxas and Th. Kolokotronis had already been active by then.[277]

The Fourth National Assembly, which convened among political disputes, took place in Argos between July 11 and August 6, 1829. It produced several resolutions addressing urgent political and national issues. The Fourth National

---

[274] V.Kremmydas: Ibid., p. 199.
[275] I. Kapodistrias Ibid., p. 48-49.
[276] Kremmydas refers to Anagnostis Kontakis, Ibid., p. 200.
[277] E.G. Protopsaltis: Ibid., p. 87.

Assembly endorsed Kapodistrias' policies to the date and set the foundations for the new organization of the state. The Assembly essentially had approved the resolutions drafted by the Governor. In replacing the Panhellenic council, which had already been abolished, a 27-member Senate was established. The Governor would select twenty-one out of the 27 senators from a pool of three times the number of candidates (81) nominated by the Assembly, while the remaining six would be appointed directly by him. The Senate's task was only to advise on all non-administrative resolutions.

The exercise of political power and organization of the state had conformed to the then-current capabilities and needs of the nation. However, the Governor's multitude of responsibilities, his appointment of many Ionians at public positions including his brothers Augustine and Viaros Kapodistrias to high offices, as well as the supersession of the dignitaries fueled an ever-increasing opposition sentiment. Kapodistrias was set primarily for service to the homeland, and through his actions, he intended to bring law and order to the organization of the state. His centralization of power and stern control form of governing, however, despite his good intentions, pushed many liberals towards the opposition, which until then consisted mainly of dignitaries from Hydra and some other regions. The great political victory of I. Kapodistrias in summer 1829 in Argos soon provoked a strong and continually escalating opposition until it led to his assassination.

The moves of the Allies

Following the departure of the three Ambassadors from Constantinople in November 1827, Russia, which was contemplating waging war against the Ottoman Empire, managed to persuade

Austria and Prussia to declare neutrality. Russia informed the other Powers, Britain and France that it could alone declare war as a representative of the Alliance of the Three Powers. Britain, who did not want to leave Russia to settle the Greek issue alone, opted to blockade the Greek coast as a way to force the Egyptians out of Peloponnese. France, in addition to the participation of its fleet in the blockade, seemed willing to send an army to Peloponnese to expel Ibrahim. It was officially declared that the above measures bore no hostile overtones against the Ottoman Empire! Indeed, the diplomatic rival of both Britain and France was not the Ottoman Empire but Russia.[278]

Based on a protocol signed in London on July 19, 1828, France, under the aegis of the Allies, undertook to send an expeditionary force for the liberation of Peloponnese. A French army with a power of 14 thousand men under General Nicolas Joseph Maison landed in Navarino in August 1828.[279] Meanwhile, Codrington, on the order of the British Government, had gone to Alexandria and succeeded in concluding the Treaty of Alexandria (July 16, 1828) with Mehmed Ali. As agreed by the treaty, Ibrahim's troops withdrew from Peloponnese in October 1828, and thus the French army, despite the intentions of its leader, did not need to engage in any decisive battle apart from a few skirmishes. However, the French military played a significant role in the clearing of the remaining Egyptian and Ottoman armies out of Peloponnese.[280]

In the meantime, at the instigation of Metternich and to isolate Russia, the Ottomans called on the two other Powers, Britain and France, to

---

[278] S. Th Laskaris: Ibid., p. 35.
[279] S. Th Laskaris: Ibid., p. 36.
[280] E.G. Protopsaltis: Ibid., p. 95.

restore their diplomatic relations. The issue was brought at the tripartite conference in London, which continued to be in session. Russia agreed, provided that they would adhere to the condition of Greece's geographic extension and its vassalage to the Sultan. It was decided that the two Ambassadors, upon their return to Constantinople, could also speak on behalf of Russia when discussing the issue of Greece.

The Sublime Porte frequently had accused Russia of being responsible for its problems, claiming that it was scheming for the dissolution of the Ottoman Empire. It threatened with the repudiation of the Ackermann Agreement (1826) and the abolition of the prerogatives of Russian nationals. In response, Russia declared war on the Ottoman Empire on April 26, 1828. The Russian army crossed Prut River on May 7, 1828, and continued its advance within the Ottoman territories.

After receiving the mandate for the demarcation of the new state, the Ambassadors of the three Powers initially went to Corfu and chose the island of Poros as their place of work, where they arrived in September 1828. The three Ambassadors conferred with Kapodistrias, who had already taken over his duties as Governor of Greece in January 1828. The Ambassadors ended up proposing borders drawn with their north line that of Arta – Volos while including the Cyclades and possibly Samos and Crete within the Greek borders. They set the amount of the annual tax tribute analogous to the former income of the Sultan from Greece and agreed that the highest executive power would be entrusted to a single person with hereditary succession and ratification with a ferman of the Sultan. The Muslims of Greece would leave and be compensated for their real estate.[281]

---

[281] S. Th Laskaris: Ibid., p. 37.

The London Conference accepted the memorandum of the Ambassadors with the Protocol of March 22, 1829, that was annexed to the Treaty of July 6, 1827, in its main points, while Crete and Samos were left outside Greece. The new ruler would be Christian; he would be selected by the three Powers after consultation with the Sultan and would not belong to British, French, or Russian dynasties. The Ambassadors of Britain and France would return to Constantinople to negotiate with the Sublime Porte the arrangements agreed among the three Powers.

The Russophile group in Greece later argued that the Treaty of July 6, 1826, among Britain, France and Russia emerged from the desire of the first two not to let Russia alone handle the settlement of the Greek issue. To this end, the Russophiles, by reference to the content of a letter from the politician and foreign minister in 1828 Lord Aberdeen to Duke Wellington, maintained that Britain undertook the protection of Greece only to prevent war between Russia and the Ottomans, and avert an exclusive Russian influence on Greece.[282] Furthermore, the Russophile group blamed Canning for setting up a Greek kingdom only in Peloponnese, while noting that the naval battle of Navarino was deemed an unpleasant event by the British foreign minister. It argued that later on, during the negotiations for the Adrianoupolis (Edirne) Treaty, Britain sought to curtail the borders of the new state as much as possible. As Aberdeen wrote to Wellington on September 24, 1829, "if Evvoia were left to the Ottoman Empire along with Crete, it would provide the Sublime Porte the ability to control Greece". Indeed, there were shots taken among the allies. Wellington referred to France as two-faced, claiming that while on the one hand prepared and organized

---

[282] Wellington Dispatches.

275

the Egyptian army, on the other, urged the Greeks to persevere on their rebellion.[283]

Metternich's views on European Powers, as noted by historian Konstantinos Paparrigopoulos, were that "the course of action of Russia was unpredictable, sometimes bearing stringency, others extreme benevolence, but it was always dubious. That of Britain was imperious, arrogant, with plenty of unforeseen ventures. That of France was reckless, ambivalent and at times seemed to waver to and fro, while that of Prussia was apprehensive and timid". For his part, Paparrigopoulos points out that the moral initiative on the Greek matter was projected by Russia, the active initiative by Britain, while France joined the two only after it was convinced that they would proceed without it. A diplomatic analysis confirms the views expressed by the Greek historian.[284]

International developments after 1829

Kapodistrias strongly protested the territorial stipulations of the March 22, 1829 Protocol and the disregard for the opinion of the Greeks on the appointment of the new ruler. He also argued the need for the new ruler to embrace the Orthodox doctrine.

The Powers dismissed his arguments, and in June 1829, the Ambassadors of Britain and France arrived in Constantinople to facilitate the agreement. Soon, however, they realized that the Sultan was adamant about the integrity of the Empire, and all that he would consent was a general amnesty, along with more or less reinstatement of the status quo before the revolt. It necessitated the defeat of the

---

[283] Study of Periklis Argyropoulos (in Greek).
[284] Letter of Metternich to baron Ottenfels of December 30, 1826.

Ottomans by Russians for the Sultan to accept the independence of Greece.[285]

After some initial difficulties, the Russian army managed to defeat the Ottomans, reaching Adrianoupolis (Edirne) in August 1829. On August 15, 1829, the Sublime Porte accepted the agreement of the three Powers favoring Greece while proposing a few amendments that were rejected. By the Treaty of Adrianoupolis of September 14, 1829, with which the Russo-Turkish War ended, the Porte acceded to the Treaty of July 6, 1827, of London and to the London Protocol of March 22, 1829, sanctioning the establishment of a tax vassal, autonomous Greek state. Britain and France were unhappy with Russia's unilateral actions, and for that reason, Russia assured them that it would not impair the Council's work in London. The Sublime Porte, for its part, testified on September 9 to the Ambassadors in Constantinople, that in addition to its adherence to the London Treaty, it will also consent with the decisions that the Council would take in London, to avoid worse sanctions from Russia.[286]

Subsequently, Kapodistrias focused his attention on two fronts: the territorial expansion through military operations in central Greece and the pursuit of total independence through diplomatic actions of the Governor. The latter goal coincided with the interests of Britain and France, who did not want a state that was vassal to the Sultan, which would be under the influence of Russia in light of the prevailing conditions. They also contemplated that the Czar might find opportunities to exploit situations developing in Greece and intervene in the Ottoman Empire, as he did with the Danube principalities. Precisely this was what the Sublime Porte had been

---

[285] S. Th Laskari: Ibid., p. 39.
[286] E.G. Protopsaltis: Ibid., p. 90.

afraid of and had initially rejected the Treaty of London of July 6, 1827.

Russia deemed befitting not to bring any further objections, reckoning perhaps that an independent Greece might be a positive outcome for its own geopolitical interests as well. In November 1829, the London Conference agreed to establish an independent Greece while limiting its western border further south, as Britain preferred the Ottoman Empire and not Greece to be on the mainland coast opposite to the Ionian islands. In this light, it proposed to cede Akarnania as compensation to the Sultan for deprivation of Greece's tribute payments.[287]

Following the already agreed content, the three Powers signed a protocol on the independence of Greece on February 3, 1830. It was also stipulated that the Ottoman nationals in Greece and Greek citizens in the Ottoman Empire would have the same commercial and maritime prerogatives as the nationals of states with which the two countries were in peace.

Regarding the appointment for the ruler of Greece, the candidacy of Duke of Namur, son of the future King of France Louis Philippe, was discussed in 1825 - 1826; but the proposal was abandoned because of the little sympathy that the reigning King of France Charles I held for his cousins. The candidacies of Otto of Bavaria, John of Saxony, Charles of Mecklenburg, and especially of Leopold of Saxe-Coburg were also explored.[288] By a particular protocol, Prince Leopold was finally selected for the throne of Greece. For Wellington, this choice also

---

[287] S. Th Laskari: Ibid., p. 40.
[288] E. G. Protopsaltis: Ibid., p. 99.

aimed at the distancing from London of the meddling prince.[289]

Sultan Mahmud, for his part, had focused his interest in the creation of a modern European state, and for that, he needed the assistance of France and Britain. He, therefore, raised no objections to an independent Greece, as it also facilitated, among other matters, in "getting rid of a troubled region and its people". Thus, he formally accepted the independence of Greece with its communication of April 12, 1830, to the Ambassadors of the Three Powers.

The Greeks, although protested for the new decrement of their liberated territories, felt obligated to accept what was agreed on, for fear of further unforeseen complications. In his letter to Leopold, Kapodistrias communicated his country's problems, particularly the financial ones, and relayed the nation's will that his ascent to the throne be ratified by a vote of the National Assembly and the wish of the nation that the new king embraced Christian Orthodoxy. Similar matters were expressed by the Senate (controlled by Kapodistrias) in a memorandum to the representatives of the Powers in Nafplio. All these issues of concern discouraged Leopold, who, after contemplating his future in Britain, submitted his resignation from the offered crown in May 1830. Certainly, if there was a sincere desire to elect a rather competent ruler such as Leopold, Kapodistrias' letter could have been avoided, or at best, should not have addressed issues proposed previously and rejected by the three Powers. Leopold eventually became King of Belgium.

Leopold's refusal to accept the crown of Greece led to new challenges. Moreover, the European interest digressed to the July Revolution in France

---

[289] S. Th Laskaris: Ibid., p. 42.

and the independence of Belgium, leading to a lack of concern for the Greek issue. The situation stagnated.[290]

Kapodistrias' efforts in restoring the borders at the Volos – Arta line were successful mainly due to the fall of Wellington and the takeover of the British Foreign Office by Henry John Temple, third Viscount Palmerston (1830). The latter aspired for the new state to be strong enough to stand on its own and not be so dependent on the Czar. The Sultan, despite his objections, was eventually persuaded, primarily by the promise of compensation of almost 30 times the annual tax revenues of the region. Besides, at the time, he was occupied with the mutiny of Mehmed Ali, whose troops had invaded the southern provinces of the Empire.

When Mehmed Ali's demands for the administration of Peloponnese and especially of Crete in a way that would provide him control of the access to the eastern Mediterranean were not met, he requested for the administration of Syria and Cilicia in return for his services fighting the Greeks. When Sultan Mahmud refused, Mehmed Ali invaded Syria. The son of Mehmed Ali, Ibrahim, defeated the Ottoman army and advanced up to Konya.[291] In a strange twist, it was France and Britain who intervened in favor of Mehmet Ali, while Russia offered support to the Ottomans!

The approach of the Ottoman Empire and Russia is indicative of the liquidity of international relations and the variability of processes in an environment of rapid developments and the light of fluctuating interests. The Treaty of Hunkar Iskelesi

---

[290] Spyros V. Markezinis Political History of Greece, 1966, Edit. Papyrus, p. 207 (in Greek).
[291] Newspaper article of Vasilis Kyrazopoulos, Politis, February 2017.

was signed in Bosphorus between the Ottoman Empire and Russia in 1833. This mutual assistance and non-aggression treaty ascertained the Ottoman effort to reach out to Russia. The articles of this eight-year Treaty referred to the details of that assistance while re-ratified the Treaty of Edirne. In a secret article of the Treaty, it was stated that in the eventuality of war between Russia and a Western state, the Ottoman state would close the Straits to the fleet of the warring Western state. However, disputes between Ottomans and Russians before long resurfaced, with the Westerners once again pulling strings.[292]

The internal political developments

Petrobey Mavromichalis' participation in the two political bodies founded by Kapodistrias, and in general, the friendly relations with him did not last for long. This was because of Kapodistrias' efforts to conform to the standards of an organized European state at the time by eliminating the influence of all clandestine powers while gathering all authorities to the central government, i.e., the Governor. This was not viable to the chieftains who believed that they, with their own forces, had defeated the Turks and therefore did not owe their obedience to the new State and that on the contrary, the State owed them its existence.

According to the British historian Walter Alison Phillips, "Although Kapodistrias' methods were authoritarian, this does not mean that he was a tyrant because a tyrant is selfish and ruthless regarding the means he employs. Kapodistrias, on the contrary, intended to govern the country and strived

---

[292] V. Moutsoglou: Turkey: The personality of the State, Ibid.

for this purpose while sacrificing his position on the Russian councils".[293]

The political character of a state is formed, among other things, by the historical circumstances of its founding, the temperament of its people, and its size. In a small country, few, unlawfully assembled collectivities can have a disproportionate influence on a central authority. The evolution of the personality of the state takes place over time, passing through various stages of immaturity.

The Greek government, which sought absolute power, could neither inspire it because of the prevailing conditions nor did it have the ability to enforce it. Moreover, it could not fulfill the financial demands of the chieftains and the dignitaries, neither of Kolokotronis nor Petrobey. The opposition to the Governor was comprised of chieftains of Rumeli under Ioannis Kolettis (French Party), the Maniates led by the family of Petrobey Mavromichalis, and finally Hydra of the Koundouriotis family (English party) that constituted the strongest contentious faction. The opposition demanded implementing the Troezen constitution in its original form and for delegates to be elected for a new national assembly.

Later on, the confrontation of Kapodistrias with the self-proclaimed Constitutionalists attained a European nuance because of the tension in Russia's relations with Britain and France due to multinational complications (Mehmet Ali, Italian States, Belgium, Poland). The Constitutionalists considered that the international events favored them, and thus, in 1830, Petrobey's brother, Tzanis Mavromichalis, led an uprising in Tsimova (Areopoli, Mani) by inciting the Maniates against the Prefect of the region. Petrobey was forced to remain in Nafplio, essentially as a prisoner, while Kapodistrias

---

[293] Spyros V. Markezinis: Ibid., p. 187.

summoned Tzanis in Nafplio to negotiate. However, when Tzanis arrived there, he was arrested and imprisoned in the Palamidi castle of Nafplio. Shortly afterward, Petrobey himself was also imprisoned pending trial for nine months on charges of high treason. Maniates raised the flag of rebellion in Limeni and awaited the return of the Mavromichalis brothers. The uprising of the Maniates could only be suppressed with the use of arms.

At the same time, chieftain Tsamis Karatasos revolted in Thebes and Atalanti, while the Hydraeans declared that they did not recognize Kapodistrias as Governor. Hydra, at the end of the great Revolution, had found itself in a dismal economic situation. Piracy was substantial revenue, and its effective suppression to which Kapodistrias had significantly contributed to had led to a major financial crisis. Income from trade could not replace that of piracy since the Greek flag was not recognized internationally, and the Hydraen ships could not reach various ports. The situation had led thousands of sailors to unemployment and hunger. The Hydraeans attributed their misfortunes to Kapodistrias, claiming that he deliberately delayed the recognition of the flag to humiliate the islanders. In Hydra, the conspiracy organization "Hercules" was, followed by that of the "Bond".[294]

In May 1831, the rebels expelled the government authorities from Hydra, and the governance of the island was undertaken by a seven-member committee, including A. Mavrokordatos, G. Kountouriotis, A. Kriezis, and M. Tompazis. This was repeated in Syros, an ally of Hydra. Kapodistrias's popularity had declined, while there were strong indications that Britain and France were harboring the anti-government Constitutionalists. Kapodistrias

---

[294] E. G. Protopsaltis: Ibid., p. 102.

decided to mobilize the fleet against the seven-member committee in Hydra. Once Hydraeans became aware of this, they charged Antonis Kriezis to seize the naval base of Poros and the ships there. Kriezis took over the naval base, and along with Karatasos, who was assisting them, captured the fortress of Poros. Crews and commanders of some ships joined the Constitutionalists' side. At the end of July 1831, Andreas Miaoulis arrived in Poros along with 200 sailors solidifying the occupation of the naval base.

On July 28, an encounter of Russian ships with the Greek ship "Spetses" took place. The rebels were defeated, and the captain of the boat, Hydraean Lazaros Pinotzis, blew it up in order not to hand it over to the authorized government. This demolition of a Greek ship morally harmed the Constitutionalists, portraying them as insurgents who destroy the national fleet. Most islanders of Poros abandoned Miaoulis following the encounter with the Russian fleet. Eventually, a Greek naval force under the command of patriot Kanaris defeated the rebels with the help of the Russian fleet.

The foiled Hydraean admiral Miaoulis was outraged and torched the frigate "Hellas" and the Corvette "Hydra", while Mykonian sailor G. Galasides saved the steam-powered "Karteria" at the last moment. Following that, Miaoulis, using explosives, blasted the fortress nearby. He, along with the other Hydraeans, promptly departed Poros returning to Hydra, where he was triumphantly received.[295] The forward-thinking Kapodistrias granted him amnesty in an effort to quell the tense atmosphere that

---

[295] Greek history issues, version 4.0 (http://www.istorikathemata.com/2012/12/the-destruction-of-the-Greek-fleet-by-Miaoulis-in-Poros-1831.htm) L (Last access 03/09/2020) (in Greek)

prevailed.[296] The conspirators against the Governor, however, colluded within and outside of Nafplio campaigning for the murder of the (supposedly) tyrant. France and Britain supported the subversive government that had formed in Hydra against "Russophile" Kapodistrias. The situation appeared hopeless.

The incarceration of Petrobey's caused the rage of the Mavromichalis family to the extent that led to the heinous assassination of Kapodistrias by Petrobey's brother, Konstantinos and his son George, on September 27, 1831. Ioannis Kapodistrias thus found a tragic death without ever receiving the official news of Greece's independence. The assassination of I. Kapodistrias was not the result of a political plot but the result of a personal – family retaliation.

Kapodistrias' work as Governor, at a very crucial period for Greece, is considered constructive overall. He attempted to set up a European state under very dire circumstances. Subsequent efforts of successive Greek governments to establish a central government with powers in all sectors and recognized by all in the same manner as those in the European states were not successful. Anarchy and civil war followed Kapodistrias' death. Makrigiannis attributed this unfortunate turn to the politicians.[297]

Indeed, the long slavery of the genus was the root cause of the inability to create in the new State the necessary institutions of power respected by all. The first Ottoman period had subdued the peoples through the force of arms. Then came a period during which the Ottoman domination had managed in being tolerated, offering some security and, despite widespread poverty, avoidance of misery. During the period of the Ottoman regression, the situation was

---

[296] E. G. Protopsaltis: Ibid., p. 105.
[297] Makrigiannis: Memoirs/2, Papyrus p.p. 210-220 (in Greek).

derailed both regarding security and economy. The disarray, the imposition of the mighty based not on law but power, led the Empire into quasi-anarchy within the Sultan's order. Riots succeeded one after another. Even the Janissaries rebelled. It was under this socio-political context that the Greek Revolution broke out.

At a time when the power of the Sultanate was sometimes not respected even by the Ottomans themselves, it was certainly not possible to expect for Greeks who were just coming out of a long period of slavery, and who had fought hard for their freedom that they each perceived differently, to promptly adopt institutions similar to those created in the West through long-standing processes. And surely no comparison could be made with Italian or German unification as the prevailing terms were different. In revolutionary Greece, defiance to central authority and its armed contestation were presumed as "justifiable", almost "standard" procedures.

In addition to the individual specificities, the chieftains' financial claims, the efforts to securing power positions before the King's arrival, as well as the sentiment that each had fought harder than he was credited for, the competition of the "protector" Powers entered dynamically into the quandary. In this context, divisive syndromes once again found their way. The Greeks sank in a sterile endless squabble, with no substantial winner but with injury to the cause.

The newspapers of the era also had a role in the political events, despite the great difficulties they faced. Several printed newspapers were issued, like the "Greek Salpinx" published in Kalamata as early as August 1, 1821, the "Greek Chronicles" issued in Messolonghi by Ioannis Mayer from 1824 and until its fall, newspapers of the opposition as "Apollo" (1831), etc., as well as handwritten such as "Aitoliki

Gazette", "Acheloos" and "the newspaper of Galaxidi", the last with fake news in its single issue that survived. In addition to technical and economic problems, a resolution limiting freedom of the press was adopted by the political power in 1831.[298]

The three-member administrative committee chaired by Augustine Kapodistrias, Kolokotronis, and Kolettis, established after the Governor's assassination, attempted to secure order and convene a national assembly. Six months after the Governor's murder, an act allegedly criticized by Petrobey, Augustine Kapodistrias, ordered Petrobey's release to avoid a new cycle of civil strife. The move, however, failed as the opposition was widespread and militarily well-organized.

In Hydra, the opposition garnered about seventy "delegates" from the surrounding areas and, with the support of the representatives of Britain and France, demanded the convening of a national conference. The administrative committee, under Augustine and with (Russophile) Kolokotronis, itself also sought the convening of the National Assembly but on its own terms. When Kolokotronis resigned from the three-member commission along with Kolettis,[299] the Fifth National Assembly elected Augustine Kapodistrias as Governor of Greece. Kolettis' faction did not recognize the election. Following Francophile Kolettis siding up with the opposition of Hydra-Rumeli, the government convened the Fifth National Assembly in Argos in December 1831, chaired by Tsamados. In contrast, Roumeliotes gathered in a special assembly and elected Panoutsos Notaras as the chair.

---

[298]Aik. Koumarianou: E-Historically "The press in the fighting Greece" p. 146, 150-153 (n Greek).
[299] Kolokotronis: Ibid.

Consequently, opposition parties with the military forces loyal to them attacked the government forces. In the clashes that ensued in the plain between Argos and Nafplio, the government forces prevailed. The National Assembly was transferred to Nafplio, where it voted the Constitution of March 15, 1832. According to this Constitution, the Greek jurisdiction is "sovereign, hereditary, constitutional and parliamentary", thus establishing a constitutional monarchy. However, the Constitution of March 15, 1832, was never implemented.[300]

The anti-governmental forces were reinforced with a political unit from Rumeli led by Th. Grivas, while Kolettis, who was supported by chieftain Makrigiannis, also joined in with 60 "delegates".[301] The Constitutionalists withdrew to Perahora and elected their own temporary three-member government with Kolettis, Zaimis, and Koundouriotis, and as Secretary the Anglophile Mavrokordatos. They decided on Megara as the venue of the Assembly. The two "governments" with headquarters, one in Nafplio and the other in Megara, found themselves confronted with a civil war.[302] In the country, total anarchy reigned with the legitimate authorities of the State having been abrogated.

The Senate, the only remaining legal body, attempted to elect a five-member Administrative Committee, but Kolettis disagreed with its makeup, fearing that the other four members would oppose him. It was decided to set up a seven-member Administrative Committee with a rotating presidency and a majority rule. This majority was always difficult to attain, resulting in the paralysis of the State's operation. The news that the "Protector Powers" had

[300]Spyros V. Markezinis: Ibid., p. 200.
[301] Makrigiannis: Ibid. p. 32-54.
[302] E. G. Protopsaltis: Ibid., p. 110.

elected the Prince of Bavaria Otto, as King of Greece (March 11, 1832) led momentarily to the two powerful men of the time, Kolettis and Kolokotronis, to agree to form a government from all parties. However, the chieftains turning immediately against the newly formed unified government pressed for their salaries while the treasury was penniless. Once again, anarchy prevailed. After a foreign intervention, Augustine Kapodistrias was forced to resign on March 28, 1832, and resort to Corfu. The government disbanded, and Kolettis seized power.[303]

Under chaotic conditions, it was decided to convene a new national assembly. The "Fourth National Assembly of the Greeks" (July 14 - August 10, 1832), which was initially convened in Argos, was not recognized as the previous ones after the Third. Nevertheless, the civil war, in which the remnants of the French army of Maison also joined in favor of Kolettis, continued. At the battle in Argolic plain, Kolokotronis' friend, Dimitrios Kallergis,[304] prevailed. Kolettis was forced to move the Assembly from Argos to Nafplio and then to its suburb, Pronoia.[305]

In Pronoia, at the request of the new King's father, King Ludwig I of Bavaria, the Assembly ratified the decision on Otto's choice as the King of Greece. The Fifth National Assembly was declared null. The representatives of the three Powers prevented the debate on the Constitution or the fundamental laws without the involvement of the royal authority. Amid disagreements over other issues, the Assembly interrupted its work "until the arrival of the Regency", the tripartite Bavarian committee that would accompany the still minor Otto - Othon and who

---

[303] E. G. Protopsaltis Ibid., p. 111.
[304] E. G. Protopsaltis Ibid., p. 112.
[305] Spyros V. Markezinis Ibid., p. 202.

would exercise the administration of Greece until the new King had reached adulthood.[306]

Meanwhile, the heroic Dimitrios Ypsilantis passed away on August 6, 1832, and the government was reduced to a six-member task force rendering the decision-making process quite challenging. The National Assembly suffered through endless debates when, on August 14, 1832, the chieftains stormed the conference room and arrested the richest delegates, including the President of the Convention, who held hostage until a large part due from their salaries was paid.[307] The resuscitated Senate substituted the disbanded National Assembly. Amidst political despair, it was thought that the Russian Admiral Ricord could be appointed as Governor of Greece. This idea did not gain any traction because of the reaction of the representatives of the rest of the Powers.[308]

Finally, the involvement of the French army, which had clashed with the irregulars and resulted in the death of many dozens of Greeks,[309] angered the chieftains who sided with Kolokotronis and prevailed in the armed conflict. Nevertheless, Kolokotronis, who took over the Argolic plain, did not enter Nafplio nor overthrew the government. Instead, he agreed on the appointment of a new government under Kolettis, Zaimis, and Metaxas, who would hand over power to the new King.[310]

---

[306] Eventually, the Constitution imposing the constitutional Monarchy was adopted as late as 1843, after the September 3 revolution under D. Kallergis, and I. Makrigiannis.
[307] E. G. Protopsaltis: Political History of modern Greece, Issue B´, Athens, 1973, p.112, Spyros v. Markezinis: Political History of Greece, 1966, Edit. Papyrus, p. 205 9in Greek).
[308] Spyros V. Markezinis: Ibid., p. 205.
[309] Kolokotronis: Ibid., p. 204.
[310] E. G. Protopsaltis Ibid., p. 112.

That was more or less the state of the impoverished country. The casualties and physical destruction during this period of anarchy between the death of Governor Ioannis Kapodistrias and the arrival of the Regency were enormous, and in some sectors, may have outweighed the losses from the Great Revolution. Likewise, the moral deprivation suffered in these turbulent years was also immeasurable. The pursuit of legal order cannot be the guiding light to the conscience of citizens unless it is respected beforehand through procedures that are considered legitimate, enforceable by law, sustainable, and prosecuted in the event of a violation. None of these existed at that time, and the natural outcome without them was the slide to anarchy.[311]

The end of tribulations

King Ludwig in order to accept the appointment of his second son, Othon, as King (and not as a ruler) of Greece, requested the extension of the borders of the new country up to the line Arta – Volos, i.e., with the addition of Akarnania district that was previously removed by the London Protocol of February 3, 1830, and the approval by the Powers of a loan of sufficient size for the organization of the state. These requisitions were accepted by the Powers while the request for the annexation of Crete and Samos to the new state was rejected. This was due both to geopolitical reasons and to the expected refusal of the Sultan that could have led to new conflicts undesirable to the Powers. As far as Crete was concerned, there was also the complication of

---

[311] Spyros V. Markezinis Ibid., p. 206.

291

Mehmed Ali's claims, who at the time was backed by France and Britain.[312]

The May 7, 1832 conference finally announced the selection of Prince of Bavaria Othon (Otto Frederick Ludwig) as King of the Kingdom of Greece. According to the Treaty of London, Greece, under the sovereignty of Otto and the guarantee of the courts of Russia, Britain, and France, would become a sovereign and independent state. [313]

The Ottomans did not readily accept not even the narrow borders of the new Greek State, especially regarding Akarnania. In the end, they were persuaded to agree to the amended boundaries in exchange for financial compensation, which Greece would pay from the loan it would receive. During the negotiations of the final agreement, the Sublime Porte unsuccessfully attempted to impose conditions to restrict the size of the Greek armed forces at sea and land and prohibit the provision of assistance to states with which the Ottoman Empire would be at war. The Allies rejected the terms on grounds they were considered incompatible with the concept of a sovereign state.

The Greek issue was settled definitively, with the Treaty of Constantinople (Kalender Kiosk) signed on July 9, 1832, between the three Powers and the Ottoman Empire and the "Arrangement between Great Britain, France, Russia and Turkey for the conclusive mapping out of the continental boundaries of Greece" signed in Constantinople on July 21, 1832. The latter defined the borders of independent Greece

---

[312] E. G. Protopsaltis Ibid., p. 114.
[313] S. Th Laskaris: Ibid., p. 46-47.

on the line Arta – Volos, under the term laid down by King Ludwig I to the Allies.[314]

All Greeks enthusiastically received the news for the decisive settlement of the Greek issue. However, the agreed borders were viewed by Greeks only as temporary, as most of the Greek population had been left outside. The effort had now shifted to the liberation of all Hellenism.

The internal armed conflict only ended with the arrival of the new King. Othon, accompanied by several ships with a Bavarian army, sailed on January 30, 1833, with the British frigate "Madagascar" and landed in Nafplio on February 6. He was welcomed by the people and the army with enthusiasm emanating from the relief and the hope that the suffering would end. The three-member regency set to govern Greece until the King reached adulthood tried to impose the European Bavarian order and organization on the newly formed Greek State. This approach, naturally, was not well received by either politicians or former fighters alike, or by the broad strata of the people.

---

[314] Ministry of Foreign Affairs of Greece: The Foundation of the Modern Greek State, Athens 1999 (in Greek).

The Greek Revolution of 1821

THE POST REVOLUTION PERIOD AND CONSTANTINOPLE

A few centuries after the Fall of Constantinople, one of the mainstream views among the Greeks was that it might be possible to Hellenize, to some degree, the Ottoman Empire. It was envisioned that this could be achieved through the cultural, social, and economic prevalence of the Greek element in the Ottoman territory, leading to the revival, in some alternate form, of the Byzantine Empire. On the other hand, the "Lament of Constantinople" that always played a significant role in the psyche of the nation was forming a consensus towards liberation by force of arms.

Later, when Russian war activities commenced against the Ottoman Empire, the hopes of the Greeks shifted towards the solution of the liberation of the city by the "Moskovus". Several Phanariotes fled Constantinople and took office in the Court, Government, and army of Russia. But the disappointment didn't take long to set. "According to the Oracle", as written by Athanasios Komninos Ypsilantis in his historical work "After the Fall" in 1774, «Astronomers and wise men and saints had referred to the need to redeem Constantinople by Moskovus and liberate the Romans from the Ottoman thralldom and resurrect the Roman kingdom. And the reign of the Romans would return in 320 years after the Fall, and those years were followed by six years of wars during which the Moskovus came close to Constantinople; they distressed it but could not

295

redeem it...[315] Thus, if at a time as prophesied by the Oracle, and after so many victories of Russians on the Ottomans, the Romans could not be emancipated, it would be difficult to envision that, hereafter, the resurrection of the Roman kingdom could happen». The "oracles", which basically mirrored the wishes of the then Roman people, should be assessed with the perspective of the events at the time.[316]

Thus, until the period that preparations for the Greek Revolution commenced, the prevailing views in Constantinople saw the possibility of a peaceful co-existence of Greek and Turkish peoples, in one form or another, within the territorial boundaries of the Ottoman Empire. The liberation of Constantinople symbolized the freedom of the Greek genus, which they believed could only be realized around the capital of Hellenism, Constantinople. The salvation of the genus could only be perceived as a continuation of the Byzantine state. The memories of ancient Greece were embedded too deep into the nation's subconscious to guide it to a different path. The only resolution that seemed reasonable and feasible to the Greeks of Constantinople was its liberation and fall of the Ottoman Empire, either by its gradual Hellenization or by force.

The appointment of Greeks in high governmental positions and, to no small extent, in the diplomatic service of the Empire, along with the prevalence of Greeks in the economic life of the country, supported the former choice. At the same time, the treatment of the Ottomans to the Christian subjects of the Empire and cold logic alluded that the liberation of Hellenism could only be realized through armed struggle. The path shown by the Friendly

---

[315] Refers to the Russo-Turkish War of 1768–1774
[316]Athanasios Komninos Ypsilantis "Historical Events After the Fall" Constantinople, 1870, 534 (in Greek).

Society proved at least partly correct. Freedom could only be achieved by the power of arms and with the support of the nation's own forces. The creation of the free Greek State was the triumph of the supporters of the latter choice, but liberation was only partial. Most of Hellenism, together with that of Constantinople, remained under the Ottoman rule, and a different resolution was needed.[317]

Throughout the Revolution, the conditions of Greeks in Constantinople were dire, and their lives always in danger. In particular, the destruction of the Ottoman fleet in Navarino had inflicted a devastating blow to the Ottomans, as did other news, real or fictional, for victories of the Greeks in Moldovlachia or massacres of civilian Turks. The wrath of the Sultan and the entire Muslim population was immense. However, despite its threats, the Sublime Porte did not proceed to the slaughter of all Greeks in the city. It detained all merchant ships flying flags of the three Powers and banned the departure of diplomatic couriers of the three embassies in Constantinople on the grounds that the international conventions from which this right emanated "had ceased to exist in light of recent events".

The decisive resolution of the Greek affairs was settled in 1832. Still, a large majority of the Greek population remained outside the narrow borders of free Greece, bearing the citizenship of Ottoman subjects. This segment of Hellenism continued its life and growth independent of the path of the Greek State while always considering Constantinople as its capital and center.

The new Greek State created by the Revolution had Hellenism as its basic philosophy and the liberation of all Greek regions as its primary goal.

---

[317] Vasilis Moutsoglou: The Greeks of Constantinople 1821-1922 (in Greek)

Not only it failed to foresee cohabitating with non-Christians, but it could barely tolerate it. Greek constitutions ruled out the citizenship of all those who "did not believe in Christ and were not of Greek nationality, except for those who took part in the struggle for freedom." The aspiration of the new State was the revival of the Byzantine Empire with its capital, Constantinople.

These perceptions were bound to lead to the alienation of the new Greek State from the Ecumenical Patriarchate, which by remaining in Constantinople, had to adopt a different perspective. The Ecumenical Patriarch was the spiritual leader of an enslaved, ethnically mixed Christian Orthodox flock. An approach that excluded non-Christians created an inherent difficulty in establishing a religiously and ethnically mixed state that Constantinopolitans had in mind as an epitome of the national problem they faced.

The Greek Revolution, as it evolved, thwarted the plans of supporters of national prevalence and control through a Greek-Turkish partnership. The appointment of Greeks in Ottoman government positions was halted. The Sultan ceased to assign Greek rulers to Danube principalities. The Ottoman diplomatic service that consisted to a large extent of Greeks was abolished, as was the position of the great Dragoman of the Sublime Porte that was primarily held by Greeks and was replaced by the Translation Office of the Sublime Porte. The idea of the Hellenization of the Ottoman Empire was supplanted by the pattern of liberating neighboring provinces by inciting revolutions as well as diplomatic manipulations to exploit any real or tangible opportunity that arose.[318]

---

[318]The permanent Ottoman Embassies abroad were restored only in 1834 by Sultan Mahmud II.

298

Throughout the period of the Revolution, to the extent of existing opportunities for emigration, there was a constant flux of Constantinopolitans of various classes, mainly of the upper, departing to the rebelled regions. The Constantinopolitans, like all other Greeks, fought for freedom and sacrificed their lives for the fatherland. After the founding of the Greek State, the Constantinopolitans, including the Phanariotes who had settled in the Danube principalities, began to descend to Greece and occupy high government positions, thanks to their political and administrative experience. In the stifling narrow space that was apportioned to free Greece, an outstanding intellectual and artistic potential was amassed.

In the first capital of Greece, Nafplio, and from 1834 onwards in Athens, along with politics, an intense intellectual activity started to flourish, an activity that was, to some extent, conveyed from Constantinople as well as from other capitals of Europe where Hellenism prospered. This dynamic and authentic trait of Hellenism, that had contributed to the initial impetus for the development of the Greek homeland, as expected was met with adverse reactions from a segment of the people of Greece, mainly chieftains, who considered themselves left out. Thus, the Constitution of 1843, included a provision, according to which Greeks who had come from abroad after 1827, the "Heterochthones" (foreign-born) as they were referred to, were denied political rights. Henceforth they had no right to occupy public posts, except for only certain military and educational positions. All Greeks who had descended in Greece after 1827 were subjected to rigorous formalities. Citizenship could only be acquired after residing in Greece for a certain period.

In addition to the sentiments that arose by such provisions of the Greek constitution, one must also add the exceedingly hostile attitude of the Ottoman administration towards the fledgling Greek State, which also weighed in against Constantinopolitans. Indeed, not only any thoughts of closer bilateral relations were out of the question, the Ottoman government refused even to sanction the Kingdom of Greece as a sovereign state. When King Othon visited Smyrna in private in 1833, he was recognized by the Greek population there and was welcomed enthusiastically. Mahmud II reacted by demanding and ensuring the punishment by the Patriarch of the Metropolitan of Smyrna Seraphim for performing a doxology in the Metropolitan church in the presence of Othon.[319]

Ambassador Zografos, who served from 1834 as Greece's Ambassador to the Ottoman Empire, strived earnestly in establishing friendly relations between Greece and Turkey, but to no avail, as the Sultan refused any communication with a representative of a state that he despised so much. After the death of Mahmud II in June 1839, Zografos, who had since been appointed Prime Minister and Foreign Minister in 1838, went to Constantinople and managed to conclude a treaty of friendship and trade between Greece and the new Sultan Abdulmedjid. This time, though, it was the Greek public that reacted adversely to it on the grounds that the Treaty could be an obstacle to national integration through the liberalization of Ottoman occupied territories. The King did not ratify the Treaty, and Zografos resigned.

All these incidents created a unique predicament between the Greeks, who were obliged to live under the Ottoman regime, and the Greeks in Greece, who were able to express themselves freely. This distinct plight was further hardened with the

---

[319] E.G. Protopsaltis: Ibid., p. 119-120.
Spyros v. Markezinis: Ibid., p. 24-26.

establishment of an independent church in Greece. The Greek State deemed that the Greek Church could no longer belong to Patriarchate, which considered being held captive by Turks, not perceiving its internationalism. The Bavarian Regency in Greece made arrangements akin to the model of the Russian Church, where the supreme command was entrusted to a five-member Synod of archbishops under the protection of the King. The Ecumenical Patriarchate did not consent to this settlement reached without the "blessing of the Great Church of Constantinople". The situation improved to some degree with the Constitution of 1843, which although proclaimed the administrative autonomy and independence of the Church of Greece, at the same time, it secured its dogmatic and spiritual unity with the Ecumenical Patriarchate.[320]

Archbishop of Sinai Konstantios I, was elected Ecumenical Patriarch in 1830 as a successor to Patriarch Agathangelos. Konstantios maintained the conservatism of the church, which was not only a result of the prevalent tenet among church hierarchy but also in the difficult era after the Revolution, it was the only system that could ensure the survival of the Hellenism of the city, and in a broader sense, the Hellenism of the Ottoman Empire. Thus, when the city's Chians asked in July 1833, three months after the death of Adamantios Korais in Paris, for permission for a memorial service, it was not granted, although at first, the Patriarch seemed undecided. Korais, of course, had criticized the church, but there were apparent national motives for honoring his memory, although, at the same time, there were others that prompted for caution. Considering the negative postures taken on by some secular dignitaries like Nicholas Logiadis and Stefanos Karatheodoris, one may infer that this refusal might

---

[320] D.A. Zakynthinos, Ibid., p. 67.

have been related to the general views of Greeks of Constantinople, reflecting their concerns with their future as a community within the Empire.

Nevertheless, the success of the Revolution, in general, also helped the Greeks who remained in the Ottoman Empire. It empowered their national spirit, elevated their confidence, and reinforced their hopes for the liberation of their own prominent homeland. Through the Tanzimat (reform) era, their communities became more organized, and economic and cultural prosperity augmented. Likewise, the Greeks themselves contributed significantly to the economic and cultural development of the Ottoman Empire that they resided in. This period was sustained until the period of the Young Turks when the Greeks of the Empire were confronted with a fierce Turkish nationalism, that was strengthened even further with the founding of the Turkish Republic, which finally eradicated them entirely in the 1960s, 150 years after the Revolution.

EPILOGUE

Despite its historical success in establishing an independent state, the end of the Revolution, did not have a "happy ending" to the degree that many Greeks anticipated in terms of their situation, especially in terms of economy. The democratic order foreseen by the constitutions of the struggle was not restored after the expulsion of the Ottomans. The Greeks were unable to organize and sustain a state of order and justice on their own, and its imposition by external forces was necessitated. There appeared many so-called commanders who wanted to claim the power for their own.

Makrigiannis said that he wrote his memoirs to narrate the misfortunes of the fatherland and religion suffered as a result of foolishness and selfishness by religious, political, and military leaders like him. He pointed out that "we have harmed our homeland significantly and lost and still losing innocent people" and spoke of a "devastation" of the fatherland.[321] He accused his political opponent Kolokotronis of getting rich. Certainly, he was echoing the views of a segment of fighters. Many members of the Friendly Society were also powerless, engaging in arguments with each other about the history of the Society while the state failed to provide aid to those in financial need. Skoufas and others found themselves in a state of dire poverty. Indeed, the end of the Revolution did not leave the people who fought so hard for their freedom in peace, but in a war-shattered nation entangled in never-ending discord. The Greeks, in the first years after their Revolution were unable to devise a program to exploit the treasure of freedom they had fought so hard to attain.

---

[321] Written in 1850

The country not only lacked state institutions but did not even possess the basic infrastructure. Kapodistrias, among other important affairs, had tried to procure a "great city clock"[322] to give Nafplio at least the civil character befitting to the capital of a European state. With his death, the political existence of the newly established State was in shambles.

Nevertheless, the situation of the Greeks at the end of the decade of 1820 was completely different from its beginning, as if an abyss divided these two periods. In ten years, the Greeks had climbed the cliff, and they could gaze at the distant horizons of their future with the confidence that their heroic struggle had empowered them with. They were committed to this, despite the controversies, the quarrels, and the passions that such strife entailed. Their slogan "freedom or death" was not just a figurative expression but blood, shed by those who truly meant it when they uttered it, and there were great many. And without doubt, the Revolution, that has already been thoroughly analyzed, did not mainly come about for social or economic reasons, with due deference to these parameters. Despite the complaints of those who lost a lot or who did not gain all that they thought they would, and one of them was Makrigiannis, there was not the slightest hint of nostalgia for the "Ottoman order".

According to British reverend Richard Burgess who traveled as a "tourist" in the spring of 1834, post-revolutionary Greece was an almost well-governed country. Burgess noted that there were no notable difficulties in Peloponnese, at least any different than those he experienced in similar tours he made to Italy and Switzerland. He pointed out that Greece was secure while also referring to the

---

[322] I. Kapodistrias: letter to A. Moustoxidis, November 1827, Texts, Ibid., p.39

prohibition of firearms that King Otto had imposed. He added that he found food of excellent quality and found shelter almost everywhere (their tent was used only in the Argolis plain). Finally, he observed that Greeks were less frugal than Italians.

The analysis in this study was mainly rationalistic. However, the Greek Revolution could not have broken out and prevailed without the heroic element, the lyricism of Rigas or Solomos and their dreams articulated by its peoples with verses "Until when are we, oh brave young men, going to live in constraint...better an hour of freedom than forty years of slavery" or "Once more, as years and time go by, once more it shall be ours... ". Moreover, not all forms of revolutionary acts can be substantiated via rational reasoning, such as social and economic demands, profits, or by cause and effect. To the Ottoman insults thrown against them, Greeks raised heroism that transcended ordinary human measures. The idea of "nation", an intangible concept, elevated the Greek spirit to the highest level, that of self-sacrifice.

The nation is the basis of the Greek State, its independence, democracy, and human rights in the country. It is the very notion that provided the distinction between the "peoples" of the Ottoman Empire and which, through struggles, led to the creation of the nation-state. A distinction that was valued worthy to a life: Freedom or Death.

After 1832, the political developments in Greece form another chapter in history. However, the foundations of the country's political, social, and cultural structure were laid in the previous period that of the Greek transition, as it was recounted. Greece of that time, with the democratic polity formed in 1843, and the adoption of a constitution replacing the absolute Monarchy, no longer bore any remnants of the Ottoman-Balkan feature, quickly assimilated

305

the themes of enlightenment and became part of modern Europe.

As Kolokotronis, vocalizing perhaps all the fighters had put it: "As long as I was able, I have done my duty unto the Fatherland, I and all my family; I saw my country free, I saw what we desired, I and my father and my grandfather and my whole generation, as well as all the Greeks."

BIBLIOGRAPHY

ENGLISH

• Richard Clogg: The struggle for Greek Independence, 1973.

• Arnold Toynbee: A study in history, Oxford, 1947.

• S.W. Sowards: The Balkans, 1996.

• The Muslim Presence in Epirus and Western Greece: http://earthlab.uoi.gr/escutis/Books/ESCUTIS_Greece_study.pdf (Last access 03/09/2020).

• Mark Mazower: The Balkans, 2000.

• Lord Byron: The isles of Greece.

• The Rev. Richard Burgess, B.D: Greece and the Levant, London, 1835.

• Bernard Lewis: The Arabs in History, Hutchinson University Library, 1968.

• Bernard Lewis: Istanbul and the civilization of the Ottoman Empire, Norman 1963.

• Paul Wittek: The birth of the Ottoman Empire.

• Savvides Alexis G.C.: «A note of the terms Rum and Anatolian Seljuk and early Ottoman times», Bulletin of Center of Asia Minor Studies, VolV, Athens 1984 – 1985.

• Ministry of Foreign Affairs of Greece: The Foundation of the Modern Greek State, Athens 1999.

FRENCH

• Jacques Ancel : Peuples et Nations des Balkans, 1930, Nouvelle Edition, Paris, 1992

• John Julius Norwich: Histoire de Byzance, Edit. Perrin, 1988.

• Dalegre, Joelle : Grecs et Ottomans, 1453-1953 : De la chute de Constantinople a la disparition de l'Empire Ottoman, 2000.

• Wladymir Brunet de Presle et Alexandre Blanchet : La Grèce depuis la conquête romaine jusqu'à nos jours, Firmin Didot, 1860.

• Guillaume de Bertier de Sauvigny : Metternich, Paris, Fayard, 1998.

TURKISH

• Ali Fuat Orenc: History Magazine Issue No. 46, 2007.

• Mehmet Seyitdanlıoglu: The Greek Revolution and the politics of Mahmud II, University of Hacettepe, http://journals.manas.edu.kg/mjsr/oldarchives/Vol 06_Issue12_2004/396.pdf (Last access 03/09/2020)

• Oral Sander: History of Ottoman Diplomacy.

• Filiz Yashar: Tetabir-i Osmaniyye, Journal of Faculty of Literature, 2015, https://scholar.google.com/citations?user=g4IPzAsA AAAJ&hl=en#d=gs_md_cita-d&u=%2Fcitations%3Fview_op%3Dview_citation%26 hl%3Den%26user%3Dg4IPzAsAAAAJ%26citation_for _view%3Dg4IPzAsAAAAJ%3AzYLM7Y9cAGgC%26tzo m%3D-120 (Last access 03/09/2020).

- Ali Fuat Orenc: Mora Turkleri, 2009.

- Lutfi: History Istanbul, 1999.

GREEK

Books

- Dion. A. Zakynthinos: Political History of Modern Greece, Athens 1965.

- Helene Glykatzi – Ahrweiler: How much Greek is the Byzantium, Athens, 2016.

- N. Svoronos: Survey of Modern Greek History, 1981.

- Kapodistrias: Texts, 1976.

- Athanasios Komninos Ypsilantis "Historical Events After the Fall" Constantinople, 1870, written circa end of 18th century (in medieval Greek).

- Manouil Gedeon: Chronicles of a Columnist, Athens 1932.

- Spyros Vryonis: The Decline of the Hellenism of Middle Ages and the procedure of Islamization, Athens 2008.

- Skarlatos Vyzantios: Dictionary of the Greek Language, Athens, publications of 1839, 1852, Publisher Andreas Koromilas.

- D.K. Vyzantios Babylonia, play.

- Vasilis Kremmydas: The Greek Revolution of 1821, Athens, 2016.

- S.T. Laskaris: Diplomatic History of Greece 1821-1914, Athens 1947.

• Dion. A. Zakynthinos: Political History of Modern Greece, Athens 1965.

• Vasilis Moutsoglou: Turkey, the Evolution of the Personality of the State, Athens, 2016.

• V. Filias: Society and power in Greece. 1. The Forged Urbanization 1800-1864, 1974.

• K. Moskof: National and social conscience in Greece, 1972.

• Eleni E. Koukou: Institutions and Privileges of Hellenism after the Fall, Publ. Sakkoula, Athens, Komotini, 1988.

• N.V. Vlahos: History of the Balkan States, 1908-1914, Athens.

• K. Paparrigopoulos: History of the Greek Nation, New Hellenism, Kaktos.

• V. Moutsoglou: The Greeks of Constantinople 1821-1922, Athens, 1998.

• Manouil I. Gedeon: References of events before my time, 1800-1863-1913, Athens 1934.

• Ioannis Filimon: Historical essay on the Friendly Society, Nafplio, 1834.

• L. Th. Houmanidis: History of Economy, Athens, 1969

• Manouil Gedeon: Patriarchal Tables, Constantinople.

• Linos Politis: History of the New Greek Literature, Athens 1979.

• K. Th.Dimaras: Neohellenic Enlightenment, 1974.

• D.Kitsikis: History of the Ottoman Empire 1280-1924, Estia, Athens, 1988.

- D. Tsakonas: Sociology of the Modern Greek Spirit, Athens 1969.

- Chr. Frangos: Athanasios Psallidas and the "Greek Nomarchia", 1972.

- A.G. Protopsaltis: Political History of modern Greece, Issue B´, Athens, 1973.

- Emm. Xanthos: Memoirs of the Friendly Society.

- Apost. E.Vakalopoulos: History of the New Hellenism, Volume V, Thessaloniki 1980.

- Apost. E.Vakalopoulos: History of the New Hellenism, Volume VII Thessaloniki 1986.

- Vakalopoulos: History of the new Hellenism, Vol. B 1964.

- P. A. Giorkatzis: The "Aphorism" of Alexandre Ypsilanti, Kavala, 1988.

- Vasilis Moutsoglou: The criteria in international politics, Athens, 2015.

- G. Zotiadis: Political and diplomatic history of the New Era, 1973.

- Theodoros Kolokotronis by hand of G. Tertsetis: Narration of events of the Greek race from 1770 to 1836.

- General Makrigiannis: Memoirs, A, 1850.

- D. Fotiadis: The Revolution of '21

- D. Kokkinos: The Greek Revolution

- Greek Parliament: Constitutional History.

- G. B. Zotiadis: Political and Diplomatic History, 1973.

- Spyros V. Markezinis Political History of

311

Greece, 1966, Publ. Papyrus.

Articles, Papers

• Delphi Conference 1988: Greek civilizations of the East. N. Sarris, G. Kamarados-Vyzantios, D. Theodoridis.

• Archimandrite Germanos Afthonidis: Foreword to "Historical Events After the Fall", Ath. Komninos Ypsilanti.

• Alexis G.C. Savvides: A note of the terms Rum and Anatolia in Seljuk and early Ottoman times, Bulletin V. of the Centre for Asia Minor Studies Athens 1984-1985.

• Modern Greek registry, Pelekanos Publications, Athens.

• Dionysios Tzakis: E-Historically, Achaia "The timid, the infamous and the vulgar».

• Efi Alamanis: The action of Papaflessas after the meeting of Vostitza, history of the Greek nation, Ekdotiki Athinon, Vol. L, (1975).

• Gregory Ars: "How the Greek Revolution began in Iasi", E-Historically.

• Anastasis Vistonitis: "To Vima" 19.3.2017.

• Iakovos Michaelides: Theodoros behind Kolokotronis, 2014.

• Thanasis Christou: E-Historically, "The declaration in Salona and Levadia"

• Aikaterini Flassianou: E-Historically, "Eruption of the revolution in Halkidiki».

• Konstantinos Papoulidis: E-Historically: "Mount Athos, when the "untrodden" of the Holy Mountain was violated».

• Annita N. Prassas: E-Historically, "Naoussa: The Revolution and the destruction of the city».

• Konstantina Adamopoulou – Pavlou: E-Historically, "Economou delivers Hydra to the struggle».

• Dionysis Dionysiou: E-Historically "Kanaris in Cyprus".

• Petros Papapolyviou: E-Historically "The Revolution of 1821 and Cyprus".

• Spyros Dim.Loukatos: E-historically "The attempts for alliances and their fate».

• A study by Periklis Argyropoulos.

• Research of the Dept. of historical archives, MFA, Greece

• John C. Loukas: E-Historically "the Greek Fireboats in Alexandria».

• George H. Orfanos: Article in Rethymno News, 2016.

• D. Dionysios E-Historically "Kanaris in Cyprus".

• Aik. Koumarianou: E-Historically "The press in the fighting Greece».

• Newspaper article of Vasilis Kyrazopoulos, Politis, February 2017.

• Greek history issues, version 4.0 (http://www.istorikathemata.com /2012/12/the-destruction-of-the-Greek-fleet-by-Miaoulis-in-Poros-1831.htm).

ACKNOWLEDGMENT

The writer is grateful to Alex Moutsoglou for his valuable assistance in translating this book into English.

From the same author

The Function of Geography in the Geopolitical Puzzle, Amazon, 2020.

"The Function of Geography in the Geopolitical Puzzle" is a multi-tasking work providing Ariadne's clue, leading the reader into the geographical and historical labyrinth of the world. Presently when the debate on geopolitics gained new resonance, this book comes to emphasize the self-evident but understated: That the geographical function is the pedestal but also the binding framework of the political act, that geopolitics is the use of the geographical factor in the service of political and state aspirations.

https://www.amazon.de/-/en/Vassilios-Moutsoglou-ebook/dp/B08JYW648K/ref=sr_1_1?dchild=1&keywords=The+Function+of+Geography+in+the+Geopolitical+Puzzle&qid=1603872358&sr=8-1

Paperback Amazon:

https://www.amazon.com/function-geography-geopolitical-puzzle/dp/B08JVLBWFD/ref=sr_1_1?keywords=Vassilios+Moutsoglou&qid=1603875577&sr=8-1

The Last Days of Istanbul, Amazon, 2021.

"The Last Days of Istanbul" is a political fiction story placed in Turkey's historical framework in the context of the events occurring around the Technical University of Istanbul in 1971. The novel unfolds on many levels, social, political, historical, psychological, and detective story. The central character, a student of this University, on the one hand, is persecuted by the police, who consider him an extremist of the Left. On the other, he is dragged by the vortex caused by the Greeks' expulsion from Istanbul during 1955-1975.

Available also in e-kindle

Vassilios Moutsoglou is a Greek Ambassador ad honorem. He has studied Mechanical Engineering in Istanbul, Political Sciences in Athens, and Diplomacy in the Greek MFA. As a diplomat, he has served in Canada, Poland, Saudi Arabia, Belgium (E.U.), and Algeria.

His previous work includes published books in the Greek language on The Greek Community in Constantinople -19th century (1998), Greek-Turkish Relations- 1955-1999 (2000), The Balkans (2002), Arab Spring (being an Ambassador in Algiers at the time) (2014), The Motives in International Politics (2015), The Personality of Turkey (2016), The Greek Transition of 1821(2018), The Geographical Function of the Geopolitical Puzzle (2019).

Made in the USA
Monee, IL
15 April 2022

56255b16-179a-4064-92eb-5e6232b44d4cR01